P9-CDL-521

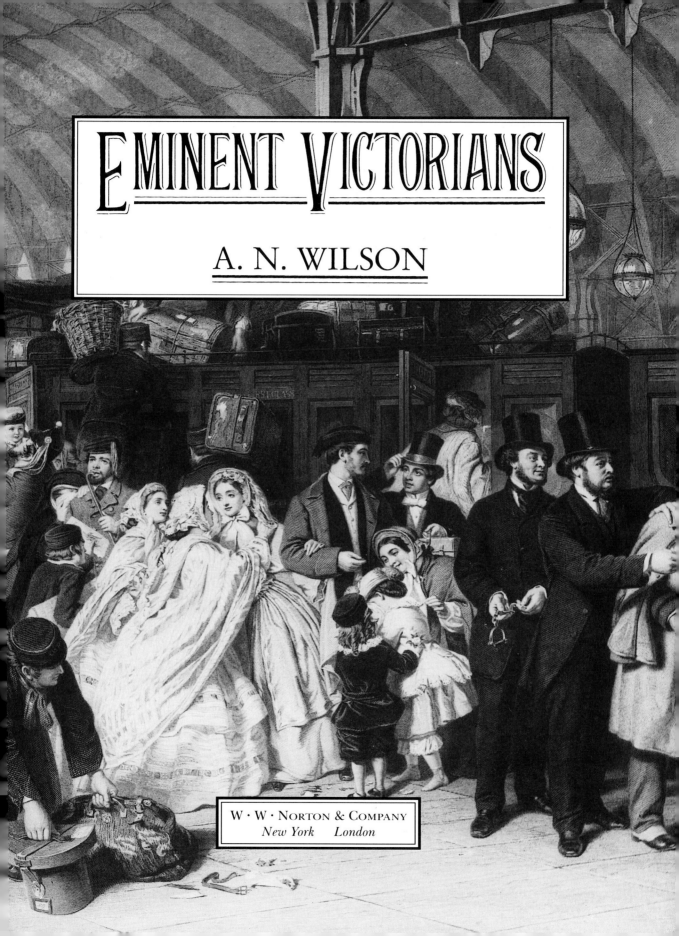

EMINENT VICTORIANS

A. N. WILSON

W · W · NORTON & COMPANY
New York   London

for John Lucas

Frith's crowd scenes give vivid glimpses of Victorian life.
His famous painting of Paddington station seethes with human activity and
reminds us of the revolutionary importance of the railways.

Copyright © 1989 by A.N. Wilson.
First American Edition 1990.

All rights reserved.

Printed in the United States of America.

Manufacturing by Arcata Graphics/Halliday.

ISBN 0-393-02848-8

W. W. Norton & Company, Inc., 500 Fifth Avenue, New York, N.Y. 10110
W. W. Norton & Company, Ltd., 37 Great Russell Street, London WC1B 3NU

1 2 3 4 5 6 7 8 9 0

Contents

Preface

'THE HISTORY OF THE VICTORIAN AGE will never be written: we know too much about it.' Seventy years have elapsed since Lytton Strachey wrote those words as the preface to his hilarious volume of essays, *Eminent Victorians*. He added, with his tongue so firmly in his cheek that it is a wonder the words came forth at all, 'Je n'impose rien; je ne propose rien; j'expose.' In fact, his highly contentious 'expositions' of four much-revered Victorian figures are full of imposition and proposition. Many of the more grotesque 'facts' he unearthed – such as the assertion that one of Dr Arnold's legs was much shorter than the other – were invented because Strachey thought they made his subjects more ridiculous. Rendering his four subjects absurd – and by implication all the values they represented – was the purpose of his volume. It was a book which had a profound effect on the minds of the whole post-1918 generation. The values of public school and imperial militarism, embodied in Dr Arnold and General Gordon, were cut down to size by contemplating the supposedly ludicrous characters of Arnold and Gordon themselves. Religion, in the person of Strachey's caricature of Cardinal Manning, was thrown overboard with equal glee. As for the opening sentence, intended ironically at the time, it has been overtaken by the more gargantuan joke of Victorian Studies – masses and masses of material about every aspect of life in the last century. Not only do we 'know too much' about the Victorian Age; we have also been treated to a series of extraordinary Victorian revivals, both in taste and in morals. Even in my boyhood (born 1950) 'Victorian' was a term of aesthetic abuse when applied to architecture or painting. John Betjeman could see beauty in George Gilbert Scott's St Pancras Hotel or the Albert Memorial. But nobody could be quite sure whether or not he was joking. His friend Evelyn Waugh, meanwhile, bought up a huge collection of Victorian 'narrative' paintings of 'The Last Night in the Old Home', 'And When Did You Last See Your Father?' genre; almost every canvas must have come to him cheap.

Then, fashions changed. As the developers moved in to every provincial town in England and began to destroy what had been regarded as

'Victorian monstrosities', people began to take John Betjeman seriously. Gothic revival architects like George Gilbert Scott, William Butterfield, or G. F. Bodley came to be the subjects of serious study. Faced with the brutalism of post-Bauhaus architects, persons of taste and refinement began to see the glories of George Edmund Street's Law Courts or even Alfred Waterhouse's Manchester Town Hall.

Victorian paintings which only a few decades earlier had been the subject of laughter suddenly became valuable. The Pre-Raphaelites now command enormous prices in the sale rooms, and even the lesser Victorians are beyond the most avaricious dreams of the private collector. Victorian furniture which had been lumpy and inelegant when it was in grandma's attic suddenly seemed full of character under the auctioneer's hammer. Button-backed chairs and chaises-longues returned to the drawing-room. Repro-Victorian wallpaper from Sandersons or Laura

Alfred Waterhouse's Manchester Town Hall is one of the most magnificent examples of civic architecture in the Gothic manner, bringing 'the last enchantments of the Middle Ages' to the industrial North.

Ashley began to transform every household in the land. And as house prices shot up, and the Georgian rectories became the preserve of millionaires, the rest of us started to discover that Charles and Carrie Pooter, of The Laurels, Brickfield Terrace, Holloway, had in fact been arbiters of the greatest good taste. Those tiles round the fireplace, which ten years before we would have paid a builder to hack out, are seen to be of the greatest beauty. Thank goodness for that little piece of stained glass window over the front door! How glad we are to have those wrought-iron railings in the garden fence.

Charles Pooter is of course the fictitious narrator of *The Diary of a Nobody* by George and Weedon Grossmith, first published in 1892 and evergreen to this day, not only as the best comic novel in the language, but also as offering a glimpse of life in an 'ordinary' household towards the close of Queen Victoria's reign. The suburbs of England were full of Pooters, and in launching his attack on the 'Eminent Victorians' it is not surprising that Lytton Strachey did not even give them a glance. Because he was born into one of the great intellectual dynasties of the Victorian Age, Strachey, and his more serious Bloomsbury or Fabian coevals, took it for granted that they could overthrow the systems erected by the patricians like Arnold and Manning. It seemed to them as though the great Victorian institutions, the public schools, the Army, the Church, had had their day; likewise, probably, the monarchy. The new civilisation, based on the values of the *New Statesman*, would create an England that was altogether different. This, to a large extent, took place – particularly in the 1945 Parliament of Clement Attlee, who, though he looked like a Pooter, was really a Fabian patrician at heart.

This reading of events failed to see that the Pooters were the really triumphant class of the Victorian period. Karl Marx, surveying England in the 1840s, became convinced that it was only a matter of time before the proletarian masses rose up against their capitalist masters. It did not happen, because almost every member of the proletarian masses was dreaming of that cosy domestic respectability which Charles Pooter, the clerk in the City, had established for his wife Carrie and his raffish son Lupin. This huge class of person, who took their holidays at Broadstairs and followed new crazes like the purchase of Christmas cards, had no interest in Marxist revolutionary programmes. But that is not to say that they were not revolutionaries. Their kind had not existed in eighteenth-century England. Once they came into being, they were an unshakeable

8

force. They wanted the best for themselves within their modest, hard-earned incomes and carefully-put-by savings. It was the Pooters who supported, or dismissed, the governments of Gladstone, Disraeli, Salisbury and Rosebery. It was they who wanted, and obtained, the vote. It was they who educated their children. In turn, they would start to enter the civil service and the business community. Because of the extraordinary class system in England, they would have to wait eighty years before they truly obtained a political voice. No wonder, that once a Pooter was established in Downing Street (and you can tell from *The Diary of a Nobody* that it would be Carrie not Charles who had the will-power for that) there was much talk of a revival in Victorian values.

While the sale-rooms paid prices for the paintings of William Holman Hunt which in a sane world would be reserved for Titians, and while Laura Ashley made her fortune, Mrs Thatcher reintroduced simple Gladstonian economics: you don't spend money you don't possess. Instead of systems, she stood for the little family with its savings, and its decent values. The result was the most successful political career in British twentieth-century history. The last laugh was on Pooter.

In the course of the Victorian revival which we have so surprisingly witnessed in our own times, there has been a lot of talk about 'Victorian values'. At the time of the Suez crisis in 1956, the British nation was quite largely divided between those who still clung to some quasi-imperial sense that 'we' had a right to invade Egypt if Johnny Egyptian was mis-behaving himself, and others who thought that the whole enterprise was mad, anachronistic, bloodthirsty. There was indeed such divide in 1982. The surprising thing was that when General Galtieri invaded the Falkland Islands he provided the Prime Minister, whose political fortunes until that juncture had seemed to be flagging, with the chance to summon up reserves of 'jingoism' in the British people that most *bien-pensant* observers would have imagined to be long since dead. The rights and the wrongs of the Falklands campaign will probably continue to be debated. What was so arresting at the time was the atmosphere in Britain. People said that it was a revival of the Dunkirk spirit; but it wasn't. At Dunkirk, there was an imminent likelihood of invasion by the most dangerous army in Europe. The Falklands War was far away, and, at least until the sinking of HMS *Sheffield*, it felt like a carnival. If it re-awoke the spirit of an earlier war, it was that of the Crimean, when the Black Sea was invaded not only by the 'task force' of British troop ships, but also by sightseers, excited by a dizzy sense of vicarious national heroism. It was a strange example of the way that our Victorian legacy has the power to return and haunt us.

Unlike Strachey, I am not close enough to the Victorians to feel superior to them. A child of my time, I have gone through periods of 'nostalgia' for an age I never knew, and a feeling that the Victorians built buildings, followed creeds, or made achievements which it was sad to discard. Viewed in another light, however, they seem so different from us that it seems farcical to hope that we could ever hope to understand them, let alone imitate them. The passage of time, which seems so cruel when one is in nostalgic or elegiac mood, is never without mercies. We might regret steam trains, but who would choose to live in a Victorian slum? Oxford was more beautiful in the days before Lord Nuffield built the Cowley works, but for me the beauty would have been hard to appreciate if, like Dr Pusey, I had believed that the majority of the human race was doomed to hell-fire throughout eternity. Men's clothes were nicer, but children were starving, and worse (see my chapter on Josephine Butler) on the streets of London. On the whole, I have come to echo Lucky Jim in his definitive lecture on the Middle Ages, 'Thank God for the twentieth century.'

My relationship with Strachey, like my relationship with the Victorians, has had its ups and downs, too. As a stylist, I used to love him too much. Set pieces, like his death of Queen Victoria (in his biography of the Queen) got into my bloodstream, with the result that for a period I rejected him as nothing but a mannerist. The Bloomsbury air of sniggering superiority to the Victorians wore very thin by the time I was about twenty-five. After all, the great Victorians have a sheer bigness about them which is impossible to laugh off. No English poet of the twentieth century matches Tennyson, even though any schoolboy can point out Tennyson's faults. For sheer improbability of plots, repetition, sloppy writing, it would be hard to find a writer as bad as Dickens on a bad day. But the achievement of Dickens remains something which makes many 'better' novelists of our century seem like pigmies.

My selection of 'Eminent Victorians' has not been arbitrary, but inevitably it fails to be comprehensive. What? No Dickens? No Darwin? No Gilbert and Sullivan? No William Morris? No Butterfield? No Lord Leighton? What kind of nineteenth century is this? I have selected the Prince Consort partly because of the multifarious range of his interests,

The nineteenth century saw a vast expansion of the lower middle classes of whom
Charles and Carrie Pooter in The Diary of a Nobody *are the archetypal examples.*
Streets like this one in London are typical of those built to accommodate them.

but partly as a symptom of that 'Pooterite' revolution at which I hinted
in an earlier paragraph. Gladstone, as well as being the greatest
statesman of the age, was also a man who contained many characteris-
tically Victorian contradictions within his nature – the Tractarian
recluse at war with the man of action; the old Tory at war with 'the
people's William'. Charlotte Brontë could, like many of the great Victorian writers, perhaps be described as a Late Romantic as much as she
was a Victorian. Her story is perpetually haunting, just as *Jane Eyre* is
endlessly re-readable, and her presence here reminds us that there is
nobody who is typical, everyone is an oddity, if few odder than she. Few,
that is, unless it be Mrs Cameron the photographer who although she
could not be described as 'eminent' in the sense that Newman or Gladstone were eminent, was one of the most stylishly accomplished
practitioners of that art-form or species of chicanery which was first
invented and propagated during Victoria's reign. Josephine Butler, on
the other hand, on the face of it the most typical of the group, showed
exceptional courage and honesty in the way she challenged the accepted
sexual mores of the day. Like my readers, I could have chosen a different
six, though I would always be sad to leave out Newman who seems, the
more one thinks about him, to have been one of the most remarkable
people who ever lived.

Like Strachey, I think it is possible to learn more from short biographies of a roughly contemporaneous nature than from some generalised know-all survey. Also like Strachey (only in my case quite sincerely), I have not tried to make a point. It has seemed to me, though, the more I have dwelt upon these six characters, that any attempt to revive 'Victorian values' in our own day would be a precarious exercise. The greatest Victorians were the ones who were on the move. 'To live is to change,' said Newman. All six of my subjects were aware of it. Newman himself did not only change his own religion. He radically changed both the Church which he left and the Church which he joined. By the very fact of his having lived, it would be impossible to return to 'Victorian values' either in the Roman or the English Churches because they are both almost unrecognisably different from their Victorian manifestations. Likewise, in the political sphere, the programme of reform and change presided over by Gladstone has meant that, except in the broadest outlines, it is impossible to think of how one might return to Gladstonian politics. Besides, having rumbled 'Victorian values', both Newman and Gladstone in their different ways were intent on destroying them, rooting them out. Mrs Butler was the same. The double standard by which a household was kept 'respectable' by the husband being tacitly allowed to visit the stews is arguably the safety-valve on which much British life depended. Once that valve was burst by Mrs Butler, it could be said that all kinds of other changes were inevitable, changes not only to the lives of poor women, but to women in general. Once women were liberated from the thraldom in which Charlotte Brontë and her sisters grew up – in which the choice of career was confined to marriage or becoming a governess, or some equally old-maidish occupation – the world was indeed going to change.

In the course of writing this book, my admiration for Strachey himself has revived. His lightness of touch, his pure elegance, is not something which I could imitate. We live in different ages, and that is the point. My initial purpose in stealing his title was to cut him down to size, to remind his ghost that there really *were* eminent Victorians, giants in those days. Now that the book is finished and laid before the public, I can only repeat his words, 'Je n'impose rien; je ne propose rien. . . .' His book is a thousand times better than mine, and it will still be read when mine is forgotten. But when both Strachey and I are forgotten, they will still be reading *Jane Eyre* and Newman's *Apologia*.

Prince Albert
1819-61

Father of the modern British monarchy

*By the end of his days no one looked more respectably middle class
than the Prince Consort, photographed here by Mayall.*

When Queen Victoria died, on 22 January 1901, few people can have felt a heartier relief than her personal physician, Sir James Reid, whom she had led a sorry dance for the previous twenty years. Deprived of the power to be a tyrant in a political capacity, Victoria as an old lady had enjoyed keeping all her courtiers on their toes. Sir James was even dragged away from his own father's death-bed to attend to the Queen's favourite, John Brown. And there was no moment of Sir James's private life which his monarch considered too private that she could not intrude upon it with bulletins of her own digestive or bowel processes.

Demanding to the last, she left Sir James with rigorous instructions for her own burial. It was, in fact, probably the first time that Sir James had ever seen the body of his patient, since in life she had a strong sense of her own dignity and only allowed him to discover the state of her health through verbal inquiry. Now, if he chose, he could look at her. His wife considered that in death 'her face' was 'like a lovely marble statue, no sign of illness or age, and she still looked "the Queen", her veil over her face and a few loose flowers on her bed – all so simple and grand.'

There was to be no embalming and no Lying in State. The Queen, as head of the Army, had asked for a military funeral, and she was to lie in her coffin wearing – as presumably heads of the Army do in death – a simple white silk dress and the Order of the Garter. What was less simple was her request that Sir James should order her coffin to be filled with mementoes. Though the Queen may very well have been in law the Head of the Established Church of Scotland and the Established Church of England, she seemed in death to be casting back to the chieftains of the Viking Age, who set sail on their funeral barges laden with the jewels, wives, armour and hens which they had managed to accumulate during a life of plunder; or perhaps she harked back to the Pharaohs, who liked to hoard in their pyramid tombs the food, the libations and the ornaments which would accompany them for their long trek through eternity. So, Sir James recorded in his journal, he was instructed to place into Queen Victoria's coffin favourite photographs of Prince Albert, and of her children; a garment worked upon by Princess Alice; keepsakes from all her favourite servants and relations – chains, bracelets, lockets, shawls, handkerchiefs. Then there were the plaster casts which she had had taken of her children's little limbs. Heaven was to be cluttered with *objets* and mementoes, just like one of the Queen's drawing-rooms at Osborne or Balmoral.

The funeral took place on 22 February 1901 and – as has very often been observed – it was one of the last great occasions when all the crowned heads of Europe were assembled together: all those kings and grand dukes and emperors whose power and manner of life, within a couple of decades, would have been blown from the earth by war and revolution. Of all the dead little mementoes which Sir James Reid had placed in Queen Victoria's coffin, surely none could have been deader, in 1901, than the concept of monarchy itself.

As we watch them today on that faded old film, in their stiff uniforms and cocked hats, the monarchs seem almost as pathetic as those other sad films of fifteen years later – the wounded returning from the Front, their eyes bandaged, their sight destroyed by the gas. Both are processions of the blind. The twentieth century was soon to be called the century of the Common Man – but it was a title more properly owing to the Victorian Age. The century which produced Karl Marx and Mr Pooter could not for long contain these medalled chests, these fluttering feathers, these spiked helmets, these proud empty heads. Monarchies are expressions of national mythology. They survive in societies which, willingly or unwillingly, place all power in the hands of one individual and their circle. It usually requires perpetual vigilance by the military, and a preparedness to put down dissent with the utmost ruthlessness for modern (post-Napoleonic) monarchies to survive. In the seventeenth century, monarchs survived by claiming that they had been put on their thrones by God. But in the nineteenth century, when God himself was dethroned, where did that leave the monarchs? Even in countries like Russia – where the news of God's death (proclaimed by Nietzsche) was slow in arriving – the divinely-appointed Emperors needed to protect themselves with savage laws and cruel intolerance. It was of no avail to them when the time came. The Romanovs, like the Bourbons and the Hapsburgs and the other great European dynasts who assembled behind that well-laden coffin of Queen Victoria, were all doomed to be scrubbed out of the history books. They were as obsolete as their clothes.

Victoria's son, Edward VII, was a popular king in England – largely perhaps because people felt sorry for him having to wait so long to inherit. In many ways, he was unlike his parents, a determined throwback to the Hanoverian days of dissipation when kings were really kings – their favourite occupations being to interfere in international politics and to sleep with other men's wives. Edward VII's love of Paris provided ample opportunity for both activities, and the establishment of the famous Entente Cordiale. But had he lived longer into the twentieth century, I wonder whether the British would have continued to like him, or even to keep him on at Buckingham Palace? The long reign of King George V and Queen Mary was a reversion to something very different. With the brief and unhappy interlude of the reign of Edward VIII, the British royal family has kept going where many another ancient dynasty has collapsed. Whereas all the famous kings and queens of Europe have been famous precisely because of their political influence, the British have decided that their monarchs 'traditionally' have no political bias or indeed interest whatsoever. How can this convincingly be argued on behalf of a family who, merely on a private level, must own half the wealth of Scotland and Norfolk, and who, in their ritualistic public display – in their State Openings of Parliament, their glass coaches, their crowns and uniforms – hark back to an infinitely obsolete hierarchical view of society?

The answer, surely, partly resides in the fact that the British royal family is *déclassé*. They certainly are not aristocratic, though they have married into the aristocracy. The Queen Mother, for example, is very evidently a Scottish aristocrat when she is met in a private capacity. But her public role is something rather different. We would not use phrases like 'the Queen Mum' about a duchess or some terrifyingly upper-class lady from the pages of a gossip column. Her Majesty Queen Elizabeth the Queen Mother has become a fantasy grandmother for everyone – for members of the working class as much as for the rich and grand. Hence her extraordinary clothes, which are less those of an aristocrat than of a charwoman who has won the football pools.

When you come to examine the irrational basis by which newspapers assess the popularity or otherwise of members of the royal family, you find that it resides precisely in the extent to which they are usable as vehicles of such fantasy. Those who conduct themselves like their de-throned royal cousins in Europe, who flaunt their wealth, or stamp their feet, or 'come the royal personage' are on the whole detested by the British public, though they provide amusement for the readers of American or European newspapers and magazines. Those on the other hand who appear like mega-versions of us, the middle or lower-middle classes, are adored. It does not really matter if the activities themselves – four-in-hand racing, shooting, wild-life preservation – would be beyond the means of many of us. Prince Philip seems essentially like Dad with his hobbies. And though it may be the case that members of the royal family have gradually begun to allow into their midst divorced persons – and even on occasion to get divorced themselves – they have maintained, throughout the century, the sort of level of morality which would have been expected not of an aristocratic family but of a family like mine – a provincial middle-class to lower-middle-class family which had never, until the 1970s, known a divorce.

How did this strange institution, the modern British monarchy develop, with its apolitical constitutional position, its fuddy-duddy morals, its concepts of public service, and its rather quaint notion – particularly among the males of its number – that they should be 'good all-rounders'? It is not in the least a natural idea, and it certainly has very little to do with any other type of monarchy which you might encounter in the history books. The answer, I suspect, is to be found in almost every big town in Britain. Either consciously or unconsciously, nations betray themselves by their monuments. When we visit the Soviet Union, we perhaps feel that the Russians are trying too hard to persuade themselves that Lenin was responsible for all the good things in the world when he was, in fact, as absolute a monarch as the Tsars, and ruthlessly imposed a political system on the people from above.

The British abundance of statuary, dating from the 1860s onwards, portrays a man whose achievement was subtler than that. If the favourite comic book of the latter end of Queen Victoria's reign was *The Diary of a Nobody*, then their favourite statue was of a prince who, by all historical rights, should have been a nobody, but whose peculiarly small-scale qualities matched the moment and created something which was to survive and outlast all the most illustrious dynasties of Europe. For the modern British monarchy is, without question, the invention of Prince Albert.

Prince Albert was born on 26 August 1819 in the tiny German Duchy of Saxe-Coburg, the second son of preposterously ill-matched parents. His father Ernest, the Duke of this diminutive domain, was an old roué whose protruding lower teeth and baggy, bloodshot eyes gave him the appearance of a lecherous bulldog. He had innumerable illegitimate children by more or less any woman who was to hand but he had chosen as his bride a girl of only sixteen years old. Not surprisingly perhaps, the Duchess Louise abandoned him at the earliest possible opportunity, eloping to Paris with an officer in the Coburg army. She died in 1831, when Prince Albert was only twelve. He did not see much of her after the age of five.

None of this really mattered, because the truly important characters in Prince Albert's story were not his parents but three other people in every way more robustly ambitious on the family's behalf – his Uncle Leopold,

*The Schloss Rosenau was the country retreat in Saxe-Coburg
where Prince Albert spent his childhood.
It always occupied a special place in his heart and he recreated
much of its atmosphere at his Scottish seat, Balmoral.*

his Aunt Victoire, and above all the family doctor, tutor and general adviser, the Baron Christian Frederick Stockmar.

First – Uncle Leopold, Duke Ernest's younger brother. It did not worry him that, as a younger son, he stood no chance of inheriting an obscure German duchy. He managed to marry, in 1816, the only child of George IV – and the heiress to the throne of England and Scotland. When Leopold married Princess Charlotte, he took the title of Prince Consort and Parliament voted him a stipend of £50,000 per annum. It was very clear from the outset that Leopold did not intend to be a mere stooge. He was determined to interfere in English political life as much as he could, and to take upon himself the power as well as the state of a monarch.

Strangely, this was not merely acceptable but positively appropriate in the entrepreneurial world of early nineteenth-century England. Just as the old Whig aristocratic dynasties were going to have to stand aside for the prosperous members of the middle class, so the British were ripe to be governed by a self-made monarch.

There was no historic or dynastic link between the throne of England and the Duchy of Saxe-Coburg. Leopold and Stockmar forged the links which were eventually to sweep away the old Hanoverian inheritance of George IV and his brothers, replacing it with what they hoped would be a Germanic autocracy of the kind favoured by Frederick the Great of Prussia. All their ambitions were fulfilled, but fulfilled in ways they did not in the least expect. Leopold, who looked so likely to produce a new royal line in England, was rather to live to see the progeny of his brother and sister ruling there in his stead.

The first blow to Leopold's ambition fell when Princess Charlotte died in childbirth after he had been married to her for only eighteen months.

Albert's Aunt Victoire had also married into the British royal family. In the scramble, not without comedy, which followed the death of Princess Charlotte, the Royal Dukes, none of them thin, none of them young, all attempted to provide themselves with the dignity of siring a future king or queen of England. To this end, Edward, Duke of Kent, third son of George III, who had previously shown no predilection for marriage, chose as his wife Leopold's sister. She had been married before to Emich Charles, Prince of Leiningen, who died in 1814. By her first husband, Victoire had produced two children – Charles, Prince of

Leiningen, and Feodora, who was doomed to marry the infinitely obscure Prince Ernest of Hohenlohe-Langenburg. Victoire's second husband was the only surviving son of George III who managed to produce a legitimate heir which is why the first-born of Victoire of Saxe-Coburg should have died as a German princeling of infinite obscurity, but her third child, by virtue of being the daughter of the Duke of Kent, should have been Queen Victoria, Defender of the Faith, Queen of the most prosperous and expansive commercial power in Europe and – in the fullness of time, through the fancy of her most fanciful and favourite Prime Minister – the very Empress of India. Not bad going for the House of Saxe-Coburg – a duchy rather smaller in size than the English county of Dorset.

But the glorification of the House of Saxe-Coburg, the unification of its two scions – Victoria and Albert – would perhaps never have happened, or never have had such momentous consequences, had it not been for the efficient stage management of Leopold's indispensable right-hand man, Baron Christian Frederick Stockmar.

Stockmar – described by Mr Gladstone in splenetic mood as 'a mischievous old prig' – was not only Prince Albert's tutor and mentor, but a perpetual presence in his life until the middle of the century. It was Stockmar who recognised that Albert's good looks and intelligence marked him out as something rather special – anyway as far as the house of Saxe-Coburg was concerned. It was Stockmar who saw that the boy received a good education – a grounding in languages, mathematics, and literature, but also an appreciation of the manner in which school-room subjects might affect the world. From an early age, Albert was trained in economics, agriculture, architecture. He learnt to paint. He was keenly musical. Stockmar made sure that Albert, together with his far less promising elder brother Ernest, travelled to Italy to study art and music; and that the boys attended Bonn University. It is quite unthinkable that any of George III's sons might have gone to Oxford or Cambridge, let alone submitted themselves to the wide-ranging academic disciplines which were expected of German students of the time. Stockmar was busy creating a monarch for the modern age – a figure who could preside with plausibility over an expanding industrial and imperial power.

Ever since it had become clear that none of Victoria's uncles would produce an heir, Leopold had been using his influence with his sister to groom the young princess of Kent for the office of monarch of England.

The Duchess of Kent was a silly, somewhat tyrannical woman, under the sway of her devious secretary and adviser Sir John Conroy. Throughout Victoria's minority, he (together with her governess Baroness Lehzen) brought appalling pressure on her to behave as they thought fit. On more than one occasion – sometimes choosing moments when Victoria was seriously ill – Conroy tried to force her to sign pledges that she would appoint him as her secretary, and in effect the Regent, if she were to succeed before her majority. Common sense, plain stubbornness and her Uncle Leopold – who at one point sent over Baron Stockmar to advise her – saved her. By the time she did succeed, at the age of eighteen, Victoria had formed her first important political alliance – with Lord Melbourne – and she was able to send Conroy, Lehzen and her mother about their business. It is one of the most liberating stories in history when their spell is broken and Victoria reigns alone.

The marriage between Victoria and Albert, the two cousins, which took place on 10 February 1840, was something which had been mooted since their childhood. It was fortunate for all concerned that Victoria, a self-willed individual, who was, in the early years of her reign, very happy in her freedom, very much enjoying power, and totally besotted with her Prime Minister, Lord Melbourne, should have fallen in so readily with the plan to get married. After all, she was only twenty and Albert just a few months younger.

It was physical infatuation which decided her, as her Journal entry for 15 October 1839 makes clear:

> I said to him that I thought he must be aware *why* I wished him to come here, and that it would make me too *happy* if he would consent to what I wished (to marry me); we embraced each other over and over again, and he was *so* kind, *so* affectionate; Oh! to *feel* I was and am loved by *such* an Angel as Albert was too *great a delight* to describe! He is *perfection*; perfection in every way – in beauty – in everything!

It has the breathless enthusiasm of a schoolgirl who has been given a new puppy. For the next twenty-two years, Albert and Victoria were to provide an ideal royal partnership and, through their nine children, exercise a vast influence in almost all the royal families of Europe. By the close of the century the blood of Albert and Victoria had provided kaisers, tsars,

This revealing photograph by Roger Fenton captures the Queen and the Prince Consort in a thoughtful mood. 'I am only the husband,' Albert confided to a friend, 'and not the master in the house.'

grand dukes, kings and queens for Germany, Russia, Schleswig Hol-stein, Hesse, Norway, Romania, Spain, Sweden, Greece and Denmark.

But, beyond providing a sort of royal stud farm from the compara-tively untried stables of Saxe-Coburg, what was the role of the Prince Consort to be? What was Albert's function? To ask a more fundamental question – what was the function of the monarchy itself?

It should not be supposed that the overweening ambition of the Saxe-Coburgs – of Leopold, of the Duchess of Kent, of Stockmar – had gone unnoticed among the Whig aristocratic families, nor among the rising new Tories who held the key positions of power in London political circles. By the same token, Albert had not been educated by Stockmar to think of himself either as an upper-class roué like his father, nor as a stuffed dummy to stand behind the Queen on ceremonial occasions.

The determination of Parliament to show the new arrival that he must not overstep the mark *politically* was clear very early on when the House of Commons was discussing the question of Albert's allowance. Deep resentment was still felt against King Leopold, who had by then taken some million pounds out of the Exchequer. Led by the Tory Opposition of Sir Robert Peel, the Commons voted overwhelmingly that the new

Prince should only be granted £30,000. It was, of course, enough to live on. But a message had been sent by Parliament to the Court, and it was one which was profoundly resented.

Victoria had grown up with the English tradition that the monarch, like most of the good families in London, was a Whig. Her atavistic distaste for the Tories turned to active dislike when she saw the way they intended to treat her beloved Albert.

But Albert himself was to change all this. When it came to the point, it was discovered that his own political views coincided much more closely with those of Sir Robert Peel than with the old Whigs. But this was not why he urged the Queen to abandon her early partisanship. Taught by Stockmar, he believed that a sovereign should be above party politics. Stockmar's reasoning was that the sovereign could thereby continue to influence events whichever party was in power. It was because he wished to extend his power, not reduce it, that Albert took the Olympian non-party view. By paradox, however, it was this which was to enable the British monarchy to survive when so many others went under. Even when the last vestiges of political power had, in effect, slipped through their fingers, the British royal family had – thanks to Prince Albert – established a role for themselves in national life beyond their political function as constitutional figureheads.

This is not for a moment to suggest that Albert wanted the monarchy to become politically emasculated. He made frequent efforts to interfere in the government of the realm. The earliest rebuttals he received were from Victoria herself. She refused him, in the initial stages of their marriage, permission to see any of the official State papers which came to the palace in boxes to be signed and approved.

'In my home life I am contented,' Albert confided to a boyhood friend, Prince William of Lowenstein, 'but the difficulty of filling my place with proper dignity is that I am only the husband, and not the master in the house.' The faithful Lord Melbourne thought that it was foolish of the Queen to be so cagey with the boxes. 'The Queen has not started on a right principle – she should by degrees impart everything to him, but there is a danger in his wishing it all at once.' In fact, Victoria did consent to allow Albert to handle some of the State papers during her first confinement barely nine months after their marriage and, in the event of her death and the survival of an infant king or queen, it was agreed that Albert should be the Prince Regent.

Little by little, Victoria learnt to rely on Albert's political judgement. For example, her violent hostility to the Tories became modified and she came to share his admiration for Sir Robert Peel. The principle of the sovereign being above party rivalry began to develop.

Naturally, given his birth and origins, Albert took a keener interest in foreign affairs than Victoria did at first, and it was usually in this area that he clashed with the politicians. Palmerston was his greatest sparring partner, and there were some embarrassingly public differences between the Foreign Secretary and the Prince Consort. For example, by the end of 1846 the Portuguese were in a state of virtual civil war. The clash was between the ultra-reactionary royal family, whose Queen Donna Maria was being, as Victoria put it, 'as foolish as ever' and a revolutionary military junta. Albert was anxious that there should be a commonsense constitutional solution, with concessions made by the Queen to the demands of the libertarians. A representative was sent in the person of one Colonel Wylde to see if there was any possibility of compromise. Wylde was sent by the Government but Albert felt that he was very much the representative of the royal family, and it infuriated him to learn that, while Wylde's private negotiations were in progress in Lisbon, Palmerston was openly instructing the British diplomats in Lisbon to support the rebels. 'The Queen of Portugal had told Wylde that the belief that England wished well to the cause of the rebels was one of the chief causes of their strength,' wrote the furiously sensible twenty-six-year-old Albert to the cheerfully belligerent sexagenarian Palmerston.

Both Victoria and Albert profoundly disliked the cynicism with which, after the 1848 revolutions in Europe, Palmerston was prepared to treat with the enemies of monarchy. When Louis Philippe was thrown off his throne in France, for example, the Queen was scandalised that Palmerston could write to her, in his bluff way, that the adventures of the royal refugees were 'like one of Walter Scott's best tales'. (Like many girls of her generation, Victoria had a passion for Scott.) Similarly, when the King of Sardinia led an army of liberation against the Austrians, the British Crown and the British Foreign Office were once more at variance. Britain, urged Albert, by which he meant himself and his wife, could not endure the creation of an independent Italian state.

But – this is where the Darwinian powers of survival by the Victoria and Albert team show themselves so strongly – they did, of course tolerate something which was totally contrary to their original wishes. In

a similar way, having expressed horror at the expulsion of Louis
Philippe, they were perfectly happy to befriend Napoleon III and to
accord him full imperial honours. Consistency is the enemy of survival in
political life. Albert showed the powers of adaptation which (as Darwin
was demonstrating with the lower species of the Galapagos islands) is
the essential ingredient in ensuring genetic success. Figures like Queen
Donna Maria of Portugal were well on their way to becoming political
dinosaurs.

One sees this most glaringly in the most exciting of Palmerston's political adventures. Throughout his career, Palmerston had been a famous
advocate of gun-boat diplomacy. Never send an ambassador if a
destroyer will do the job, seemed to be his approach. When trouble blew
up in the Black Sea, and the Russians occupied Balkan territories which
by right belonged to the Ottoman Turks, there was an international
outcry. The Cabinet in London was in general in favour of finding some

"DANGEROUS!"

This Punch *cartoon of 7 January 1854 makes play with Albert's
known love of skating and shows the suspicion with which his
desire to intervene in foreign affairs was regarded.*

peaceable solution to the problem. However, egged on by Palmerston, the Prime Minister of the day, Lord Aberdeen, prepared for the British Fleet to enter the Black Sea. They did so without consulting the Queen, who was on holiday at Balmoral. Albert was furious. He wrote to the Cabinet that it was 'morally and constitutionally wrong' for the Cabinet to act without consulting the Sovereign. 'We ought to be quite sure', he wrote that 'they do not drive at war while we aim at peace.'

But war fever and anti-Russian feeling swept the country. The news that Albert was opposed to the war was carefully leaked to the Press by his political enemies – very likely by Palmerston himself. By the end of 1853, the papers were full of suggestions that Albert was a pro-Russian. The *Daily News* complained that 'The nation distrusts the politics, however much they may admire the taste, of a Prince who had breathed from childhood the air of courts tainted by the imaginative servility of Goethe.' *Punch* carried a cartoon of the Prince nervously skating by a board labelled 'Foreign Affairs, very dangerous'. (The point of the drawing was that Albert was a keen skater, who helped to popularise the sport in England.)

But it is entirely typical of this adaptable monarchical species that Albert, far from maintaining an anti-war line, became, once the Crimean hostilities had broken out, a keen patriot.

Moreover, the war became a magnificent excuse for him to exercise his uncontrollable urge to suggest reforms and reorganisations of inefficient British institutions. None was worse organised than the Army itself. He had a chance to see this at first hand by observing the antics of his own regiment, the Eleventh, or Prince Albert's Own Hussars – better known in history as the Light Brigade. Lord Cardigan, who had bought his command of the regiment for £40,000, had transformed, at huge personal cost to himself, the Hussar blue of the uniform to crimson, the colour of the Saxe-Coburg livery; the motto of the regiment was changed to Prince Albert's own – *Treu und Fest*.

Not all Albert's attempted Army reforms were particularly happy. *Punch* described his own design for new helmets for infantrymen as 'a cross between a muff, a coalscuttle, and a slop pail'.

Albert watched the spectacle of the Crimean War with a mixture of excitement and horror. Sixteen thousand British troops died of dysentery and disease before a single shot was fired. By the time the Russians had withdrawn from the disputed territories in the Balkans, there was no reasonable ground for the war to continue. But the newspapers at home were crying for blood. They wanted their army to 'lick the Russians'. The Prince was gravely suspicious of the Press. He had suffered enough at their hands, and he felt that far too much about the war was let out by the gossips who masqueraded as 'war correspondents'. 'The pen and ink of one miserable scribbler', he wrote, 'is despoiling the country of all the advantages which the hearts blood of 20,000 of its noblest sons should have earned.'

Both he and the Queen were profoundly impressed by the work of Florence Nightingale at Scutari. 'Such a head!' said Victoria when she heard of the organisational skills of the Lady with the Lamp. 'I wish we had her at the War Office.'

Perhaps the most famous moment in the war, however, occurred when, as a result of misheard misdirections, the Noble Six Hundred of the Light Brigade charged to their deaths, the inevitable victims of the Russian guns. Tennyson's famous lyric sanctified the blunder:

Honour the charge they made! . . . Noble six hundred! . . .

Prince Albert's Colonelcy-in-Chief of the regiment helped to dignify it.

At Deene Park in Northamptonshire, the seat of Lord Cardigan, there hangs a famous picture which depicts Lord Cardigan at Windsor Castle explaining the Charge to Prince Albert and his family. It is a strange icon, which speaks volumes. On the one hand we observe that Cardigan, who was a bad man and a bad soldier, has been transformed into a military hero. He had returned to England after the Crimea to the strains of 'See the Conquering Hero comes!' And already, by the time this picture was painted, all over Britain, streets and squares and villas were being named after him. So it is that we find Prince Albert by his side – and with him, the royal children. But there is one very noticeable absentee from the canvas – someone we should expect to have been beside Prince Albert's side when the heroic story of Balaclava and the Light Brigade was related: Queen Victoria herself. The apocryphal story, which I rather like, is that the Queen was in the original painting but that she had herself painted out when she discovered the profligacy of Lord Cardigan's lifestyle: that Deene had for years been the scene of wild parties, attended by London prostitutes, and that Cardigan himself had for years openly lived with a woman half his age before making her his second bride.

As the *Punch* critic was supposed to have remarked when attending Shakespeare's *Antony and Cleopatra*, 'How unlike the homelife of our own dear Queen.'

Albert, from the moment he arrived in this country, brought with him an atmosphere of respectability and 'family values' which – like his political views – owe far more to Baron Stockmar than to his own dissolute parents. It may be that both Albert and Victoria were consciously repelled by 'aristocratic' dissipation because of the lifestyles of their parents and uncles. It may be that their reaction against all 'that kind of thing' was instinctive, each generation naturally behaving differently from its parents.

Albert was a keen huntsman and showed courage in the saddle which impressed his early hosts in England who had not expected him to be equal to riding to hounds in the Quorn hunt. He is pictured here with his beagles.

Deene Park is a good place to reflect on that fact. Cardigan had been one of the first English noblemen to welcome Albert to England and the Queen and Prince Consort had visited Deene Park in the very early days of their married life. The Queen was acutely conscious of the fact that the English aristocracy wanted to put Albert to the test, and one obvious way of discovering the man's mettle was to see whether he was brave enough to hunt.

He followed the Belvoir Hunt in 1843 at a meet when the going was so rough that even his secretary, George Anson, fell off. 'Albert's riding so well and so boldly, and so hard has made such a sensation that it has been written all over the country,' said the Queen in an enthusiastic letter to Uncle Leopold. It was true. Whatever else he was, the man was no milk-sop. 'It has put an end to all sneering for the future about Albert's riding.'

But unlike her father, and all her royal uncles, Victoria was never to move freely among the aristocracy, nor to belong to any fast set. Both lonely in childhood, both naturally demure, both passionately fond of one another, Victoria and Albert wanted to be homemakers rather than guests in the great houses of England.

Albert was a punctilious administrator, and he soon set to work reorganising the royal households. He thoroughly overhauled the chaotic administration of Buckingham Palace. At Windsor Castle, which had lately been refurbished by George IV, Albert made a true home, adorning the walls with paintings which he had discovered in the vaults of Hampton Court, and with modern masterpieces by his favourite painters Landseer and Winterhalter. At Windsor, too, he experimented in the establishment of a model village on the estate, and a dairy was set up according to his own plans and run according to his own specifications. Back at the Castle, he could watch his children grow, and indulge his inherent love of family which, throughout his own childhood, had been so much frustrated. It was he who, in 1840, first popularised Christmas trees here. If it was Charles Dickens who might be said to have invented the English Christmas three years earlier in *The Pickwick Papers*, it was surely Prince Albert who gave the English Christmas some of its more distinctive features.

But tireless as he was at making sure that Windsor and Buckingham Palace were organised as befitted royal residences, Albert was really always hankering after a *schloss* on the German pattern. He had enormously enjoyed his time spent in childhood among the quiet simplicities of Schloss Rosenau, a neo-Gothic country retreat, near Coburg, the place where for five brief years – before she was banished – Albert had known the company of his mother. It was the atmosphere of the Rosenau which he and Victoria wished to recreate for themselves in their two family residences in Scotland and in the Isle of Wight.

As lovers of late Romantic art and literature – the poetry of Sir Walter Scott, the paintings of Landseer, the music of Mendelssohn – it is no sur-

The royal family at Balmoral, 29 September 1855. Left to right, Prince Alfred, Prince Frederick William of Prussia, Princess Alice, the Prince of Wales, Queen Victoria, Prince Albert, the Princess Royal (Vicky) who on this day became engaged to Frederick William (Fritz), the first of the great dynastic matches forged by Queen Victoria.

prise that Victoria and Albert should have fallen in love with the Highlands of Scotland. Their initial intention was to find or build a Highland home on the West Coast. But although they were in raptures at the beauty of Argyll – of the Crinan canal in particular and the seaviews of the Hebrides – they concluded that the west was too wet and too fly-blown. After several delightful visits to Scotland they finally, in 1848, alighted upon Deeside, one of the driest and sandiest parts of the north-east. Balmoral Castle had been rebuilt in the 1830s by Sir Robert Gordon in the Scottish Baronial manner. Victoria and Albert greatly added to it. A ballroom, where they could both learn to dance reels, was to be one of the necessities of life here: as well as dozens of extra rooms where guests, relations, and even members of the Government could be accommodated.

The royal link with Deeside continues to this day unabated. It was not merely the hunting, the painting in water-colours, the invigorating walks, the peace which the Queen and the Prince Consort enjoyed when they came to Balmoral. That, after all, could have been had in Wales or Yorkshire. As the yards of tartan carpets in Balmoral testify, the Queen and Prince Albert actually wanted to be Scottish. They wanted to dance reels, to wear the tartan, to attend the Kirk – thereby causing considerable offence to those members of the Church of England who took seriously her titular headship of that body – to hear the pipes played in the heather, and to sing old Scottish airs. Balmorality, as it came to be known, had an enormous effect on nineteenth-century taste.

Not on aristocratic taste, so much as on that of the middle and the lower middle classes. The Scottish Baronial style crops up in the unlikeliest settings. Purely suburban places like Great Malvern and Leamington Spa can boast their turreted middle-class versions of Balmoral. Even the thistle-festooned pubs and tartan biscuit tins which became a part of any Victorian man and woman's life owe their existence to Prince Albert's Deeside dreams.

The Scottish theme is carried on, too, in one of the most distinctive domestic interiors in the South of England – in the Horn Room of Osborne House on the Isle of Wight. This was Victoria and Albert's English country retreat, and once again, as you look about Osborne, you see how it is merely a big version of a style of house which might have accommodated not a duke or an earl but perhaps a doctor or a bank manager. Osborne was paid for by the sale of the Brighton Pavilion.

Victoria had refused to use her uncle's seaside fantasy house as her country residence. Ostensibly, there were good reasons for this. The Pavilion was on a public road, and there had been attempts on her life. More deep seated reasons must have had to do with her feeling about her uncles. The Chinoiserie and exotic interiors of the Brighton Pavilion had been the backcloth for a lifestyle which Victoria and Albert would assiduously avoid imitating.

Osborne was very dear to them both. When she purchased the estate in 1845, the Queen wrote to her Uncle Leopold: 'It sounds so snug and nice to have a place of one's own, quiet and retired.' That is what it felt like – a place of her own. She who ruled over the British Empire wrote with all the eagerness of a young wife whose husband – a bank clerk, perhaps, or a jobber on the Stock Exchange – having been compelled to share their early days with relations, had at last found an independent abode in the suburbs.

It was fitting that the Queen was to die here – for she had spent many of her happiest hours at Osborne. Her very accomplished water-colours of the place breathe lightness and happiness. The bright splash of the 'Hay Harvest at Barton Farm' – on the Osborne estate – is captured with all the colours in the royal paint-box. The seaviews of the Solent could be used for a holiday poster. How could she be anything but happy on the Isle of Wight? For this is where she came to be with her family, and it was very much the creation of Prince Albert.

Osborne reflected Albert's good taste and modernity. Since, for many years, Victoria lived there as a widow, we need to discount her additions to the place if we are to catch a glimpse of Albert's original conception. Clutter, which she loved so much as an older woman, did not fill the rooms as Albert conceived them. The beautiful corridor, leading to the Audience Chamber, houses his collection of fine sculpture. At the same time, the clear, stately interiors planned by this Enlightenment Prince, contain jarring surprises, explicable in terms of his homesick childish self which he never outgrew. The chandelier in the Audience Chamber, florid with glass convolvulus, exactly echoes the motif of the bedroom in the Schloss Rosenau where his mother gave birth to him. And the spectacularly hideous Horn Room, in which every single item of furniture – sofas, tables, lamp brackets – is made from antlers, would be more in place in some German hunting lodge than in the house of a modern British prince. The imperial exotica which Victoria added in her

LEFT The Horn Room at Osborne. All the furniture, lamp fittings and other features are made out of antlers and horns, as in some German hunting-lodge. Some of the more aesthetically surprising interiors reflect Albert's profound nostalgia for his German childhood.

RIGHT Osborne House on the Isle of Wight, designed to Prince Albert's specifications. Its Italianate style reflects Albert's love of the Renaissance.

widowhood – in particular, the splendid Durbar Room, which feels like the state apartments of an Indian nabob – ironically suggest a throwback to her uncle the Prince Regent's love of the oriental. One wonders whether Albert would have liked it.

When Osborne was still a dream in his mind, Albert planned out every bit of the place. He discarded all the architect's plans for the conversion of the original house and chose a master builder – Thomas Cubitt who had lately impressed him by his grand reconstructions of Belgravia, not far from Buckingham Palace. He planned the towers, the asymmetrical skyline, the bow windows with their superb views of the sea. He also planned that the place should have every modern comfort. Most unusually for the 1840s, Osborne had hot running water in the bathrooms. The Prince Consort's bath is presided over by two vast naked figures – is the man Albert or is it Hercules? The nudes which look down from the walls of Osborne with such uninhibited voluptuousness reflect the early married happiness of the royal pair.

If their parents had been strange and remote, Victoria and Albert took a close interest in the lives of their own children from an early age. Prince Albert appears at his most attractive as the young father of young children. When he had died, Victoria remembered for example how 'If he was not ready, Baby [Princess Beatrice] generally went into his dressing room and stopped with him until he followed with her at his hand

coming along the passage with his dear heavenly face. . . . Poor darling
little Beatrice used to be so delighted to see him dress and when she
arrived and he was dressed she made dearest Albert laugh so, by saying,
"What a pity!".'

Stockmar's nursery prodigy from the Schloss Rosenau became, very
easily and happily, the president of the nursery at Osborne. It is nowadays taken for granted, not only by the British public but by a much
wider public in the world at large, that the royal family is a sort of
emblem of family happiness, a picture of what it should be like in all well-
conducted households. If this is so, it is the legacy of Prince Albert. No
one held up the Prince Regent or George III as ideal fathers. Most
British monarchs have had private lives which did not bear too close a
scrutiny.

*A royal group on the terrace at Osborne. From the first, Albert planned
Osborne as a family house, where his children could grow up with the
wholesome influence which had been largely lacking in his own childhood.*

There is a paradox here with which the modern royal family is still
living. It is frequently insisted upon that they have a private life which
deserves to be respected. True enough – and all persons of good taste are
offended when stories, usually untrue or wildly exaggerated, about the
marriages and love lives of the royal family become the subject for
splashy headlines in the newspapers. But the matter is complicated by
the fact that, on one level, it is for their private lives that we now value the
royal family. Royal weddings, which used to happen in private, are now
big public events. Royal films give us tantalising glimpses of life behind
the scenes at Balmoral or Windsor.

Such phrases as 'The Royal Soap Opera' reflect the actual function
which the royal family occupies in the imagination, as well as in the
newspapers, of the world. This is very much the legacy of Prince Albert,
who longed to be a king, and a great political figure, but provided the
British people instead with an image of family life.

This, incidentally, explains – I think – why so many British people feel comfortable with a matriarchal ruler. Their favourite monarchs – certainly their most long-lasting ones – have been women: two Elizabeths and Victoria. As for politicians – well, in the history of female politicians, it is early days. . . .

Strange psychosexually determined prejudices underlie our attitudes to the archetypal family-projection which the British have set up in Buckingham Palace. Instinct appears to tell many people that it is right and proper to have a Queen. But where does that leave the male members of the royal family? In asking this question, we are not merely asking what is the function of princes, but what is the function of males. When they have done their work as studs, and supplied the world with the next generation, is there not an element of pathos about most men as they sink into middle age? Few of them do 'work' which really needs doing. Are all the great schemes promoted by royal men – the concern for good causes, the sporting life, the interests in art and science – just a glorified version of Dad and his hobbies? The royal equivalent of the pigeon hutch at the end of the back yard?

If so, Prince Albert led the way with some very distinguished pigeon hutches indeed. The most splendid of them all was the Crystal Palace, the site of the Great Exhibition in Hyde Park in 1851. The idea originated with Henry Cole, a leading light of the Society of Arts, of which Prince Albert was the patron. Cole had visited the Paris Exhibition of 1849, and fired Prince Albert with the idea that London could go one better – hold a vast international exhibition, displaying all the best achievements of modern art, science and technology, and at the same time advertising British supremacy and boosting British trade. Launching the appeal for subscriptions to pay for the exhibition, Prince Albert said, 'The distances which separated the nations are rapidly vanishing before the achievements of modern invention, and we can traverse them with incredible ease. . . . The publicity of the present day causes that no sooner is a discovery made than it is already improved upon and surpassed by competing efforts. The products of all quarters of the globe are placed at our disposal and we have only to choose which is best and cheapest for our purposes and the powers of production are intrusted [*sic*] to the stimulus of *competition and capital*.' (His italics.) He could have been a modern Prince speaking of the competition from Japanese technology in the age of the micro-chip.

London had never seen anything like the Great Exhibition of 1851. There were 13,937 exhibitors – 6556 of them foreign, the rest British. There were over 100,000 exhibits, and all housed in the vast, airy spaces of what came to be called the Crystal Palace, a huge glass construction, designed by Joseph Paxton with many hints from Prince Albert himself. Everyone remembers the crisis when the birds inhabiting the elm trees of Hyde Park encased within the glass began to cause havoc to the exhibits below. What could be done? The Queen consulted the aged Duke of Wellington, who knew the answer to everything. 'Sparrowhawks, ma'am', was his solution.

But it is sometimes easy for us to forget the extraordinary visual and emotional impact of the Crystal Palace. Now the name just refers to a football team, for the reason that after the exhibition, the Palace was reconstructed in the suburbs of South London on Sydenham Hill. The local team took its name from the Palace which was destroyed by fire in 1936. Now that it's no longer visible, we easily forget how magnificent it was. Queen Victoria recorded, 'The sight as we came to the centre where the steps and chair was [sic] placed, facing the beautiful fountain was magic and impressive. The tremendous cheering, the joy expressed in every face, the vastness of the building, with all its decorations and exhibits, the sound of the organ (with 200 instruments and voices, which seemed nothing) and my beloved husband, the creator of this peace festival "uniting the art and industry of all nations of the earth", all this was moving, and a day to live forever. God bless my dear Albert, and my dear country, which has shown itself so great today.'

On the day it was opened, 700,000 people lined the route from Buckingham Palace to Hyde Park. Over 30,000 got inside the Crystal Palace to see magnificent achievements of art and science – the statue of the Queen made out of zinc, the group of stuffed frogs, one of them holding up an umbrella, the patent pulpit fitted with gutta-percha tubes to the pews of the deaf, or the doctor's walking stick which contained an enema. Charles Kingsley, author of *The Water Babies*, wept when he stepped over the threshold to see so united a display of human ingenuity. So did the Prime Minister, Lord John Russell, and the Home Secretary. And, when it was all over, nobody wept to discover that the Royal Commissioners who had patronised the exhibition had made a profit of £180,000, which Albert could use to erect a permanent exhibition-centre in South Kensington.

The Great Exhibition of 1851 was one of Prince Albert's finest achievements.
The exhibition was housed in the Crystal Palace, the first prefabricated building in history,
and was the brainchild of Joseph Paxton who had designed the glasshouses at Chatsworth.

He wanted his Albertopolis, as it came to be known, to be a vast structure with four institutions devoted to raw materials, machinery, manufacture, and the plastic arts. Modern industry should be shown to be as important as Geology and Zoology, which both had societies in London patronised by royalty. In the event, the Albertopolis did not quite get off the ground in the form that the Prince wished, but the South Kensington museums – particularly the V and A – survive as a permanent reminder of his patronage of the arts and sciences.

His artistic taste is interesting. We tend to associate him exclusively with the glossy, tranquil canvases of Winterhalter, and the set-piece doggy or hunting scenes of Landseer. Certainly these represent one side of Albert's nature. But the paintings which he actually bought with his own money reveal a broader range of sympathies than that. There is comedy (inextricably connected in our minds with Dickens whose novels he illustrated) in George Cruikshank's *Disturbing the Congregation*, bought by the Prince in 1850. There is the stagey but decidedly erotic passion of Augustus Egg's *L'Amante*, which Albert hung in his dressing-room at Windsor. Most striking of all, perhaps, is Albert's taste for the work of John Martin, the visionary landscape painter whose *Eve of the Deluge* Albert purchased in 1840.

But it would be paradoxical not to recognise the German-born Winterhalter as the Prince's great *trouvail* and creation. As so often happens with the relationship between an artist and a painter, Albert himself became Winterhalter's greatest work, whether as the paterfamilias, surrounded by adoring and adorable children who appear to have been moulded – like something in the Brothers Grimm – out of candy or coloured marzipan, or as the serious, slightly tubby, slightly balding uniformed statesman, arrayed in the uniform of the Colonel of the Rifle Brigade.

In Winterhalter's most revealing royal canvas – *The First of May 1851* – we see Albert's creation, the Crystal Palace, in the background. But the foreground is uneasily reminiscent of the iconography of Christian art. The subject is notionally the Duke of Wellington who is kneeling to present a gift to his godson and namesake Prince Arthur (later to become the Duke of Connaught). The baby holds out to the grand old soldier a bunch of lilies of the valley, emblems – like the Palace in the background of the picture – of universal peace. Anyone who has ever visited a picture gallery cannot fail to be reminded of an Adoration of the Magi by one of the Italian masters. No wonder Albert looks, somewhat pensively, out of the canvas and away from the Mother and Child. For what part does St Joseph have in such a scene, except to stand politely, or reverently, in the background? Winterhalter did not wish us to identify the infant Prince Arthur with the Incarnate. But he was making a rather wistful point about Prince Albert himself.

What was his role to be, as the children grew up? Like many parents who are besottedly fond of their children as young infants, Albert rather

A sketch of Prince Albert by the German artist, Franz Winterhalter.

resented their reaching maturity; and he and the Queen had, in particular, an abhorrence of the Prince of Wales growing up like any normal young man. There was so much 'bad blood' in the family. They so desperately did not wish their first-born son to take after the dissolute bulldog Duke Ernest of Saxe-Coburg, or after any of Victoria's fat, lecherous, greedy old Hanoverian uncles. The programme drawn up by Prince Albert for the instruction of the Prince of Wales was dauntingly worthy. This was how the young Prince had to divide his day when he was seven years old.

RELIGION	half an hour at a stretch
ENGLISH	one hour
WRITING	half an hour
FRENCH	one hour
MUSIC	half an hour
CALCULATING	half an hour
GERMAN	one hour
DRAWING	half an hour
GEOGRAPHY	half an hour

No wonder, by the time that he grew up, that 'Bertie', as they called the boy, was determined to stretch his wings and enjoy himself. Unlike his father he was not clever, and he did not enjoy his enforced attendance at the Universities. They tried sending him to Oxford which he did not like. Then they tried sending him to Cambridge, which he liked even less. This was an embarrassment to Albert who had allowed himself to stand for election as the Chancellor of Cambridge University, and who took his position there extremely seriously.

The more they watched him grow, the more the Prince of Wales appeared to his parents like a reproachful throwback to the bad old days. Prince Albert's elaborate programme of education seemed to have no discernibly beneficial effects whatsoever on the young man. Unsure what to do with him next, they packed him off (like so many royal princes after him) to do a stint in the Army.

In the summer of 1861 Lord Torrington, 'that arch gossip of all gossips' as he was called by the Prince Consort, brought to Albert's attention what was being said in the London clubs. The Prince of Wales had, it seemed, formed a liaison with . . . an actress! What was more, he had brought her over . . . to Windsor Castle itself!

Albert was the father of nine children and, as the Queen's journals make abundantly clear, the royal pair continued to enjoy conjugal relations to the end. At the time when the Prince of Wales's liaison with the actress, Nellie Clifden, was uncovered, Albert was only forty-two years old. And yet he wrote to his son in terms which would have seemed prissy coming from a maiden aunt of seventy-five. The strongest passion of Albert's life, one feels on reading this letter, was a passion for respectability. Why should he have felt that royal families must be respectable? They never had been before. But the spectre of Prince Albert's puritanism has hovered over them ever since. It was Albert, through old Queen Mary and Stanley Baldwin, who put paid to Mrs Simpson's chances of becoming Queen of England. To George IV, she might have seemed an admirable bride. It was surely Albert's ghost who made it impossible for Princess Margaret to marry Group-Captain Townsend, at a period when large numbers of 'respectable' people did in fact condone divorce. It is surely the puritanical shade of Prince Albert who inspires the prurient and vulgar gutter-press of today in their constant vigilance to guard the moral standards of the royal house.

Bertie, his father wrote, might try to deny any association with Nellie Clifden:

'If you were to try to deny it, she can drag you into a Court of Law to force you to own it and there with you (the Prince of Wales) in the witness box, she will be able to give before a greedy multitude disgusting details of your profligacy for the sake of convincing the Jury, yourself cross-examined by a railing indecent attorney and hooted and yelled at by a Lawless Mob!! Oh horrible prospect, which this person has in her power, any day to realise! and to break your poor parents' hearts!

It is an extraordinary letter to have penned to an officer in the Grenadier Guards, as Bertie was at the time. Probably there was not a fellow officer in his entire mess who had not from time to time had some association with the likes of Nellie Clifden, and the idea of anyone being shocked by it is the purest Pooterism.

It was a sign of Albert's failing powers that he wrote in quite such immoderate terms. There is no doubt that the Prince Consort was under stress. In the spring of that year he had had to cope with Victoria's excessive grief on the death of her mother, the Duchess of Kent. His tireless overwork, his neuralgia, and his toothache had all helped to age him prematurely. The Adonis of Landseer's early canvases had been cruelly transformed by the passage of years into the paunchy balding figure of the photographs and the last Winterhalter renderings.

But it was not overwork which killed Prince Albert. Like so many of his wife's subjects, he was killed by typhoid, probably bred in the drains of Windsor Castle. It is astonishing to us, who are aware of the dangers of typhoid, cholera, polio and the like, to see how long it took our ancestors to guess the connection between water-supplies and disease. Prince Albert had encouraged Sir Edwin Chadwick in his life-work of providing England with proper drains. He did not realise that from the point of view of sanitation, Windsor Castle was as dangerous as a slum in one of the northern cities. His already overstrained constitution gave in to the fever, but its early symptoms went unrecognised. Albert was too busy. His preoccupation with his son's moral welfare, and his concern for the administration of government policies – Army reform, a crisis in British relations with the United States – continued unabated. But suddenly there entered in a new and premonitory note of resignation. 'I do not cling to life,' he had once said to the Queen. 'You do, but I set no store by it. I am sure if I had a severe illness I should give up at once, I should not struggle for life.' Isn't this a strange thing for a man hardly in early middle age to say to his wife? It surely reveals unhappiness, a sense that for all his business, his organising skills, his so-called 'interests' in art, music, the state of industry, he really felt his life to be totally pointless.

On 22 November 1861, Albert inspected the newly-opened Staff College and Royal Military Academy at Sandhurst, and took the opportunity to give a further dressing down to the Prince of Wales. It was a pouring wet day and Albert returned to Windsor drenched and feverish.

Anxiety about the American situation seemed to make his condition worse. The Civil War there had been going on for nearly a year. The Northern States had seized a British ship, the *Trent*, on the high seas and arrested two Confederate diplomats who were travelling under British protection. This act of aggression was just the kind of thing which delighted Lord Palmerston, the Prime Minister, and arrangements were made to withdraw the British Ambassador from Washington. Albert, shivering on his bed of sickness, was appalled by the intemperance of the diplomatic despatches and did in fact intervene. He couldn't eat. He was hardly strong enough to hold a pen. But he insisted on toning down the despatches sent by Palmerston and Lord John Russell and to withdraw Great Britain from the very brink of war with the Northern States. It was his last political piece of interference, but it was very effective.

It was against this background that Palmerston's medical advice to his sovereign must be seen. The Queen, and both her doctors, Sir James Clark and William Jenner, insisted that Albert was suffering from no more than a feverish cold. When the Prime Minister urged Victoria to take another doctor's opinion, she rejected his proposal as mere impertinence. On 3 December she wrote, 'Dreadfully annoyed at a letter from Lord Palmerston suggesting Dr Ferguson should be called in as he heard Albert could not sleep and eat. Very angry about it. In an agony of despair about my dearest Albert and crying much, for saw no improvement and my dearest Albert was so listless and took so little notice. Good kind old Sir James . . . reassured me and explained to Dr Jenner too that there was no cause whatever for alarm.'

As the illness progressed, Albert's diarrhoea got a little better, but his temper worse. Although still calling her Weibchen (little wife) he started to display violent anger against her. 'He is so kind calling me gutes Weibchen [excellent little wife] and liking me to hold his dear hand.' Nevertheless, if he felt that she was bossing him, he lost his temper again. It is surely not fanciful to see in these outbursts of rage a crucial element in their whole relationship, and indeed in Albert's life. He was a frustrated man, a man whose cleverness and talents were all made subservient to his rather absurd role as the Queen's toy man. With a part of himself, he must have hated being Prince Consort, and hated his wife for forcing him into this ignominious role. Perhaps if he had not hated either, with a part of himself, he would not have been so eager to lay down the burden of life. No wonder, when he died, that her happiest relationships were with male servants. They obsequiously provided what Albert was not temperamentally equipped to give.

By the middle of December, the Queen at last began to realise what was happening. On the morning of Friday 13 December, she found him awake, with blank, staring eyes, and his breath coming in shallow gasps. When the Prince of Wales arrived, summoned from Cambridge by his sister Princess Alice, he found his father almost dead and his mother

Queen Victoria is pictured here perusing State papers in 1893. Her beloved friend the Munshi stands in attendance. He was an adviser in whom she reposed absolute confidence, even though he was subsequently unmasked as a fraud.

distraught. 'I prayed and cried as if I should go mad,' the Queen confided in one of her ladies in waiting.

Albert's symptoms were too obvious to ignore – a brown tongue, shivering fits, extreme weakness, diarrhoea. This did not prevent Dr Watson, the specialist sent in at Palmerston's insistence, from telling Victoria that 'I never despair with fever.'

The next day, 14 December, Dr Brown, another of the Prince's medical advisers, woke her at 6 am with the good news: 'I've no hesitation in saying . . . that I think there is ground to hope the crisis is over.'

An hour later, the Queen entered the Blue Room to find Albert awake, his eyes unusually bright and staring. In the course of the morning, Albert was got out of bed, and wheeled out for a change of air in another room while they changed his bedding. The Queen stayed with him, though from time to time she walked out on to the terrace, but the sound of military music, playing in the distance, reduced her to tears. She noticed that Albert's face had a 'dusky hue'.

Gradually, throughout the day, a succession of visitors trooped through the Blue Room. The Queen was afraid that it would agitate the patient to see Bertie, but the Prince of Wales, followed by the other children, all came in to take their leave. Their father was too weak to say anything to them. The Keeper of the Privy Purse came, and the Master of the Household.

When, yet again, they had to change his bedding, the Queen went next door and lay down, exhausted. Then she heard heavy breathing from the Blue Room, and ran back in. 'Es ist die kleine Frauchen,' she said – it is your little wife. She asked him for 'ein Kuss' and with her hands she moved his head so that he could kiss her. Then, in anguish, she ran from the room again.

The agony was lingered out a little more, as with almost instinctive formality, the royal household gathered around the bed: Princess Alice and the Prince of Wales kneeling. Princess Helena was there, Dean Wellesley and General Bruce. The gentlemen of the household stood in the corridor. The next time the Queen entered the room, the obvious fact, which she had not quite been able to face until then, dawned on her with hideous clarity. 'Oh, this is death,' she murmured. 'I know this, I have seen it before.'

'Two or three long but perfectly gentle breaths were drawn, the hand clasping mine, & (oh! it turns me sick to write it) *all all* was over. . . . I stood up, kissing his dear heavenly forehead & called out in a bitter agonising cry, ''Oh my dear Darling!'' & then dropped on my knees in mute, distracted despair, unable to utter a word or shed a tear.'

Victoria's life was shattered by the removal of Albert from the scene. She was only forty-two years old, and her reign had another forty years to run. There can be no doubt that, on her side at least, the marriage had been a passionate love affair. In Albert, she lost her lover, her friend, the father of her children, and an invaluable political adviser. It is very unlikely, for example, had Albert lived (he the great Peelite and sympathiser with many views which were to be promoted by Gladstone) that the Queen's feud with the great Liberal leader would ever have happened. It is certainly unlikely, had Albert been alive, that she would have had quite so close or so flirtatious a relationship with Disraeli. Disraeli's worldly glossiness, his grandiose forms of flattery – such as getting her to call herself the Empress of India (a name somehow better suited to a pig or a railway engine than to a person) – would presumably have had no chances of success had Albert's moderating influence been to hand.

Victoria's cult of Albert has something ghoulish about it, no doubt, but even in death, Albert managed unintentionally to be a useful projection of national fantasy. He had failed to become the modern dictatorial monarch which Stockmar and Uncle Leopold had wanted him to be. But he had become, with his essentially meritocratic views, his interest in industry, his cultivation of home virtues, the soap opera monarch of modern times. If the middle classes, and even the lower classes, could somehow identify with Albert the good, the hen-pecked family man, could they not also see that he, like so many of them, was subject to avoidable death by something so unmonarchical as the drains? These were times when in some northern towns, the average age of death was twenty-six. To us, with antibiotics and indoor toilets, the young family who has suffered the death of a child or a young parent is a tragic rarity. It happens, because we are all mortal. But it is unusual. For the Victorians, it was the norm. Though the long seclusion of the Widow Queen made her increasingly unpopular, the initial bereavement linked her to her people far more intimately than anything which she would have been able to do in her own rather haughty Hanoverian person.

It is not entirely fanciful, therefore, to see the abundance of Albert memorials which sprang up all over Britain as monuments not simply to a very remarkable man, but also to one with whom they could identify. You do not much come across the Christian name Albert among the upper classes, the upper ten thousand with whom Albert in life never had much to do. Miners, station masters and foremen were called Albert.

As the forty-year mourning proceeded, Albert became a sort of divinity to the Queen. But, as I have said, she was not without consolation. Her happiest friendship was with the Highland ghillie, John Brown, with whom she could spend days on the moors near Balmoral, or walking in the grounds of Osborne. The exact nature of their happy relationship will probably never be known. They liked drinking whisky together. Brown was one of those who got on well with royalty because he could be natural – even brusque – in the Queen's company without for a second surrendering the sense that he was her inferior, her servant. When he died, she was desolated. Her Indian servant, the Munshi, provided some substitute for Brown's company, and indeed she allowed the Munshi more confidential knowledge of her State papers and the mysterious red boxes than she had allowed to Albert. Her doctors and advisers had great difficulty in persuading her of the (regrettably true) reports that he was a con-man.

It was appropriate, then, that when she came to die, Victoria should have been placed in her coffin with mementoes not only of her children and friends, and not only of the Prince Consort, but of her beloved servant John Brown, whose photograph, if we are to believe Sir James, was put into her left hand before the coffin lid was placed over the curious collection of bric-à-brac with which she chose to be laid in Frogmore. There she lies, beside Albert, to this day.

CHARLOTTE BRONTË
1816-55

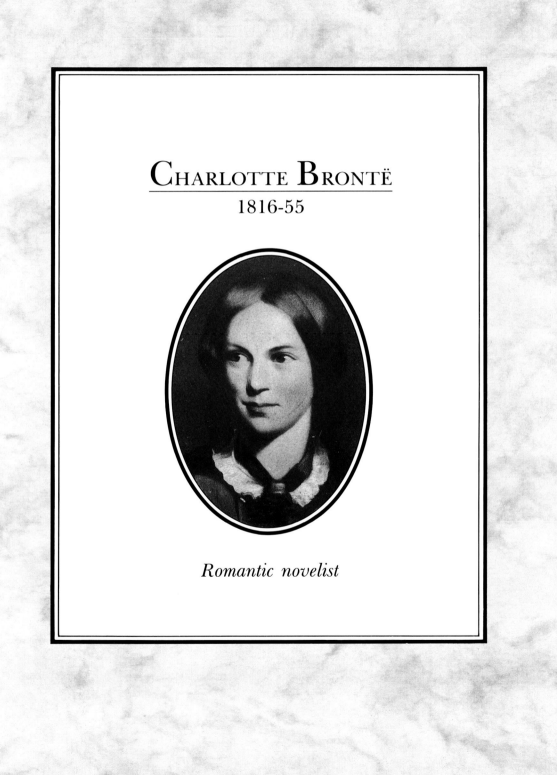

Romantic novelist

George Richmond sketched and prettified nearly every famous person of the mid-nineteenth century in England. His portrait of Charlotte Brontë was especially dear to her husband, Arthur Bell Nicholls. When he died, in 1906, his coffin rested the night beneath Richmond's portrait, as he had asked.

In 1847, Messrs Smith Elder and Co. published a novel by a new author of whom no one had heard. The author's name was Currer Bell. The book was called *Jane Eyre*. It caused an instant sensation, not least because some of the reviewers considered it so extremely wicked. Queen Victoria herself was thrilled by the novel, and recorded in her Journal:

> Finished *Jane Eyre*, which is really a wonderful book, very peculiar in parts, but so powerfully and admirably written, such a fine tone it is, such fine religious feeling, and such beautiful writings. The description of the mysterious maniac's nightly appearances awfully thrilling, Mr Rochester's character a very remarkable one, and Jane Eyre's herself a beautiful one . . .

People have been raving about *Jane Eyre* ever since. It is one of the most readable and exciting novels in the language. It is the story of how a tiny, outwardly unremarkable girl (the daughter of a clergyman) suffers the indignity of an early nineteenth-century education, the cruelty of a bad school and of insensitive religious grown-ups, the loss of dear childhood friends through death, and is rendered thereby fit only for the life of the school-ma'am or the governess. She seems to be doomed to become, like Miss Prism in *The Importance of Being Earnest*, 'a female person of repellent aspect remotely connected with education'. But then the real drama and excitement of the book begins. Jane goes as a governess to Thornfield Hall, the seat of the mysterious Mr Rochester. In spite of being a man of the world, with a little string of mistresses in his past, and the rich daughters of the local gentry wanting his hand in marriage, Rochester falls in love with 'Our Jane'. It is the ultimate fulfilment of romantic fantasy – popular novelettes, from Smith Elder and Co. to Mills and Boon in our own day, have been feeding the public ever since with fantasies of this kind.

Into *Jane Eyre*, however, there creeps a feeling of real tragedy and darkness. Queen Victoria, who doubtless responded warmly to a story in which the diminutive, plain heroine is found so alluring by the hero, was right to point to the passages where the maniac appears as the most gripping in the tale. For, as everyone knows, the mysterious Mr Rochester is not in a position to marry. Upstairs in the attic is his mad Creole wife Bertha, whom he had married for mercenary reasons before having time to discover that she was a dissolute person with madness in her blood. All the subsequent passages in the book – the destruction of Thornfield by fire, the maiming and temporary blinding of Rochester, the mysterious moment when Jane, who has run away from him, hears his voice in the winds, lifts us out of the world of novelettes – romances with a small 'r' – and into the world of Romance, as in Romantic movement, as in the paintings of John Martin, as in Goethe, as in Byron. The themes of love and death – the two being so closely linked with inescapable pain and religious awe, which the novel-reading public of the 1840s enjoyed in the work of Currer Bell – were to delight the opera-goers at the close of the century in the works of Wagner.

But who was Currer Bell? The most famous English novelist of the age, William Makepeace Thackeray, wished that he knew. He also wished that the publisher had not sent him the book: 'It interested me so much that I have lost (or won if you like) a whole day in reading it at the

The first page of Jane Eyre *in Charlotte Brontë's own handwriting. Most readers of the novel shared Queen Victoria's sense that it was 'a really wonderful' book.*

busiest period with the printers I know waiting for copy. . . . I don't know why I tell you this but I have been exceedingly moved and pleased by "Jane Eyre". It is a woman's writing, but whose? Give my respects and thanks to the author, whose novel is the first English one . . . that I've been able to read for many a day.'

William Smith Williams, Smith Elder and Co.'s reader, passed on this highly complimentary report to the unknown author. As it happened, Currer Bell was a devoted admirer of Thackeray's and asked if the second edition, published in 1848, might be dedicated to the great man, and this was done.

What an excitement that caused in the gossipy world of literary London! Currer Bell, whoever she or he was, was living in the provinces. Mr Williams corresponded with Mr Bell by writing to a post office in an obscure Yorkshire mill town. How could Currer Bell know all the London gossip about Thackeray, how he himself was married to a lunatic whom, in the most painful circumstances, he had been obliged to put away? Moreover, he was notoriously a highly susceptible man where the opposite sex were concerned, and those engaged as nurses or governesses for his two daughters were known to be capable of exciting his devotion. Before long, the rumours were flying around. *Jane Eyre* had been written by a woman who had worked as a governess in Thackeray's house, become his mistress, and been discarded.

It is a curious episode in literary history. Almost everything in *Jane Eyre* – the size and appearance of the heroine, her educational history, her hopeless love for a married man older than herself, her decision (before her reunion with Rochester) to find happiness, if at all, within the innocent circle of her own family, in running a village school, all these things were directly based on 'real life'. The only thing which was purest melodrama and fabrication was the mad wife. This one fantasy was what the knowing public seized upon as the most flagrant example of putting real life into fiction!

Currer Bell wrote in some distress to Mr Williams of Smith Elder, regretting the embarrassment which the whole episode had caused Thackeray:

It appears that his private position is in some points similar to that I have ascribed to Mr Rochester, that thence arose a report that 'Jane Eyre' had been written by a governess in his family, and that the

dedication coming now has confirmed everybody in the surmise.
. . . I am very, very sorry that my inadvertent blunder should have
made his name and affairs a subject for common gossip.

But now, another drama blew up in the life and career of the novelist
Currer Bell. Not long before, in 1846, there had been published a slim
volume entitled *Poems by Currer, Ellis and Acton Bell*. It had made no
impact whatsoever, even though, if readers had had the wit to spot the
fact, one of the poets, Ellis Bell, was a person of unique genius. The
poems had been printed by a religious publisher called Aylott and Jones.
As was often the case in the nineteenth century, the cost of publication
was borne by the author. There was therefore no loss for Aylott and
Jones when the poems failed to make any impact whatsoever. In fact,
though Currer Bell had unwisely ordered a print run of a thousand, only
two copies of the poems were sold. Amazingly, almost none of the
thousand copies survive. The volume which one can see today at the Parsonage in Haworth is a priceless bibliographical rarity. Aylott and Jones
could not foresee that, and when the Bell brothers offered them novels,
they were able to decline on the grounds that, as religious publishers,
they did not deal in anything so frivolous. But, business and principle do
not always marry, even in the most religious souls. When Smith Elder
and Co., a much cannier publisher, had accepted *Jane Eyre* Aylott and
Jones saw their chance to make a killing. They could sell the *poems* of the
three brothers by putting it about that in fact there was only one author,
masquerading as three, and that was Currer Bell, the author of *Jane Eyre*.
It was this confusion, and the same claim being made by an American
publisher, which made George Smith write to Currer Bell and insist that
'he' came clean. Smith himself was one of the great Victorian publishers.
We can now see, more clearly than a generation ago, since the
unearthing of Smith's letters, what care he took with his author, advising
against the publication of *The Professor* and encouraging, as a good editor
should, the writing of more mature novels. He was one of the first
publishers who made a figure in society, the forerunner of many a social-
climbing modern counterpart.

Wuthering Heights by Ellis Bell was published (by yet another
publisher, T. C. Newby) in the same year as *Jane Eyre* and, very surprisingly to us, it made very little impression on the public. It was re-
printed in 1850 because Smith Elder had been persuaded to take over

An extract from a letter written by Charlotte to her life-long friend, Ellen Nussey. The sketches at the foot of the letter are particularly revealing of Charlotte's rather poor image of herself as opposed to that of her more glamorous friend.

publication of 'Acton' and 'Ellis' Bell's books – Acton Bell's *Agnes Grey* had also been published by Newby in 1847 – but its great qualities seemed to have passed everyone by in the midst of the *Jane Eyre* mania which swept London in 1848.

Who on earth *were* this mysterious family? Acton, Ellis and Currer Bell were obviously some sort of pseudonym. The scandalous rumours about Thackeray and Mrs Rochester only fuelled speculations about the identity of the authors – or author. Yes, author. Wasn't it really only too probable that Acton, Ellis and Currer Bell were truly one and the same person? Matters came to a head in July 1848. *Jane Eyre* had been hugely successful in the United States, and Newby had seized the opportunity to publish Acton's second novel – *The Tenant of Wildfell Hall* – there, claiming it was an early work of Currer Bell, in order to cash in on this success. George Smith wrote a hurt letter to Currer asking if it was true that he had allowed another publisher to publish his work.

He could have no idea of the flurry and the anguish his letter was to cause his correspondent in Yorkshire. But it was prompted by under-standable anxiety. Not only did he have a business to run; but, as a publisher who had brought before the world the novel which everyone was talking about, it was only natural that he should want to be assured about its author.

A little while later, George Smith was busy at his desk one Saturday morning in the bookshop and publishing company at 65 Cornhill, London, which he ran on behalf of his father. Work was piling up, and he did not particularly welcome an interruption from his clerk who informed him that he had two visitors – ladies who had come on private business, but refused to give their names.

A little unwillingly, he asked that they should be shown into his office. 'Two rather quaintly dressed little ladies, pale-faced and anxious-looking, walked into my room.' Others who knew them have remarked on the fact that they were really very small indeed – under five feet in height. One of the ladies (we learn from other sources that she had a poor complexion, and was acutely conscious of being spotty and plain) held out a letter to George Smith, written in his own handwriting. It was addressed to 'Currer Bell Esq'.

With some sharpness, he asked, 'Where did you get this from?'

'From the post office,' was the reply. It was a striking accent. Years before, one of her school friends had been struck by her blighting timidity and her Irish brogue. But it was a Northern Irish voice, almost like a Scottish Lowland accent. She continued, reverting to the letter, 'It was addressed to me. We have both come that you might have ocular proof that there are at least two of us.'

With extraordinary excitement, and some incredulity, George Smith realised that he was in the presence of his best-selling author. She then presented herself with her real name, Charlotte Brontë. Her companion was her sister Anne.

Mr Smith immediately proposed that they should come to stay with his mother and sister in Bayswater. The shy sisters had already established themselves in a hotel near St Paul's Cathedral. Their father had taken Charlotte and Emily there before, *en route* to Belgium six years earlier. Emily had so hated the earlier journey to Belgium that thereafter she refused to leave Yorkshire; and this was the reason that Charlotte and Anne were in London without her. They excused themselves Mr Smith's kind hospitality, but they could not escape altogether. Although Charlotte was exhausted by her journey south, and by a blinding sick headache, she consented to the suggestion that Mr Smith and his partner

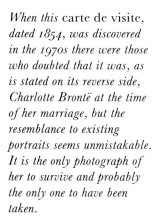

When this carte de visite, dated 1854, was discovered in the 1970s there were those who doubted that it was, as is stated on its reverse side, Charlotte Brontë at the time of her marriage, but the resemblance to existing portraits seems unmistakable. It is the only photograph of her to survive and probably the only one to have been taken.

Mr Williams – 'a pale strapping man of fifty' – should take the sisters to the Opera. Charlotte and Anne went back to the hotel to be sick, to lie down, and to take a strong dose of sal volatile. Towards evening, Messrs Smith and Williams arrived, with George Smith's mother and sister in tow, all elegantly clad in smart evening dress. The Brontë sisters had only their travelling clothes, and felt self-consciously dowdy as they were led into the splendours of the Royal Opera House. Charlotte bravely decided to 'put her headache in her pocket', and gave herself up to the excitement of the occasion. The opera – Rossini's *The Barber of Seville* – was 'very brilliant, though I fancy there are things I should like better. We got home after one o'clock; we had never been in bed the night before and had been in constant excitement for twenty-four hours. You may imagine we were tired.'

During the evening, Anne Brontë had expressed an interest in hearing the famous Dr Croly preach, so next morning, Mr Williams arrived at their hotel and took the two sisters off to Morning Prayer at the lovely Wren church of St Stephen Walbrook. Dr Croly, the rector, was not there that morning. The next item on their programme was dinner in Bayswater with the Smiths – just a family affair with Mr Smith's mother, sisters and little brother. 'We had a fine dinner which neither Anne nor I had appetite to eat, and were very glad when it was over,' Charlotte recorded. The next day was devoted to sight-seeing and shopping. They saw the National Gallery, the Royal Academy, and bought as many books as they could carry. In the course of these days, Mr Smith and Mr Williams were able to discover that Charlotte Brontë, this infinitely shy, tiny woman, was by no means a weakling. She had a strong, even forceful personality, a good sense of humour, and high intelligence. She also had, without being a flirt, the gift of sympathetic intimacy. It is apparent in the thank-you letter which she wrote to William Smith Williams, whom, having met on the Saturday, she left on the Tuesday to return to her home in Yorkshire. It is the letter of a vigorous human being who has struck up a true friendship with another human being.

> It was a somewhat hasty step to hurry up to town as we did, but I do not regret having taken it. In the first place mystery is irksome, and I was glad to shake it off with you and Mr Smith and to show myself to you for what I am, neither more nor less – thus removing any false expectations that may have arisen under the idea that Currer Bell had a just claim to the masculine cognomen he, perhaps somewhat presumptuously, adopted – that he was, in short, of the nobler sex.

This humorous, but easily intimate tone, is highly characteristic of Charlotte's letters. As well as being one of the great novelists of the nine-teenth century, she is also one of its great letter-writers. And it was in her letters that Williams began to learn some of the extraordinary circum-stances of Charlotte Brontë's life.

At this date, she was thirty-two years old, by nineteenth-century standards a spinster who was almost certain to remain an old maid for the rest of her life. And what sort of life had that been? By almost any standards, it had been quite staggeringly uneventful; and yet, as generations of readers have demonstrated, the lives of Charlotte and her sisters are, in their way, quite as fascinating as their work.

As Charlotte left London, on that hot July day in 1848, she was returning to a Yorkshire parsonage where she had lived ever since she was four. Her father, the Reverend Patrick Brontë, was a self-made man of unusual accomplishments. His birthplace in County Down, in the North of Ireland, is today a heap of stones, but one can still make out its tiny dimensions. Twelve hens, if they inhabited the space, might well feel constricted. Hugh Brunty (Patrick's father) filled the space with twelve human beings – his wife and ten children. Purely by his own wits, Patrick

Brunty emerged from this peasant background, became a schoolmaster, and eventually went to St John's College, Cambridge. People have mocked him for dandifying the ordinary name of Brunty into Brontë. The spelling is taken from one of Lord Nelson's titles, the Duke of Brontë – just such a vein of fantasy was to lead Charlotte, when a child, to people her imaginary world of Angria with the Duke of Wellington and the Marquess of Douro. But Patrick Brunty was probably the first member of his family who was able or desirous to write the name down; as a pioneer in the art of handwriting, why should he not have spelt his own name as he chose? He, and probably his children, would have continued to pronounce the name in the Irish way, *Brunty*.

It is a very important ingredient in Charlotte's emotional history that her father was purely the product of education. If it had not been possible through cleverness to rise through the ranks of society in this way, Patrick Brontë would have lived, as most of his relations did and had done, the life of an agricultural labourer. Cambridge, ordination as a clergyman in the Church of England, the eventual cure of souls which came his way at Haworth in Yorkshire – all these advantages (regardless of their social and religious significance) released him and his family to live the life of the mind, to inhabit the world of books. This was something which he had done, from the moment circumstances allowed it. The fact that he was not a good writer does not detract from the important point – that he assumed that one might want to be a writer. Those 'thoughts which wander through eternity' – the evanescent fancies of an average brain, are things which the writer (unlike the generality of people) wishes to immortalise or hold. Most people are story-tellers on some rudimentary level; most, presumably, have had some consciousness of the inner life, have fallen in love, have confronted the awfulness of nature. The unusual thing is to confront these experiences with pen in hand, and this was what Patrick Brontë had done in his pamphlets *The Cottage in the Wood: or the Art of becoming Rich and Happy* and *The Maid of Killarney*. In his own life he never displayed the art of becoming either rich or happy, but he passed on to his children the habit of getting through life by means of literature-as-drug.

He married a Cornishwoman called Maria Branwell. They had six children in fairly swift succession (Maria born 1814, Elizabeth born 1815, Charlotte born 1816, Patrick – called Branwell – 1817, Emily Jane 1818, and Anne 1820). Their mother Maria Brontë died of cancer in

Haworth Parsonage. Note the preponderance of flat, imperfectly drained tombs: the place stank habitually of the dead.

1821, the year after they had all moved to Haworth. Her sister, a some-what austere lady of Calvinistic outlook, came to live in the Parsonage to look after the motherless children.

Haworth in the first half of the nineteenth century was a semi-industrial village with a handful of mills, built on a steep gradient on the edge of the moors. When Patrick Brontë and his young family went to live there it must have been very remote. The railway had not yet been built – that would come in 1867. All the village's water supply flowed through the overcrowded graveyard, contaminating every mouthful imbibed. A report by a public health inspector in 1850 considered Haworth to be one of the least sanitary villages in England. There were no water closets in the place in the Brontës' day. Half the population died before they were six years old, and the average age of death was twenty-six.

Not only was it unhealthy. It was also a place where congenial society for a man such as Patrick Brontë would have been hard to find. There were not many reading men thereabouts, nor many churchmen. Brontë himself was only just a churchman, as far as his theology went. His wife Maria had been a Wesleyan Methodist in Cornwall, and Patrick himself, when his curate was there to substitute for him at the service in Haworth parish church, used sometimes to attend the local Methodist chapel. One of his own predecessors at Haworth parish church had been a famous friend of the Wesleys called William Grimshaw. He was noteworthy for the

William Grimshaw, a former vicar of Haworth, was a friend of Wesley's and a leading evangelical. His teapot, emblazoned with the words of St Paul, was one of the Brontës' most treasured possessions; it is preserved at the Parsonage.

manner of his dying. He left strict instructions in his will that however wild the weather, they were to carry his dead body ten miles across the moors to a place called Luddenden to be buried beside his wife. The rather ghoulish tale was a favourite of Tabitha Aykroyd, the Brontës' family servant, who was doubtless the source of that scene which was eventually, when filtered through the imagination of Emily Brontë, to become the story of Heathcliff digging up the corpse of his beloved Cathy. A teapot belonging to William Grimshaw was kept at the Parsonage (it is there today). Emblazoned with the legend, *To live is Christ, To die is Gain* – a text which however uplifting in its proper place must have been disconcerting to observe as the brown steaming fluid poured from the spout into the teacup – it was no doubt used by Aunt Branwell, and suggests something of her relentlessly theological preoccupations.

To be a churchman in such a Methodistical heartland was only one of the many things which isolated Patrick Brontë. He did loyally uphold church principles against the chapel – even though he did so with a strong sense of how attractive the chapel was. Within his own church, he was entirely unsympathetic either to the Calvinism of the Evangelical party or to the crypto-Catholicism of the Puseyites. Likewise in politics, he was in favour of moderate reform, and had supported the Reform Bill of 1831/32. But as the local representative of Church and State he had felt obliged to side with the mill-owners against the rioting workers at the time of the Luddite protests against the introduction of machinery.

When these violent bands descended on the mill towns to destroy the new mechanical looms (scenes memorably evoked in Charlotte's novel *Shirley*) it was said that Patrick Brontë had been armed with a gun, and that his own life was threatened (nevertheless he buried Luddite rioters in secret). All this was scarcely the way for a parish priest to make himself feel at home among his people. Add to this the fact that he continued to speak with a strong Ulster brogue, and that he suffered from failing eyesight, and the isolation of Patrick Brontë at Haworth becomes the more conspicuous. The small, neat Parsonage at the top of the village was destined to become an isolated imaginative world.

They were an extraordinarily close family. Strangers would observe how, in the presence of visitors, these nervous, small people would hug one another like timorous animals huddling together against predators. The children inhabited a curious imaginative world of their own creating, partly culled from their wide and miscellaneous reading and partly from dreams. Emily's imagined world was called Gondal. It appears to have been a more passionate mystical place than Charlotte's imagined kingdom of Angria (the crossness suggested by the homophone is surely revealing) which was a strange blend of fantasy about high society with erotic and emotional dreamings. Tens of thousands of words were, over the years, composed in stories and poems based on these secret kingdoms. As she grew up, Charlotte began to be suspicious of her own need to create such dreams. Her hope that she might be adored by some demonic figure like Zamorna ('his face whitened more and more, something like foam became apparent on his lip – and he knitted his brow convulsively'), a figure who had started life in her Angria tales as the Marquess of Douro, developed into more ordinary erotic fantasies about the men she actually knew. Emily, by contrast, as she grew up, inhabited a world which had less and less in common with her discernible surroundings. She became ever more inward-looking and mysterious. This difference is seen very strongly when Charlotte's very patchy, uneven achievement as a novelist, with her gossipy and frequently comic interest in human character and eccentricity, is compared with the white-hot intensity and self-contained brilliance of Emily's masterpiece, *Wuthering Heights*.

Another difference was that Charlotte's spirit was always contriving ways to escape Haworth, whereas Emily's spirit never left the place even when, as inevitably happened, she was compelled to go away to seek

In her childhood Charlotte, like her brother and sisters,
wrote many poems and stories
in tiny books like this one.

education or employment. The moorland itself is the first thing to confront us in Lockwood's difficult walk to Wuthering Heights. It is the place which gives life and freedom to the anarchic, quasi-incestuous love of Cathy and Heathcliff. It inspires much of Emily's greatest lyric poetry. Though, as has been said by her best modern biographer, Charlotte was less inclined than Emily to spend as many of her waking hours as possible outdoors, the moorland around Haworth became a perpetual and important part of her inner landscape. The almost Wordsworthian moral significance the landscape held for all the Brontës is thinly fictionalised in *Jane Eyre* when Jane seems to be on the point of settling with her cousins Diana and Mary Rivers.

They loved their sequestered home. I, too, in the grey, small, antique structure, with its low roof, its latticed casements, its mouldering walls, its avenue of aged firs – all grown aslant under the stress of mountain winds; its garden dark with yew and holly – and where no flowers but of the hardiest species would bloom – found a charm both potent and permanent. They clung to the purple moors behind and around their dwelling – to the hollow vale into which the pebbly bridlepath leading from their gate descended; and which wound between fern-banks first, and then amongst a few of the wildest little pasture-fields that ever bordered a wilderness of heath, or gave sustenance to a flock of grey moorland sheep, with their little mossy-faced lambs: they clung to this scene, I say, with a perfect enthusiasm of attachment. I could comprehend the feeling, and share both its strength and sweep – on the wild colouring communicated to ridge and dell, by moss, by heath bell, by flower-sprinkled turf, by brilliant bracken and mellow granite crag. These details were just to me what they were to them – so many pure and sweet sources of pleasure. The strong blast and the soft breeze; the rough and the halcyon day; the hours of sunrise and sunset; the moonlight and the clouded night, developed, for me, in these regions, the same attraction as for them – wound round my faculties the same spell that entranced hers.

And yet, to judge both from her fiction and her letters, Charlotte seems to have felt from the beginning that her childhood was a dream from which she would one day wake up. Her siblings never came to terms with this, and some of them, sadly, never needed to do so.

Charlotte wrote in 1835:

> *We wove a web in childhood,*
> *A web of sunny air;*
> *We dug a spring in infancy*
> *Of water pure and fair;*
>
> *We sowed in youth a mustard seed*
> *We cut an almond rod;*
> *We are grown-up to riper age –*
> *Are they withered in the sod?*

Although the poem sets out to deny any such mortality to the workings of the imagination, Charlotte shared with her siblings the knowledge that something died forever when they grew up; and since she was destined to be the last survivor of this ill-starred dynasty, she also had a painful sense of how frail was their physical hold on existence itself.

Education, which had been the making of the Brontë father, was to be
the undoing of the Brontë children. Charlotte, at the age of eight, was
sent to the Clergy Daughters' School at Cowan Bridge, near Tunstall in
Lancashire. Her sisters Maria and Elizabeth were already in residence
at this recently founded establishment, and little Emily, not seven years
old, was due to follow by the end of 1824. This school was the 'Lowood' of
Jane Eyre, a place of great physical austerity, run by an Evangelical
clergyman called the Reverend Carus Wilson, the model for Mr Brocklehurst in the novel. One can tell instantly, when reading *Jane Eyre*, that
Brocklehurst is based on a figure in real life. Just as Mr Rochester has all
the solid reality of a perfectly realised fantasy figure – he is so well-
rounded because he has become so fully what his creatrix wanted him to
be – so Brocklehurst, like a photograph not quite in focus, comes before

Cowan Bridge School was the model for Lowood in Jane Eyre, *where the conditions were
insanitary and the regimen cruel. All the Brontë sisters attended this place until the deaths of
Maria and Elizabeth, aged 10 and 11 respectively, as a result of tuberculosis contracted here.*

us distorted by the author's hatred. His cruelty and his religious humbug seem too extreme to be real. It is only when we read about the real Mr Wilson that we discover, of course, that 'Brocklehurst' is really rather a benign portrait of a man who was far more monstrous than any novelist could paint. Not only did he force the children to live in insanitary conditions (one privy for over seventy people); not only were they cold, hungry, exhausted much of the time. But Wilson's morbid belief in a Calvinistic system of predestination made him believe that death itself, if it overtook the children in his care, was to be seen as a positive blessing. He was one of those Christians who believed that only a very few have been designated for Heaven in God's scheme. Most – and these unfortunately included Charlotte Brontë – were in the dubious position of not having been elected to glory. It gives force to the joke in *Jane Eyre* when the infant is asked how she is to avoid the pains of hell. 'I must keep in good health, and not die.' This really was the only way of avoiding hell in Mr Wilson's school, and if he thought that you were elected to glory, then he was quite cheerful about the prospect of your early demise, even if you were only eleven. Readers of Wilson's monthly magazine *The Children's Friend* were able to peruse many an edifying yarn about little children happily going to their maker or – if they belonged to the infamous majority – being snatched by such playground misfortunes as skating on thin ice or being bitten by a dog into the flames of immortal perdition. But this was not just written for show. Wilson really meant it. One of Charlotte's companions, Sarah Bicker, died at the age of eleven. She made a pious end; though suffering from the last agonies of typhoid, with inflammation of the bowel, she was compelled to spend her last minutes being catechised by Mr Wilson to make quite certain that Christ had died for her sins. 'And He will save all men?' asked Wilson. 'No, Sir,' said Sarah, 'only those that trust in him.' 'I bless God,' Wilson wrote in *The Children's Friend*, 'that he has taken from us the child of whose salvation we have the best hope and may her death be the means of rousing many of her schoolfellows to seek the Lord while He may be found.'

Not all parents would find this a reassuring item in a school curriculum. The combination of insanitary conditions and crazed Calvinistic theology were to carry off two of Charlotte's sisters. Maria was taken home to Haworth 'in ill health' in February 1825. She was the model for Helen Burns in *Jane Eyre*. She died of consumption on 6 May 1825, aged eleven. Her sister Elizabeth died about a fortnight later.

Mr Brontë immediately removed Charlotte and Emily from Cowan Bridge, but the terrible experience of being there was something from which the girls never escaped. The pure anger which she felt about the deaths of Maria and Elizabeth sharpens every word of the opening chapters of *Jane Eyre*. But, as happens to Jane Eyre at Lowood, Charlotte had begun to guess at Cowan Bridge that life for such as her, at that particular date, offered an alarmingly restricted range of options. The sickly daughter of an impoverished clergyman had only the option, if she failed to secure a husband, of staying at home or entering the world of education. And not education as we understand the phrase – not colleges, not institutes, not universities. The best she could hope for was a post as governess in a pleasant household, or as an assistant mistress in some such school as Cowan Bridge. It was with this in mind that Mr Brontë decided, after a delicious period of five years in which Charlotte and Emily did not go to school, that they should once more be sent off to the classroom – this time to the much more benign establishment at Roe Head, presided over by Miss Wooler. Charlotte was evidently a born academic. She flourished at Miss Wooler's and had the kind of brain which would have benefited from further education at a university – quite out of the question at this date, of course. Emily, who had cocooned herself in the world of her own private dreams, was not happy at Miss Wooler's and soon enough left. Anne, the youngest child, also came to Roe Head while Charlotte was there and seems to have flourished.

The two most important things which happened to Charlotte at Roe Head were the forming of friendships and the improvement of her French. The two friends she made there – Mary Taylor and Ellen Nussey – remained friends for life, and the letters Charlotte wrote to them for the rest of her days are among the most valuable sources for her biography. In particular, I think, one is interested in Mary Taylor whose family had a genuinely modern outlook on things, and whose feminism was a noticeable influence on Charlotte's thinking. Just as Charlotte, while unmarried, found it difficult to find a place in English society, so did the independent-minded Mary Taylor, who ultimately emigrated to New Zealand rather than follow the male-dominated rules set down for the way Englishwomen should behave.

The French – begun at home and brushed up at Miss Wooler's – enabled Charlotte, in her late twenties, to have her only sustained experience of life outside an English parsonage, schoolroom or governess's

Charlotte was a ready and fluent letter writer and formed an intimate pen-friendship with her publishers. One of her letters is shown here.

parlour. The experience of being a governess – not quite a servant, but certainly not the equal of the family for whom she worked – was mortifying to one of her sensitivity. When she left one family for whom she worked, the Sidgwicks, Charlotte wrote that 'I was never so glad to get out of a house in my life'; and she told her future biographer the novelist Mrs Gaskell that, 'None but those who had been in the position of a governess could ever realise the dark side of "respectable" human nature.' Anne, her sister, was having an almost equally miserable time with a family called Ingham, near Mirfield, and collecting the experience which would enable her to write *Agnes Grey*.

But between these unpleasant experiences, all four surviving Brontë siblings – Branwell, Charlotte, Emily and Anne – were much together, much at home. Their teenage years were perhaps their happiest: by day, happily absorbed in the routines of the Parsonage (they were passionately house-proud, so that polishing and cleaning took up much of their time), the livestock (two geese called Victoria and Adelaide, and a succession of dogs) absorbed much of their emotional energy as well as the delights of Nature and Art. All were accomplished sketchers and painters. All four were musical. Emily was a brilliant pianist – the piano which Mr Brontë bought for her still survives at the Parsonage – and Branwell developed a particular facility on the church organ. And all four were writers. At the end of an average day, Mr Brontë, his sight already fading, would have retreated to his study, an austerely furnished room immediately to the right of the front door, while, a few feet across the passage-way, his children would assemble to read aloud from their voluminous written works, the chronicles of Angria and Gondal.

Charlotte's memory was of their pacing about the room with excitement as they spoke of their creations. When you see the room, which is really quite small, this circumambulation seems all the more peculiar. But then you remember two things. One is that all the siblings but Emily (who was five feet six) were really very tiny indeed. Peering into their dining room, which itself has a somewhat doll's house quality, you have to imagine people of almost doll-like size themselves. The second thing to recall is how still you were expected to sit, right up to the period of the 1950s, in genteel English society – at least in the sort of provincial society to which Charlotte Brontë (or I) belonged. Children were taught to sit and sit and sit. One was meant to sit with a straight back, too. I imagine that the Brontë children, when they were not scrambling over the moor, or completing the household tasks they were set from an early age, were expected to sit still for most of the day. They would certainly not pace about the room in the presence of a servant, nor of their father or aunt. So, when they were on their own, this slightly frenetic movement began.

The three girls' devotion to their brother Branwell has been made the subject of endless speculation. In particular, it has been hinted that Emily's passionate nature nursed incestuous feelings for him, or that the story of Heathcliff and Cathy Earnshaw might conceal an actual incestuous affair between the two. Of course, no one can ever know the truth of these rather wild speculations, but I should be amazed if any such thing ever existed at the conscious level. The success of the Brontë novels, and in particular of *Wuthering Heights*, derives from Emily's and Charlotte's instinctive knowledge that sex is something in the head. Such knowledge, when translated into art, very rarely derives from experience. For some reason or another, real sexual experiences or feelings produce a kind of imaginative taboo in all but the most relentlessly auto-biographical of pens. Novelists tend to write about the experiences they did not have, not the ones which they had. Besides, Branwell Brontë appears to have been an altogether jollier and more genial companion than Heathcliff.

The wonder is, when we consider how much trouble was devoted to the girls' education, that he received so little. Probably his poor father depended too much on his society. The loneliness of Mr Brontë is one of the underlying sadnesses of the whole story. He evidently taught Bran-well, in his fashion, to a much higher level than many schools of the time would have done. Branwell's translation of *The Odes of Horace* (Book One) for example, has been thought worth reprinting in this century. It is true that Mr Brontë had very little money. But that is more than *no* money, which his own father had had. He, with no money or position, had managed to get to St John's College, Cambridge. Branwell never came near such heights, though it was not until the 1840s that he formed that attachment to alcohol and laudanum which was to have such a disastrous consequence.

His chosen field, after much family discussion, was painting. He was sent off to the Royal Academy in 1835, but we don't even know if he got there. When he came home again, however, he made an occasional living as a portrait painter. The Bradford worthies whom Branwell commem-orated cannot have been particularly pleased by his amateurish daubs. Only occasionally did he rise to a sort of brilliance with the brush. The most noticeable example of his talent is his most famous picture, the depiction of his three sisters which now hangs in the National Portrait Gallery in London. It is a haunting picture, one of the most inescapably emotional portraits in the whole gallery. Even if we knew nothing about their work, we should know as we stood in front of it that an extra-ordinary story lay behind the picture. On the extreme left is Anne – she looks as if she is about to say something, but beginning to think better of it. Her eyes are particularly well painted, the charming, very faint sug-gestion of a squint is immediately recognisable as authentic. Next to her is oval-faced Emily. Her overpowering strength of personality, and her beauty, strike us. So does the difference between Emily and the other two sisters. If they might conceivably be about to entertain us with a pot of tea, Emily's features suggest something altogether more mystical and arcane. The smile playing on her lips is not sociable; it hints of ecstasy.

She is staring beyond us to some unseen Presence. Because Emily is there, the group ceases to appear domestic; we start to think of three Norns, three sybils – even semi-mythical figures like three Furies. There is no nonsense about the figure on the extreme right, the figure of Charlotte. If Anne looks as if she is about to say something, Charlotte looks as though she just *has* said something, and is now wondering whether it was somewhat too acerbic. It is the most Irish of the three faces, and in the curl of the lips we discern the humour that could give us wonderful sentences like the opening passage of *Shirley*: 'Of late years, an abundant shower of curates has fallen upon the north of England: they lie very thick on the hills; every parish has one or more of them . . .'

Perhaps the most alarming face on the canvas is the fourth, the one which is not there. Between Emily and Charlotte, Branwell painted himself. Then, with a gesture of self-abnegation, if not self-hatred, he painted himself out. With similar despondency in life, he drifted from one position to another, usually tight, and always short of funds. Once a life has started to go downhill in the way that, from an early stage, it was indicated that Branwell's should go, it is difficult to single out any particular moment as the lowest ebb. In terms of embarrassment, it would have been hard to match the time that he lost his job as station master at Luddenden Foot railway station for an alleged irregularity with the petty cash; or the sad culmination of his career as a private family tutor to the Robinsons at Thorp Green. He was passionately in love with his employer's wife. Charlotte persisted in believing (perhaps rightly) that it was Mrs Robinson who had made the running in the affair. Twenty years Branwell's senior, she had flirted with the young man 'in the very presence of her children, fast approaching to maturity; and they would threaten her that if she did not grant them such and such indulgences, they would tell their bed-ridden father "how she went on with Mr Brontë".' It was from this incident, Charlotte averred to her friend Ellen Nussey, that Branwell's real decline could be dated, when 'he began his career as an habitual drunkard to drown remorse'. When one visits the Parsonage at Haworth today, one wonders whether it was as simple as that. One sees the small bedroom which Branwell shared with his myopic father; the tiny dining-room where he sat with his loving sisters. Anything he did would be forgiven. Their love for him was unconditional and, one suspects, smothering, emasculating. When short of funds and low in spirits Branwell would threaten suicide. It would usually produce a sovereign from his father. The local pub, the Black Bull, was only a few yards from the house, and the apothecary – ready supplier of opium (in the form of laudanum) without prescription – was just opposite in the village square.

One of the things which makes Charlotte remarkable is that one suspects she shared much of Branwell's pessimism of outlook. It was not given to her to be consoled, as Emily was, purely by dreams and the inner life. While Emily continued to weave the tales of Gondal in her head throughout her life, Charlotte firmly brought an end to her Angria fantasies when she entered adulthood (though she allowed herself to rework them in *The Professor*). She saw as clearly as Branwell did that life offered very little for such as them. She also knew at first-hand that poverty and boredom, and the humiliation of the near-servant status 'enjoyed' by tutors and governesses in those days, were not the worst that life could offer. Like Branwell, she was to discover the misery of an impossible love for a married person. But unlike Branwell, she stared all these bleak realities in the face. One sees it so clearly in his painting of them all. He has taken the easy way, by scrubbing his face out of the picture altogether. Charlotte is doggedly staring, her jaw set, her courage and her sense of humour diminished but not extinguished by the reality of things.

The love-misery came to her in Belgium where, very enterprisingly, she had gone with Emily to escape the tedium of governessdom and curates falling on the Yorkshire hills, thick as snow. Mr Brontë accompanied Emily and Charlotte to Brussels in February 1842. Her school friend Mary Taylor, and her brother James Taylor, went with them. The two sisters attached themselves to the Pensionnat Heger, a girls' school in a handsome seventeenth-century building in a quiet part of the Belgian capital. Emily hated the school. She felt uncomfortable with her fellow-pupils. She had a profound horror of Roman Catholicism. As always, when separated from Haworth – the warmth of the family circle, the freedom of the moor – Emily was homesick. When they came home for Aunt Branwell's funeral, it was decided that Emily should remain at Haworth to take care of her father. Charlotte, however, went back to Belgium for another year, this time not as a student, but as a teacher at M. Heger's Pensionnat: or rather, as a sort of student teacher, for she was paid a salary of £16 per annum, out of which money was deducted for her German lessons and her laundry.

In 1842 Charlotte and Emily went to Brussels to study, subsequently to teach at the Pensionnat Heger. Charlotte fell in love with M. Heger, the Principal of this establishment, who is photographed here many years later in the 1870s with his pupils.

Whereas her first year in Brussels had been dominated by looking after Emily's needs, and by something like a friendship which could develop between the two sisters and Monsieur and Madame Heger, the second year was very different. Madame Heger could not fail to be aware that the young English *gouvernante* had fallen helplessly in love with her husband, *le professeur*. Seven years older than Charlotte, and five years younger than his (second) wife, Constantine George Romain Heger was a man with a melodramatic history. He had fought in the Belgian Revolution on the side of the nationalists. His brother-in-law had been shot, at his side, on the barricades. His first wife had died of cholera, as had his first child. In temperament, he had much in common with Mr Rochester and even more with Paul Emmanuel, the fascinating hero of *Villette*, Charlotte's Belgian novel. He had a furious temper ('he fumed like a bottled storm', Charlotte lovingly remembered), but he could simmer down and be kind and generous. He was an inspired and brilliant teacher. He possessed (as an obituary notice said of him) 'a kind of intellectual magnetism with children'. Like Charlotte, he combined an emotional intensity and an intellectual rigour with a deeply religious temperament.

Love for him was to become the dominant and searing emotional fact in Charlotte's life – at least for the next few years, perhaps forever. It is quite obvious that he did not return her love, although he found her companionship entertainingly intelligent. As soon as the situation became apparent, his wife jealously kept the pair apart. It meant that there were many moments of desperate loneliness, such as the occasion in the summer of 1843, when the Hegers took their children on holiday to Blankenburg, and left Charlotte behind at the *pensionnat* – all the children being also on vacation – with no companionship but the domestics. In her misery, she found herself going into the cathedral and muttering her secret love to a priest through the grille of one of the confessionals: an incident vividly written up, first in a letter to Emily and then, more famously, in one of the most poignant scenes in *Villette*. 'Of course the adventure stops there,' she wrote to Emily, 'and I hope I shall never see the priest again. I think you had better not tell papa of this. He will not understand that it was only a freak, and will perhaps think I am going to turn Catholic.'

The sheer emotional and intellectual impossibility of this is apparent to anyone who has read even briefly in Charlotte's correspondence. The moment in the confessional was nothing to do with religion, it was a desperate cry for help, like a modern person ringing up the Samaritans. It is true that living in Brussels had its compensations. She came to like the place. And there were amusing interludes, such as Queen Victoria's visit to her Uncle Leopold. Charlotte went out into the street to see the royal personage 'flashing through the Rue Royale in a carriage and six . . . a little stout vivacious lady, very plainly dressed, not much dignity or pretension about her'. But the horror of her situation deepened. Rather cruelly, M. Heger valued her as a teacher – and, very likely, as a companion – and would not hear of her leaving. It was only the forceful advice, given by post by her friend Mary Taylor, which finally enabled Charlotte to do the sensible thing. When she was back at Haworth, she inscribed a book called *Les Fleurs de la Poésie Française depuis le Commencement du XVIᵉ Siècle*. She wrote, 'Given to me by Monsieur Heger on the 1st January 1844, the morning I left Brussels.'

Dotted through the stout volumes of Brontë correspondence and memorabilia are the four surviving letters which Charlotte wrote to M.

Heger. It was said by his children that he was in the habit of destroying her letters as soon as he received them, and these four were retrieved from a waste-paper basket and stuck together by his wife. They are the most painful things Charlotte ever wrote. Yet, without the sheer misery of unrequited love which Charlotte suffered, it is doubtful whether we should have had her masterpieces, *Jane Eyre* and *Villette*. The first attempt she made to come to terms with her pitiful situation was in writing *The Professor*. But it is a dull book, and Smith was right to reject it. She skirts round her unhappiness, writes well about children and classroom life, but gives the teacher in love with the Professor too easy a ride. It is in *Jane Eyre* that she comes to terms with (among so many other things such as the unrelieved awfulness of her schooling at Cowan Bridge) the difficulty of M. Heger's character. But the ending of that novel – hence part of its enduring appeal – is sentimental. It is the ending we all want. Only in *Villette* does she dare to face up to the fact that life does not offer consolation or happy endings. We can weave a happy ending for Lucy Snowe and Paul Emmanuel if we wish, but Charlotte Brontë will not do it for us.

> That storm roared frenzied for seven days. It did not cease till the Atlantic was strewn with wrecks: it did not lull till the deeps had gorged their full of sustenance. Not till the destroying angel of tempest had achieved his perfect work would he fold the wings whose waft was hunger – the tremor of whose plumes was storm.
>
> Peace, be still! Oh! a thousand weepers, praying in agony on waiting shores, listened for that voice, but it was not uttered – not uttered till, when the hush came, some could not feel it: till, when the sun returned, his light was night to some!
>
> Here pause: pause at once. There is enough said. Trouble no quiet, kind love; leave sunny imaginations hope. Let it be theirs to conceive the delight of joy born again fresh out of great terror, the rapture of rescue from peril, the wondrous reprieve from dread, the fruition of return . . .

It may have been the case that when Messrs Williams and Smith first met 'Acton' and 'Currer Bell', some such happy ending to their troubles was writing itself in all their minds. The success of *Jane Eyre* could hardly fail to bring delight. Charlotte even confided in her father that she had written a book. Thinking she merely meant written one out in her own hand, he declined at first to read it, knowing that his eyesight would not be strong enough to decipher a manuscript. But then she presented him with the bound, finished copy. When he next appeared at tea, Mr Brontë remarked to Anne and Emily, 'Girls, do you know Charlotte has been writing a book, and it is much better than likely?'

It was a comparatively happy time in the life of the household. None of them could possibly guess how short a period it was to be. All four suffered from tuberculosis and Branwell, weakened by drink, was the first to be killed by it.

In their deaths, Charlotte's three siblings all displayed something of their essential character. Branwell, though looking terrible with unkempt hair ('the thin white lips not trembling but shaking', a friend remembered) had been out and about in the village until a few days before the end. He had looked in on friends at the Black Bull, drunk some brandy, and even managed a bite to eat. Then he took to his bed, and by Sunday morning, 24 September 1848, he realised that the end had come. It was rumoured in the village that he insisted on standing up to die, his pockets stuffed with letters from Mrs Robinson, to whom he had remained besottedly attached.

Mr Brontë's grief was extreme: 'he cried out for his loss like David for that of Absalom,' Charlotte tells us. Charlotte herself, always the victim of nervous stomach disorders, took to her bed with 'bilious fever'. The day of the funeral was raw, and Emily caught cold at it. The persistent cough, the loss of all appetite, the feverish, sleepless nights which she endured soon filled Charlotte and Anne with alarm. Charlotte poured out her anxieties in her letters. She had begun to treat Mr Williams, her publisher, as a confidant. Williams, a fervent follower of the fad for homeopathic medicine, urged them to bring a homeopathic physician to 'Ellis Bell''s sofa. But Emily refused to see a doctor of any kind.

At this point, two further reviews of *Wuthering Heights* appeared (it had been published the previous year). The *Spectator* was particularly hostile, driving Charlotte into outraged fury on her sister's behalf. 'Blind is he as any bat,' Charlotte wrote, 'insensate as any stone to the merits of Ellis.' The *North American Review* was even harsher. Emily greeted it with a smile. She was already preparing herself for a sphere where they neither review nor give in reviews.

But (no coward soul, hers) there was nothing resigned about the manner of her death. She refused to go to bed. She refused even to acknowledge that she was ill. It has been several times noticed that in her death, Emily Brontë showed kinship with the animals with whom she so profoundly empathised. She resisted death for as long as she needed to do so. Then she went, without fuss.

She died on 19 December 1848. On Christmas Day, Charlotte wrote to Mr Williams:

> Emily is nowhere here now. Her wasted mortal remains are taken out of the house. We have laid her cherished head under the church aisle beside my mother's, my two sisters' – dead long ago – and my poor hapless brother's . . . Well, the loss is ours, not hers, and some sad comfort I take, as I hear the wind blow and feel the cutting keenness of the frost in knowing that the elements bring her no more suffering; their severity cannot reach her grave; her fever is quieted, her restlessness soothed, her deep hollow cough is hushed forever; we do not hear it in the night nor listen for it in the morning; we have not the conflict of the strangely strong spirit and the fragile frame before us – relentless conflict – once seen, never to be forgotten.

Charlotte Brontë's desk at Haworth parsonage.

Charlotte was surely right to emphasise that the loss was ours, not Emily's. The lives of artists, whether cut short by death or merely fizzling out in youth, do not have to be long, and there is nothing necessarily 'tragic' about the death of someone who has achieved in the course of their life a corpus of highly distinctive poems and a novel upon which it would be impossible to improve. The same could be said of Lermontov, who was even younger than Emily Brontë when he died, and who had also, interestingly enough, developed the narrative experiment, as she had done, of a story told by several different first-person narrators.

Charlotte's destiny was very different. She was marked out as the survivor. 'My father says to me almost hourly, "Charlotte, you must bear up, I shall sink if you fail me"; these words you can conceive, are a stimulus to nature. The sight too of my sister Anne's very still but deep sorrow, awakens in me such fear for her that I dare not falter.' The fears were fully justified. By January 1849, Anne had developed the ominous honking cough which was indelibly associated in their minds with the last days of Emily. Unlike Emily, she declined slowly, quietly, one might almost say modestly. It was hoped, when spring came, that a period by the sea would improve her condition. She died there, at Scarborough, 'a quiet Christian death' which, Charlotte told Mr Williams, 'did not rend my heart as Emily's stern, simple, undemonstrative end had done.' To spare her father the agony of a third family burial service at Haworth in so short a space of time, Charlotte arranged for Anne to be buried at Scarborough. Her grave can still be seen there, the only one of the immediate Brontë family not to be buried in the family vault at Haworth. 'Papa has now me only – the weakest, puniest, least promising of his six children.'

Perhaps in the lives of all great writers, there comes a moment when they feel compelled to put their childhood behind them, to try something new. For some, such as Proust, this is the whole business of their writing lives. For others, the psychological readjustment is more compartmentalised. Tolstoy, having written his pseudo-autobiographical pieces, *Childhood*, *Boyhood* and *Youth*, is prepared for the work of his maturity. Dickens, with *David Copperfield* behind him, sets forth with a new voice to write the masterpieces of the later period.

Charlotte's severance with her past could not have been more violent or savage. Indeed, for a great many people with only a smattering of knowledge about the Brontës, it is the most important fact about them –

that they all died prematurely. It has given the surely false sense that life in the Parsonage was gloomy, miserable, a reflection of the stormier passages in Emily's poems and fiction. In fact, for much of the time, it was idyllically happy and – like the lives of many largish families in remote or provincial places – entirely self-contained. All through her adult life Charlotte had struggled to make an independent life for them all since they would be left with nothing – not even a house to live in – when their father died. Now, without Anne, Emily and even Branwell to consider, she was left to confront the great question alone – what did she intend to *do* with her life?

It all came at a time when the success of *Jane Eyre* enabled her to hope that the pattern of her life would be shaped by her celebrity as an author.

In July 1849, Charlotte wrote to W. S. Williams:

> The hush and gloom of our house would be more oppressive to a buoyant than to a subdued spirit. The fact is, work is my best companion – hereafter I look for no great earthly comfort except what congenial occupation can give – for society – long seclusion has in a great measure unfitted me – I doubt whether I should enjoy it if I might have it. Sometimes I think I should, and I thirst for it – but at other times I doubt my capability of pleasing or deriving pleasure. The prisoner in solitary confinement – the toad in the block of marble – all in time shape themselves to their lot.

It was in this frame of mind that she took up again the writing of *Shirley*, begun before the deaths of her siblings, a book which, if you come to it fresh from *Jane Eyre*, is bound to disappoint, but which has merits of its own. It has comedy. And in its accounts of the industrial troubles of the earlier part of the century, it has a much broader and more self-consciously serious subject. While waiting for proofs Charlotte read the new Dickens, *David Copperfield*. People were already talking about the affinity between Dickens's novel of childhood and *Jane Eyre*. It is indeed unlikely that the one would have been written without the other. She saw this, but added – 'only what an advantage has Dickens in his varied knowledge of men and things!' Novelists need material to feed on. Unlike poets, they should not have an undiluted diet of solitude. Charlotte was acutely conscious of the danger that if she wrote too much, the ore would run out.

But there is a paradox about her reverence for Dickens's 'knowledge of men and things'. Dickens's characters – and even his scenes – may be regarded as creatures of pure fantasy. It may be the case that he needed the stimulus of society and London life to have invented them, but nothing in literature is more obviously the product of the imagination than the works of Dickens. The people in his books are the creatures of his brain. Charlotte's characters in the fiction of her maturity are very recognisably more realistic than anything Dickens attempted. Realism was not his mode, as it was to become hers. Indeed, one could almost say that Dickens would have written better novels, very likely, if he had been compelled to live in Haworth and look after Mr Brontë, while Charlotte, with her acute eye and her commonsense vision of current affairs (ever the avid reader of contemporary periodicals) might have profited much more than Dickens did from prolonged exposure to London. Still, lives of artists as of others, are what they are, and not what they should be, and we must take the nineteenth-century writers as we find them.

One issue which begins to become very apparent in *Shirley* and which probably owes something to Charlotte's friendship with Mary Taylor, is that of feminism. The naive conversations between Caroline Helstone and Shirley Keeldar must echo sentiments which had passed between Charlotte Brontë and Mary Taylor:

"Men and women, husbands and wives quarrel horribly, Shirley".
"Poor things! – poor, fallen degenerate things! God made them for another lot, for other feelings".
"But are we men's equals, or are we not?"

In an extremely gentle, low-key way, the novel challenges the conventional, Biblical view of women as expressed in the story of Eve, or Milton's great interpretation of that myth. Shirley says that Milton tried to see the first woman, but 'it was his cook that he saw; or it was Mrs Gill, as I have seen her, making custards in the heat of summer.' Shirley's vision of woman is something different – of 'a woman Titan . . . Jehovah's daughter'.

There is a conscious farewell to the *Jane Eyre* style of writing in the novel's conclusion, when Martha (the servant who is clearly based on Charlotte's own Tabitha Aykroyd) describes the district where they live.

Lytton Strachey, whose book Eminent Victorians, *published in 1919, did so much to puncture the inflated regard in which 'Victorian values' were held.*

Franz Winterhalter, the German artist who painted so many of the royal heads of Europe in the middle years of the nineteenth century, had a particular feeling for Prince Albert.

ABOVE 'The First of May, 1851', by Winterhalter. It is an Adoration scene. A Wise Man (the Duke of Wellington) presents his gift to his godson, Arthur. The Mother is the Queen. Albert, cast in the St Joseph role, stares away from the scene with some wistfulness.

RIGHT Lord Cardigan explains the Battle of Balaclava to the royal family. It is said that the Queen had herself painted out when she discovered Cardigan's dissolute manner of life.

ABOVE A watercolour by Anne Brontë of her dog, Flossy. All the Brontës were devoted to animals and birds, and many of their paintings have animals as their subject.

RIGHT Branwell Brontë's famous portrait of his sisters in the National Portrait Gallery. Left to right they are Anne, Emily and Charlotte. The blank smudge in the centre of the canvas is where Branwell attempted a self-portrait, and then scrubbed himself out, a potent image of his urge for self-destruction.

her father and
mother was very
rich Mr and Mrs
~~Wood~~ were there
names and she
was there only
child but she
was not too
indulged on ~~a~~ ~~so~~
little ~~Ann~~ and
her mother
went to see
a fine castle
near ~~the city~~
London about
ten miles

from it Ann
was very much
pleased with

*ABOVE An extract from
Charlotte Brontë's Stories of
Angria, the imagined world
she invented during her
childhood.*

*RIGHT An alcove at the top
of the stairs in Haworth
Parsonage, in which may be
seen some of Charlotte's
possessions, including the
trunk she took to Brussels.*

BELOW Sydney Prior Hall's portrait of Gladstone shows him at the end of his life in his study, still mulling over literary texts and ruminating on the problems of the day.

ABOVE Christ Church Hall at Oxford, where generations of undergraduates have dined. A high proportion of Christ Church men have always been aristocrats and many young men who sat here went on to become bishops, judges or high-ranking statesmen. Wealth and the Church of England here reside side by side; it is appropriate that Gladstone should have been educated here.

RIGHT Charles Stewart Parnell in a caricature for Vanity Fair.

A triumphal icon (from the Illustrated London News*) of the advances in sea and land transport, and in street lighting, that marked the 60 years of Queen Victoria's reign. The 'Whig' view of history, and the Darwinian view of nature, alike persuaded the Victorians that history had been a perpetual process of improvement, each age better than the last.*

'This world has queer changes.' Martha can remember not only the early industrial days of Yorkshire, but also the days before that, the days when such supernatural happenings as occur in *Wuthering Heights* or *Jane Eyre* are part of the common folklore. 'I can tell, one summer evening, fifty years syne, my mother coming running in just at the edge of dark, almost fleyed out of her wits, saying she had seen a fairish (fairy) in Fieldhead Hollow; and that was the last fairish that ever was seen on this countryside . . . A lonesome spot it was – and a bonnie spot – full of oak trees and nut trees. It is altered now.'

If the young Brontës were the heirs of the Romantic movement, Charlotte in her maturity was preparing to be something different: a modern realist. The subject of her developed fiction is what women are meant to *do* in a world whose limited tedium was determined for them by men. The 'abundant shower of curates' at whom she pokes such fun in *Shirley* were Charlotte Brontë's only real hope of escape from her clergy-man father, who in any case required her increasing attention as his sight failed. As for love, and the bleak prospects for those who fall into it, *Villette* is her soberest and saddest development of that theme. All the wretchedness she had felt in Brussels, and the hopelessness of her attachment to M. Heger was poured into the experiences of Lucy Snowe, and her love for M. Paul Emmanuel. '*Villette* touches on no matter of public interest. I cannot write books handling the topics of the day; it is no use trying,' she wrote to her publisher George Smith in October 1852. Like John Keats, she was 'certain of nothing but the holiness of the heart's affections' which, of course, is why her public loved her.

Her fame could not console her for the loss of those she best loved – either by death or unrequited affection. Nevertheless, it provided her with welcome moments of diversion and new friendships, it offered more excuses to escape Haworth and the difficult companionship of her father, and it introduced her to one of the most important figures in her life, her biographer. The novelist Mrs Gaskell, the wife of a Manchester Unitarian minister, wrote to express her admiration of *Shirley*. It is clear from Mrs Gaskell's letters that she was fascinated by the idea of Currer Bell before ever meeting Charlotte. The high-minded agnostic feminist Harriet Martineau (the author of *Deerbrook* whom Charlotte had long admired and had met in London) had, Mrs Gaskell wrote to a friend, 'sworn an eternal friendship with the authoress of "Shirley".' When they did meet Mrs Gaskell was surprised to find Currer Bell 'a little, very little bright-haired sprite, looking not above 15, very unsophisticated neat and tidy'. From the earliest, Mrs Gaskell adopted Charlotte as a 'character' whom she would feel compelled to write up – whether in a work of fiction or as the subject of a biography was not yet clear.

It was in the August of 1850 that the two women got to know one another while staying at the house of a mutual acquaintance near Lake Windermere. Mrs Gaskell was struck by Charlotte's tininess, by her plainness ('large mouth and many teeth gone') and by her social awkwardness. While in the district, the two women went over to Fox House, the home of Dr Arnold, the famous headmaster of Rugby, and still inhabited by his widow. Charlotte, who had been profoundly affected by Arnold's biography by Dean Stanley ('where can we find justice, firmness, independence, earnestness, sincerity, fuller and purer than in him?'), was impressed by Mrs and Miss Arnold. To her son Matthew (already the published author of two volumes of poems), she talked about French novels and her father's curates. He found her 'past thirty and plain'. His manner displeased her by its 'seeming foppery' and his 'assumed conceit' but she was prepared to believe those who told her that 'Mr Arnold improved upon acquaintance'.

It was open to Charlotte, from this point in her life, to have entered the world of Victorian intellectual society. James Taylor, a partner in Smith Elder, fell in love with her and repeatedly proposed marriage. But as she confided in Ellen Nussey, 'if Mr Taylor be the only husband fate offers to me, single I must remain'. She did not love him; in fact, she found him physically repugnant. She went on loving M. Heger. Perhaps more importantly than love, the world offered by a London publisher was not one where she could have survived. The crushing loneliness of the Parsonage, her father's difficult character, the provincialism of Haworth – it was by now too late for her to escape these things. Her nature had grown used to them. And, as the lighter passages of *Shirley* show, she did not entirely hate them.

Fate, in the event, offered her more than one partner to choose from. He was the latest in a line of her father's curates, an Irishman called Arthur Bell Nicholls. A follower of Dr Pusey in doctrine, his manner of reading the services annoyed Charlotte's father. Charlotte found him 'good, mild, uncontentious' as he came in and out of the Parsonage to report on the doings of the parish. Then, just before Christmas 1852, he proposed.

This rather ineffectual young man had been in the parish for eight years now; beyond providing Charlotte with a comic vignette for *Shirley*, he had hardly intruded at all upon her consciousness. Everything that had happened – her falling in love with M. Heger, the deaths of Emily, Branwell and Anne, the illness of her father, the discovery of her fame – had been so much stronger experiences than anything which Mr Nicholls seemed to be offering. Now he revealed, in a potentially embarrassing outburst, that he had been in love with Charlotte 'for months', and that he 'could endure no longer'. Very bravely, Charlotte went into the study to inform her father of the conversation which had just taken place. There was a characteristic explosion of Ulster rage. In Nicholls, Mr Brontë now saw the man who proposed to take away from him his last surviving child and he resisted with ferocity. How could they marry on Mr Nicholls's paltry £100 a year? The upshot of the quarrel was that Mr Nicholls was asked to leave the parish and seek alternative employment.

But this dull, amiable man had offered Charlotte something which she was not prepared to forgo. Perhaps with the love of her sisters and brother around her, she would have been content to sit at home, and dream of fantasy figures like Mr Rochester, and write painful love letters to M. Heger. But now she was alone – painfully lonely and depressed. She was not in love with Mr Nicholls, but she desperately needed what he offered to her.

Another curate was engaged – a Mr De Renzy – and they began to count the days before Nicholls's departure. The last time he celebrated the Communion, on Whitsunday, Mr Brontë stayed away, even though it is one of the Sundays in the year when members of the Church of England are obliged to receive the sacrament. When Nicholls approached Charlotte, kneeling at the altar rails to receive, he 'struggled, faltered, and then lost command over himself, stood before my eyes and in the sight of all the communicants, white, shaking, voiceless!'

This was a story which was gradually unfolded to Mrs Gaskell when she came to stay in the Parsonage later that year. Mr Brontë took a liking to Mrs Gaskell and reminisced expansively. 'He had a sort of grand and stately way of describing past times,' she recollected, noting that 'he never seemed quite to have lost the feeling that Charlotte was a child to be guided and ruled when she was present.'

It was undoubtedly Mrs Gaskell's goodness of heart and practical common sense which determined her to do something for Mr Nicholls and Charlotte. But perhaps, too, instinct was already prompting her that she should write Charlotte's story, and that this story should have (as seemed possible then) a happy ending. Though no Anglican, Mrs Gaskell worked out how it was possible to get some extra money from the Additional Curates Society to supplement a curate's salary were Nicholls to be allowed back to Haworth by Mr Brontë. Then at least, the financial objections could be overruled.

It would appear that Nicholls's devotion to Charlotte was unwavering, and by early 1854, she confessed to her father that she had been continuing to correspond with the man. As she admitted to Mrs Gaskell, her father's were not the only objections to the match which had to be overcome. 'I cannot deny that I had a battle to fight with myself: I am not sure that I have even yet conquered certain inward combatants.' Mr Nicholls's apparent religious bigotry, his devotion to Puseyism, his lack of interest in literature or the arts were all handicaps. It had been said that when he was a curate in Haworth he would not speak to Nonconformists. What would he make of Charlotte's friendship with the Unitarian Mrs Gaskell and the lapsed Unitarian, now agnostic, Harriet Martineau?

But she had time to think it over. She was thirty-eight years old (Mr Nicholls two years younger). Mr Brontë's objections were at length overcome. A back room at the Parsonage was refitted as a small study. Charlotte, who had a domestic genius as well as a genius for writing novels, saw how to make the room attractive, by knocking through a fireplace and papering it with a light floral pattern. The wedding was fixed for 29 June.

Mr Brontë stayed indoors and did not accompany them to the church. The ceremony was conducted by the vicar of nearby Hebden Bridge. Her faithful friends Ellen Nussey and Margaret Wooler had arrived to stay the day before; and, in the absence of any suitable male, Miss Wooler gave away the bride in marriage. There was something purely apposite about this. For Miss Wooler, who had been her mentor at Roe Head, represented all that was best about her spinsterhood, and its one hope of usefulness, the educational profession. There was no one in the church at 8 a.m. on that day to represent the 'Currer Bell' side of Charlotte's life – no fellow-authors, no publishers, no London literary folk.

*Charlotte Brontë's marriage lines. She and Arthur Bell Nicholls were,
somewhat to her surprise, extremely happy together, but she died after only
nine months of marriage as a result of excessive morning sickness.*

Charlotte wore a white muslin dress with a motif of ivy-leaves, and a bonnet which is still preserved at the Parsonage. When the little party returned for the wedding-breakfast, they found that Mr Brontë had recovered his spirits and he was 'the life and soul of the party'. When Charlotte had changed into her shot-silk travelling dress – it still survives in her bedroom – she and her bridegroom planted evergreen trees at the bottom of the garden.

The honeymoon was spent in Ireland, and it was a great success, although it began with Charlotte nursing a nasty cold. The despised Mr Nicholls turned out to have rather grand relations – the Bells of Cuba House; and Charlotte enjoyed staying there, as well as seeing the haunts of his student life at Trinity College, Dublin. It is obvious, too, that the physical aspects of marriage brought unexpected delight. The next six months found Charlotte happy in a way that she had never been happy before. Although when they returned from Ireland, Mr and Mrs Nicholls found Mr Brontë rather unwell, their lives were unclouded. It appeared that the two men, who had quarrelled so much about the prospect of Charlotte's marriage, settled down together perfectly happily once it had happened. Mr Nicholls was now 'my dear Arthur' and 'my dear boy'; and Charlotte was pregnant.

None of them realised how debilitating the pregnancy would be to Charlotte; she was thirty-nine and very small. Her lingering 'cold' was never quite shaken off, and she made it worse in January 1855 by walking on to the moors in thin shoes and coming home with wet feet. Her usually minimal appetite diminished to pure anorexia. 'A wren could have starved on what she ate during those last six weeks,' wrote one observer.

On 21 February, her much-loved servant Tabby Aykroyd died, and was buried just beyond the garden gate in the churchyard. Mr Nicholls took the service. Charlotte was by then confined to her bed. When, some weeks later, she realised quite how seriously ill she was, she exclaimed to her husband: 'Oh, I'm not going to die, am I? He will not separate us – we have been so happy.' She died on 31 March 1855. Her father lived for another six years, Mr Nicholls remaining with him as his faithful nurse and companion. When Mr Brontë died, Nicholls returned to Ireland where he married again – to a cousin. He did not die until 1906. A photograph of him in old age survives. It is clear that he never quite recovered from the loss of Charlotte. The lively Richmond drawing of her always hung on the wall of his dining-room at Hill House, Banagher. When he died, his wife had the coffin carried so that it was placed beneath Charlotte's face. It was said by his nephews and nieces that often, in those last few days before he died he would fall into abstracted thought, meditating upon the reunion with Charlotte: 'I wonder how it will be?'

By then, the Brontë cult was flourishing. Only four months after Charlotte's death, Mr Brontë had written to Mrs Gaskell, asking her to Haworth to discuss the possibility of a biography. *The Life of Charlotte Brontë* is one of the great biographies of the nineteenth century, as well as being the basis for all subsequent studies of the family. Mrs Gaskell was criticised for sensationalism; and inevitably, she got some details wrong. She blamed Charlotte's near-anorexic eating habits, as she had observed them at first-hand, on a supposed regimen of old Mr Brontë's, claiming that he had deprived his daughters of meat. But she was handsome enough to correct this and other mistakes in her second edition. She was punctilious in her research, and she interviewed everyone who might have known her subject – everyone, that is to say, except the husband. Mr Nicholls (very understandably) refused to co-operate in the enterprise. Otherwise, villagers, schoolfriends, pupils in Yorkshire and

This studio portrait of Arthur Bell Nicholls was perhaps taken at the same time as Charlotte's carte de visite *(page 57). He was Patrick Brontë's curate and, after initial difficulties, was allowed to marry Charlotte Brontë.*

Belgium, publishers – all were quizzed for their evidence of this remarkable genius.

But the *Life* which emerged probably had an effect which Mr Brontë did not intend. The fact that a memorial was written helped to console him for the appalling misfortune of losing all six of his offspring. Something was salvaged from the destruction wrought by time. He was vividly aware, as such an intelligent man could not fail to have been aware, that his children had been exceptional people – at least one and possibly two geniuses, and all four who survived childhood of remarkable talents. To preserve their memory, he was bravely prepared to have the sad story told of his son's alcoholism. There were, of course, great protests from the Clergy Daughters' school – now moved from Cowan Bridge to Casterton – at the revelation that Charlotte had based Lowood in *Jane Eyre* so closely on Mr Wilson's educational mode. But the protest was not truly justified, even though it was generally recognised that, since the move to Casterton, the Clergy Daughters' school had 'improved'. A year after Charlotte's death, a Miss Dorothea Beale taught there. She did not find it as monstrous as Lowood, but she left, and went on to become the first great headmistress of Cheltenham Ladies' College. It is a symptomatic little link between the hopeless absence of opportunity for women which existed at the beginning of the century and the very considerably improved standards at the end. Figures like Miss Beale, and her counterpart at the North London Collegiate School, Miss Buss, provided as high a standard of education for girls as was then available for boys. They were closely involved with the foundation of women's colleges at the Universities under women like Elizabeth Wordsworth.

It was all a far cry from the kitchen at Haworth, where Emily tried to teach herself German from a grammar propped up among the bread-dough; or from the miserable 'daughters of the clergy' school from which the Brontë sisters could only hope to emerge as potential governesses or, if they were lucky, as curates' wives. The pupils of Miss Beale and Miss Buss could hope to become doctors, scientists, lawyers, civil servants, engineers. There was of course the inevitable taunt that such ideals were not 'feminine':

> *Miss Buss and Miss Beale*
> *Cupid's darts do not feel.*
> *They are not like us*
> *Miss Beale and Miss Buss.*

But once started, the movement for women's education became a self-perpetuating process.

Mrs Gaskell's *Life of Charlotte Brontë* was a study of people of the highest talents and capability who were compelled, merely by virtue of their sex, to live in a sort of protestant purdah. The genius of the Brontës set them apart from humanity. Their lives, in many particulars, were like the lives of thousands of provincial men and women throughout England, Scotland, Wales and Ireland. Those who read Mrs Gaskell's book could discover a mirror-version of their own tedious, limited existence. That is part of its intense fascination.

But only part. Though many provincial people – no telephone, no radio, no electricity, miles from anywhere and with few, if any, congenial neighbours – led lives which by modern standards would be considered intolerable, one can confidently say that none were quite like the Brontës. The social isolation of their lives, as well as the shocking brevity, make them all the more dramatic. But we would not be so interested if Haworth Parsonage had not produced *Jane Eyre* and *Wuthering Heights*.

Nor – it has to be said – would all the advantages of an enlightened modern society have necessarily done the Brontë sisters much good. Because they were people of high imaginative genius, they would doubtless be producing wonderful books; but they would certainly not have written *Wuthering Heights* or *Jane Eyre*, books which depend for their huge success on the isolation and innerness of their creators. Charlotte was sad that no one liked her later books as well as they had liked *Jane Eyre*. It is the element of fantasy, of suppressed eroticism, of isolation from humanity, which gives the great scenes of that book their power.

That is why people all over the world continue to read it. It is also the reason, presumably, why millions of tourists or pilgrims flock each year to Haworth and stream through the little Parsonage house which, since 1928, has been owned by the Brontë Society and run as a museum. Here may be seen Charlotte's tiny gloves and shoes; the daubs which unhappy Branwell made; the piano where Emily played, the sofa where she died. It is one of the best-run museums of its kind in the world, rivalled only perhaps by the Tolstoy museum in Moscow or the Carlyle House in Cheyne Row, London. In spite of the huge crowds flocking through it all the time, the house retains its private feeling. Have all the millions who go there read *Jane Eyre*? Many have, one suspects, though more have seen the film. Is it the thought of the premature deaths of the Brontës which makes them such haunting figures? Or is it that their books are so inescapably linked to the place? Step out above the village, with all its souvenir shops, its *Villette* tea room and Heathcliff Café, and you will very quickly be exposed to the same wild and rather alarming moorland which confronts us in *Wuthering Heights*.

If people suppose that the early deaths of the Brontës are *tragic*, however, they are wrong. Certainly, from the purely selfish point of view of the reader who admires their work, there is no reason to suppose that they would have produced much more of the same quality had they lived longer. Charlotte was writing more *maturely* – but that was just the trouble! And Emily might well have fizzled out altogether. To have written *Wuthering Heights* and some of the best poems in the language is enough. It doesn't matter that she was only thirty when she died. Her life was in a sense complete.

Charlotte's was not. From a literary point of view, had she lived, we would, I suspect, have witnessed her getting further and further away from the things she was truly good at. There would have been plenty of good characterisation, social comedy, bleak observation about human life; but the intense drama of Bertha Rochester bursting from her locked-up room was never to be repeated. It is not because we want to read any more of her unsatisfactory fragment *Emma* that we wish Charlotte had not died so soon. It is because, as she said herself, she had just begun to be happy. It is because we wish that she had been able to have her baby, and had lived to enjoy it. Such a happy eventuality would have ruined Mrs Gaskell's biography, and would, I suspect, have reduced the future number of pilgrims to Haworth by a thousandfold.

WILLIAM EWART GLADSTONE
1809-98

The great Liberal Prime Minister

William Ewart Gladstone, photographed in old age. By then he was the Grand Old Man, the 'People's William'. His handsome face is marked by the moral toughness with which he confronted his essentially divided nature.

When I think of Victorian England, I think of energy: irrepressible physical energy, intellectual, industrial, moral energy. I think of a place where machines are perpetually turning, where factories belch smoke, where canals and railways, laden with produce, carry freight to warehouses and ports. I think, too, of the great ships, setting out from Liverpool and Hull and London to destinations all over the world. I think of the merchants, the explorers, the colonisers, the evangelists and the engineers all self-confidently taking abroad their skills and prejudices and calling the result of their endeavours the British Empire.

At home, I think of the stupendous engineering achievements of Brunel; I think of the literary fertility of Carlyle, Ruskin or Browning, filling volume after volume of the library shelf. I think of all the movement and life of the Victorian city – the crowds, the street-cries, the clatter of wheels on cobblestones, the plight of the poor, and the adventures of the criminal. I think of the London of Mayhew, Dickens, and Sherlock Holmes.

In the very heart of London's Kensington Gardens, G. F. Watts's statue of *Physical Energy* (1904) is a reflective meditation on a prosperous industrial and imperial power at its zenith. The horse, with brawny flanks and upraised hoof, tugs at the reins in the direction of Kensington Palace, where Queen Victoria herself was born. The barefoot rider, rather more wistfully, looks down the avenue of trees towards the Albert Memorial. Is he wondering what all this expenditure of energy was for? Has the horse got out of control, and taken him into a world he does not either trust or understand? Spirit and matter, morality and desire, money and romance are torn in this divided emblem.

Of all the great Victorians, no one demonstrates this sort of ambivalence more dramatically than the greatest of their Prime Ministers. He spans the century like a colossus, never quite knowing what he makes of it, nor what it makes of him. Like Watts's statue, Gladstone's was an essentially divided nature. Few men have been more intimately involved in the world. Yet his deepest longing was unworldly. Though one of the

G. F. Watts's statue, 'Physical Energy' in Kensington Gardens, London. Spirit and matter, morality and desire, money and romance are torn in this divided emblem. The rider gazes in one direction, while the horse strains in another.

longest-serving of all Cabinet ministers, he had originally yearned to be a minister of religion. Moreover, the shift in his political views – one of the strangest stories in the history of statecraft – follows a most unusual pattern.

When he was an old man of eighty-two, a friend remarked to him, 'You know the saying that nobody is worth much who has not been a bit of a radical in his youth, and a bit of a Tory in his fuller age?' Gladstone laughed and replied, 'Ah, I'm afraid that hits me rather hard. But for myself I think I can truly put all the change that has come into my politics into a sentence; I was brought up to distrust and to dislike liberty, and I learned to believe in it. That is the key to all my change.'

He began his political career, in Lord Macaulay's famous words, as 'the rising hope of those stern and unbending Tories'. He ended his days as 'the people's William', dreaded by the Queen, and by the landed classes as the father of radicalism and the fomenter of social discord at home and in Ireland. But for others, there was something more appropriate in his journalistic nickname – the G.O.M. He was the grand old man whose sheer bigness, and grandeur, and moral weightiness was never to be repeated on the political scene.

William Ewart Gladstone was born on 29 December 1809. The place and timing of his birth are both important. He was born in Rodney Street, Liverpool. His father, John Gladstone, was a self-made Scottish merchant, who had come to Liverpool to further his fortune in trade. And much of that trade was conducted with the West Indies, and much of the trade in the West Indies was not in sugar or rum, but in human lives, in slaves. In 1795, John Gladstone was worth £15,000 – a considerable sum in today's money. By 1799, he had more than doubled it and was worth £40,700. By 1820, he was worth £333,600 and by 1828, £502,550. This was serious money.

Like many devout Evangelical families, the Gladstones attributed the steady accumulation of their capital to the loving favour of the Lord, and they built two churches as a testimony to His goodness. Anglican churches, of course, for in coming south and becoming a gentleman, John Gladstone had abandoned the Presbyterianism of his youth. William Gladstone, therefore, together with his five brothers and sisters (he was the fourth son), was born into an inheritance of vast prosperity; but he was never to forget from what that prosperity derived. He was too complex, and ultimately too Protestant a figure, to be able to separate the guilt from the blessing. You might have thought that a man who felt awkwardness about inheriting a fortune from money made in the slave trade would have supported the Yankees in the American Civil War, but Gladstone was a firm, and indeed tactless, supporter of the Confederation, his outspoken utterances on the subject at the time of the American Civil War leading to an international incident. Though he never appears to have had the 'conversion experience' which characterises so many Evangelical lives (such as that of Cardinal Newman) Gladstone believed in justification by faith. Guilt was an essential condition of life, washed by Grace, but always there. Money and Anglicanism are Mr

Gladstone's two great wet-nurses, sustaining him throughout his long moral adventure in the 'vale of soul-making'.

He was sent to Eton in 1821. His elder brothers were already there. Nothing but the best for the new money of the northern merchant. By the mysterious alchemy of money, Gladstone, whose grandparents had been peasant-proprietors in the Scottish borders, was instantaneously propelled into a world where he mixed as an equal with the sons of great scholars, churchmen and aristocrats. Being large and athletic, boarding school held no terror for Gladstone. It was here that many of his most distinctive habits and talents were developed: at the Eton Society (later in the century known as 'Pop') he revealed himself as a powerful debater, always arguing from the 'stern unbending Tory' point of view.

No less remarkable than his energy in debate was his academic prowess. It was at Eton that he developed his lifelong addiction to Homer. The *Iliad* remained Gladstone's favourite book, with Dante's *Divine Comedy* running it a close second. As the years of his grown-up life passed, with such time-consuming distractions as being Prime Minister four times, he was always trying to spare time for Homer. He wanted to prove Homer's essential kinship with the Divine revelation in the Hebrew scriptures. In the 1860s, for example, when he was Chancellor of the Exchequer, we find him laying aside the Budget to snatch a few hours with the manuscript of his book, *Studies in Homer*. 'If it were even tolerably done', he wrote, 'it would be a good service to religion as to literature and I mistrustfully offer it up to God.' At the same period, the Chancellor of the Exchequer was observed, having changed trains at midnight, sitting in the station waiting-room at Crewe, struggling with his translation of the *Iliad* into English verse.

At Eton, too, Gladstone was confirmed in the Church of England, and there began that lifelong pattern of extreme piety which was so marked a feature of his character. He wanted to be a parson, but his father who had got himself elected as a Tory MP for a pocket borough, wanted the monied interest of the Gladstones to continue to be represented in the House of Commons. William's powers of oratory, meant by Nature, if not by God, for the pulpit, were destined to echo in the secular chamber, and in the drawing-room of his hostile monarch. Meanwhile, ever 'mistrustfully' wondering whether he should not have given his life completely to God, Gladstone attended church every day of his life – sometimes twice, sometimes three times. In all the multifarious business

As a priggish High Church young man, Gladstone was described as the rising hope 'of those stern unbending Tories'.

of his existence, church business occupied the most emotionally exciting role – whether it was the establishment in London of the Margaret Street Chapel, or the use of Gladstone money for the founding of the Episcopalian seminary at Glenalmond in Scotland. However busy he was, Gladstone usually found time to write a sermon each week which he declaimed to his servants at family prayers on Sunday morning.

At Eton, Gladstone also began his habit of a daily diary, or journal as he himself termed it. He kept it up for seventy more years – over 25,000 entries with hardly a day missed. There is a certain degree of soul-searching in Gladstone's diaries, at key moments in the year, when he reviews his sins and accomplishments. But for the most part, the volume after volume of Gladstone's diary, the gradual publication of which is even now keeping an Oxford academic in full-time employment, is more a diary of doing than one of being. It is a chronicle of prodigious, one might almost say manic effort and activity, an extraordinary compilation of books read, committees attended, journeys made, speeches declaimed (often of several hours duration), of money invested, land cultivated, arguments won or lost. He was a giant – a Titan of emotional, physical and mental energy.

As a schoolboy, he does not appear to have had much homosexuality in his make-up; but he was highly-sexed and given to profound emotional attachments. His Eton friendships meant a lot to him. Greatest among the Eton friends was Arthur Hallam. This figure, destined to become legendary in our literature, was evidently, emotionally speaking, a flirt. In 1826, Hallam told his sister that he had been 'walking out a great deal, and running the changes on Rogers, Gladstone, Farr and Hanmer'. While Hallam 'ran the changes', his friends agonised for the chief place in his affections. Later, when he was an undergraduate, Gladstone wrote down a brief history of his friendship with Hallam. It is typical of the two sides of his nature – the efficient administrator who wanted to keep minutes of everything, even the changes of the heart's affections; and the figure who was all passion, the man who underscored all the most fervently emotional passages in Dante's *Paradiso*, and who really did believe that it was Love which moved the 'sun and other stars'.

Here is the friendship with Hallam, as minuted by Gladstone:

It began late in 1824, more at his seeking than mine.
It slackened soon, more on my account than his.
It recommenced in 1825, late, more at my seeking than his.
It ripened much from the early part of 1826 to the middle. In the middle Farr rather took my place . . .

And so on, until the last sad stage: 'At present, almost in uncertainty, very painful, whether I may call Hallam my friend or not.'

What appears to have made Arthur Hallam so attractive to his friends was a combination of innocence and intellectual intensity. He was a Whig, but he did not – in life at least – manage to shake Gladstone's Toryism. When they left Eton, the two boys went their separate ways. Hallam went to Cambridge, where he befriended a boy at Trinity called Alfred Tennyson. When Hallam died at the age of twenty-two, he left a whole generation bereft. Tennyson, in a long cycle of lyrics, mourned:

My Arthur, whom I shall not see
Till all my widow'd race be run.

106

Arthur Hallam was one of Gladstone's closest friends at Eton. At Cambridge he befriended Tennyson and after Hallam's death at the age of 22 the poet mourned him in the elegy In Memoriam.

These lines prompted Dickens, who read the anonymous poem, to speculate that it was written by the young widow of a naval officer, lost at sea. But the elegy, with its haunting sense that young death makes life meaningless, with its tormented religious doubts, its fascination with and fear of science was to be of huge importance. It was called *In Memoriam*, one of those poems, which – like *The Waste Land* of T. S. Eliot – seems to speak for all its generation. The Queen, deep in grief for the Prince Consort when her friendship with Tennyson was at its height, found that his sonorous expressions of despair had 'helped her much'.

Gladstone, however, was not destined to go to Cambridge – Cambridge of poets, Cambridge of speculative meditative scholars, Cambridge of the inner life. Instead he went to politicking, pious, public-life Oxford. And, being John Gladstone's son, he went to the best that money could buy, the aristocratic foundation of Christ Church. Nearly all the Prime Ministers of modern times went to Oxford, rather than to Cambridge, and this is no accident. In the hall at Christ Church today you see, beside the portrait of Gladstone, a host of lord chancellors, archbishops and elder statesmen. The place feels like the very embodiment in stone and wood and canvas and marble of the Establishment. In splendidly palatial quadrangles and rooms around, the young gentlemen were accommodated. It feels closer to one of the great London houses or one of the big stately homes than a place of scholarship and learning. And in the middle of it all, instead of a mere college chapel, there is a cathedral, with a dean and an archdeacon and a bishop's throne. What a perfect allegory of Gladstone's early life! What a parable of the way that the young Gladstone saw England. He was a Tory, not because he believed in privilege, but because he believed in duty – the God-given duty of the few to preserve the Crown and the Church for the many.

To us, in the last decades of the twentieth century, the Church of England may be one of many things. Larkin called it

> *That vast moth-eaten musical brocade*
> *Invented to pretend we do not die.*

When the poet died in 1985, rather than denouncing these lines, the Sub-dean of Westminster Abbey quoted them with reverence at Larkin's memorial service. It seemed the ultimate expression of how 'marginalised' the Church had become: no longer even one Christian denomination among many, but a fusty piece of old furniture of which even its paid-up custodians seemed to have forgotten the significance.

For Gladstone's generation, the Church of England was something quite different; particularly for those, like Gladstone, who were Tories. Nineteenth-century England is difficult enough to understand. But we will never begin to do so unless we grasp the importance, in the Victorians' scheme of things, of the Church of England. When Gladstone came up to Oxford in 1828, he was obliged to subscribe to the Thirty-Nine Articles – the rule-book or party manifesto of the National Church. Those who were unable to subscribe – Jews, Catholics, Methodists – were not admitted to Oxford. As Samuel Johnson had remarked when this was deemed unjust: 'Sir, we permit cows in a meadow but we drive them out of the garden.'

Was this merely Privilege defending Privilege? Was it merely a spiritual department of state keeping the riff-raff out of the Church just as their hopelessly corrupt and antiquated political system, with its rotten boroughs and limited franchise kept the *hoi polloi* out of Parliament, and the system of purchase made it impossible for any but the rich to serve as officers in the Army? Or was it, as Oxford Tories believed, something quite other? Was the Church not merely a national institution founded by Henry VIII, but a divinely founded society, purged but not destroyed at the Reformation, and protected by the Holy Spirit to enshrine the

Truth? If this was the case, then anything which smacked of pluralism, of toleration, would imply that the truth of God was not true. If you *tolerated* the heresies of the Non-conforming sects, such as Roman Catholicism or the Countess of Huntingdon's Connection, were you not implying that the Thirty-Nine Articles were wrong?

This argument – esoteric by today's standards – first came Gladstone's way in a manner which was to be full of portent for his future career – in the national debate concerning Ireland and the Roman Catholic Church.

The Duke of Wellington, who grew up in Ireland and was in any case a pragmatist, knew that the Irish would go on practising their faith, Thirty-Nine Articles or no Thirty-Nine Articles. There was about as much chance of getting them to become Anglicans as there was of making them into Muslims. Liberals of various complexions felt that it was a simple injustice to deny franchise to fellow-Christians who could not, for reasons of conscience, support the National Church. And not just the *vote* – that was a privilege reserved for few enough in any case. Before 1829, Catholics could not practise at the Bar, could not attend the Universities, and could not really play any serious part in the practical running of their nation's affairs.

The Catholic Emancipation Act of 1829 went some way to remedying this state of things. It was the first stage in a monumental change which was overtaking the whole country, and which would culminate in the Great Reform Bill of 1832.

But for the Church Tories of Oxford, all this constituted, in the famous words of their leader John Keble, a 'national apostasy'. Keble and his followers were only an inch away from believing that God had appointed the Tories and the Landed Class to govern England in perpetuity. In a series of pamphlets, known as *Tracts for the Times*, they poured out their worry about the increasing secularisation of the age and their insistence that the Church by Law Established was divine – the same Holy Catholic and Apostolic body which had sustained the early fathers of Christendom. It was only the second generation of 'Tractarians', as believers in these Tracts came to be called, who saw that Catholicism insists not only upon truth, but upon justice – a distinction which enabled Tractarians like Gladstone to shake loose from the Tory party.

But throughout his early years, Gladstone believed – or sort-of-believed, for his religious beliefs are never crude, however peculiar they may seem to us – in John Keble's Church Toryism. With the advanced Catholicism of its theology, Gladstone, in adopting this creed, had come a long way from his boyhood Evangelicalism.

Nothing before or since has ever remotely resembled the Oxford Movement. The medieval revival which, in the previous Romantic generation, had been primarily an aesthetic matter, became cerebral and political. Sir Walter Scott had created a vastly popular medieval fantasy world in novels like *Ivanhoe* and *The Talisman* which were adapted in endless operas, circus performances and paintings. Keats and Coleridge had sung of La Belle Dame Sans Merci and Christabel. Architects had rediscovered the beauties of Gothick. But it was only really in Oxford, and particularly in Oriel College, that men like John Keble had begun to think that the Catholic theology of the Middle Ages might actually be true. Until Newman, some decades later, took the logical step of joining the Church of Rome (the church of St Thomas Aquinas, St Albert the Great and the other medieval schoolmen) there was no thorough-going attempt to undermine the Reformation. Rather, Keble, Pusey and his friends believed that the truths which had been enshrined in the medieval Church had not been lost at the time of Henry VIII's divorce from Catherine of Aragon. The Church of England, far from being a botched-together quasi-political compromise, was in Keble's eyes the very body of Christ Himself, a holy society of Divine foundation. It followed that when Church matters were discussed in Parliament, far more than politics were at stake. Since only the Ascendancy families in Ireland were adherents of the Anglican Church there, it made sense to the Whig Parliament in London to reduce the number of Irish bishoprics. But from the perspective of Oriel, where the fellows had refashioned the established Church in a stained glass medieval glow of their own imagining, this essentially practical question was full of religious significance. Members of Parliament had no authority in the Body of Christ. To reduce the Irish bishoprics was to imply an unbelief in the full, catholic and apostolic character of the National Church. So issues which, with the perspective of history, seem almost inconceivably petty and unimportant, were test cases to show forth the truth that God Himself was directly involved with all the issues of the hour.

Within a generation, all the best minds in Oxford had rejected these High Church preoccupations. Some had gone off to join the Church of Rome – among them, Gladstone's close Oxford friend Henry Manning, destined to become the Cardinal Archbishop of Westminster. Others – the greater part – such as Mark Pattison, J. A. Froude, Benjamin Jowett, Matthew Arnold – had drifted into some form of 'liberal' Christianity, or rejected Christianity altogether. It was mere chance, or destiny, which determined that Gladstone was at Oxford when the religious revival in the Church was just about to begin. It was to colour the way he viewed the world, and his own political career, for the rest of his days.

Gladstone entered the House of Commons in 1833, the very year that Keble first denounced national apostasy in his famous Assize Sermon preached from the pulpit of St Mary's, Oxford, the University church. By 1841, when Peel was Prime Minister for another term, Gladstone, aged thirty-two, felt aggrieved not to be offered a Cabinet post. There was never any fake humility about him. He knew himself to be remarkable, and he put his talents at the service of the nation. It was therefore remiss of the Prime Minister not to offer him what God had obviously intended. But he had not long to wait; appointed Deputy-President of the Board of Trade, he had soon become President, and was then transferred to the Colonial Office.

This photograph was taken during Gladstone's second term as Chancellor of the Exchequer, when his political ambitions and his psychosexual tensions were at their height.

From the first, Gladstone was a tireless administrator. He had a tremendous eye for detail. Rather like Mrs Thatcher, he always knew – throughout his life – exactly what everything cost, and while having largeness of vision he retained the ability, essential in any government minister, to concern himself with small things, too.

Throughout this period, when he was finding his feet as a Cabinet minister, all his Church Toryism was being undermined by the pressure of events. Keble's vision of a theocracy – of not just the Church of England, but England itself, being the Tory Party at Prayer – did not correspond to the facts of things as they actually were and, as Gladstone's favourite philosopher Bishop Butler observed, 'things and actions are what they are, and the consequences of them will be what they will be.' The Tractarian position was considerably weakened in 1845 when its most brilliant exponent, John Henry Newman, became a Roman Catholic. In Gladstone's undergraduate days, Newman had been regarded as rather suspiciously Protestant and Low Church. How fast things were changing. It was not long before Henry Manning, perhaps Gladstone's closest Oxford friend, was to follow Newman into the Roman Catholic Church. It was a crushing emotional blow to Gladstone, made worse when his own sister Helen was also converted to that creed. Like many sick people in that period, Helen Gladstone also became addicted to laudanum. In his hectoring disapproval of her, it is sometimes hard to know whether Gladstone thought her drug addiction or her Romanism the more insufferable deviation.

As a young Cabinet minister, he had tried to keep alive his old Anglo-Catholic or High Church view derived from Keble. When the Government increased its grant to the Irish seminary of Maynooth – more or less the only place of higher education available to the Irish – Gladstone resigned from the Cabinet. The absurd 'logic' behind this resignation was the idea that the young Irish seminarians, instead of preparing for the Catholic priesthood, should all become Anglicans. But as a practical young Peelite economist, Gladstone the MP was a different being from Gladstone the minister. Though resigning on principle in protest against the Maynooth grant, he *voted for it in the House of Commons*. This was because common sense and common humanity told him that you could not continue to lay burdens on the Irish without some form of explosion. The famines which had wiped out so many Irish people in the 1840s were beginning to create the inevitable political backlash.

Violence was threatened. For where people are repressed and justice is violated, violence would inevitably break out. It was the matter of Ireland which broke Gladstone's Toryism. Though he remained a Peelite Tory until such a thing became obsolete, he knew, after 1845, that his position was untenable.

There was, besides, another side to Gladstone which quite differed from the parochialism of his Oxford Tory self. There was Gladstone the lover of Italy. His first visit to Rome in 1831 had made an overwhelming impression upon him. The sight of St Peter's had made him see what 'unity in the Church' might mean. 'May God bind up the wounds of his bleeding church,' he wrote in his diary on that occasion, adding, of course, an explanation to God, that the blame for schism rested entirely upon 'Rome itself'. This lofty sense of a truly universal or catholic church never left Gladstone. Paradoxically, it was what fired his violent hostility to the Papacy. When, later in the century, Pius IX declared himself to be infallible, Gladstone furiously denounced the measure as an encouragement to unbelief.

In 1850, Gladstone went to Naples and was able to see for himself what religious absolutism was like when given its head. It completely changed his own rigidly Tory attitude to political authority. Here was a Catholic kingdom which, *mutatis mutandis*, was not so very unlike what Gladstone and his young Oxford friends had hoped to establish in England. Gladstone visited Poerio, the recently deposed Liberal leader in Naples, and found that he had been sentenced to twenty-four years in irons. The prisoners were chained two and two in double irons with murderers and violent thieves.

There followed Gladstone's written outburst to the British Prime Minister of the day, the famous *Letters to Lord Aberdeen* in which he denounced the Bourbon kingdom of Naples as 'the negation of God erected into a system of Government'.

Gladstone was never to be the same man again. Both political parties were fractured in the middle of the last century – old Whigs divided from the new radicals; old Tories from Peelites and the rising new Conservatives who looked to Disraeli as their leader. It was inevitable in the midst of these new alignments that Gladstone would ally himself with the party which would eventually take the name Liberal, the party which identified itself with freedom and independence. Free Trade was the watchword economically – a market unshackled by tariffs or government interference. Minimal taxation was necessary in those days. As Chancellor of the Exchequer in Aberdeen's ministry, Gladstone would have liked to abolish income tax altogether. As it was he was never able to reduce it below the scandalously high figure of 2.5 per cent – sixpence in the pound. From these freedoms – and from the natural consequence of such economic freedom, the growth in power and importance of the urban trading classes – Gladstone learnt to believe in other freedoms. By the end of the century the young Tory die-hard had become a believer in the ballot box; in one man one vote; even, most extraordinary of all, in religious freedom, and the disestablishment of the Church in Wales and Scotland.

Freedom of morals, in sexual matters, was something rather different. Gladstone was happy in the choice of his wife. Like many Victorians, he married the sister of a great friend. And, like many rich mercantile families, he married into the aristocracy. Catherine Glynne was the sister of Sir Stephen Glynne, whose country seat, Hawarden Castle in Cheshire, became Gladstone's most treasured refuge. Here, even when Prime Minister, he would retreat for anything up to four months of the year. Forestry was his passion. When he was not digging or cutting down trees, he was going for long walks and ruminating on the rights and wrongs of things. And one of the most notorious wrongs of Victorian England, one with which Gladstone was obsessed, was prostitution.

It is symptomatic of the extraordinary double standards of the age that, only a stone's throw from the front door of Gladstone's palatial town house – 11 Carlton House Terrace – was the Haymarket. Today, it contains nothing more racy than shops and theatres. In the days of Mr Gladstone, the Haymarket was swarming with prostitutes, plying their trade. Most nineteenth-century men took their existence for granted. In a world where divorce was almost unthinkable, and sex had to be buried, a case could be made for believing prostitution to be a social necessity. The Russian novelist Tolstoy, no stranger in his youth to the pleasures of the *bordello*, defended the existence of prostitution even after his own conversion to a form of ethical Christianity. 'Imagine London without its 80,000 Magdalens!' he wrote. 'What would become of families? How many wives or daughters would remain chaste? What would become of the laws of morality which people so love to observe? It seems to me that this class of woman is *essential* to the family under the present complex forms of life.'

ABOVE *Gladstone's wife was Catherine Glynne, a merry, intelligent Welsh aristocrat who was his devoted companion for more than half a century.*

RIGHT *The Glynne family seat in North Wales, Hawarden Castle, was Gladstone's most cherished retreat and refuge. Here he could escape for four months of each year from the hurly-burly of London to read, to pray, to write and to chop down trees.*

Gladstone took a more austere view. In his encounters with dozens of women, and men, who undertook this form of work, he endeavoured to persuade them to desist. Together with other High Church friends, he set up the House of St Barnabas in Soho as a refuge for prostitutes as early as the 1840s. His obsession with prostitutes continued throughout the coming decades; and there can be no doubt that he was deeply attracted to the women whom he attempted to save. In order to curb his passions he procured a special whip, donated for the purpose by Dr Pusey at Oxford who was supplied with these disciplines by a continental convent. From the 1860s onwards, Gladstone made a habit of scourging himself with the discipline after conversing with a prostitute.

Prostitutes were to discover what the Queen, and the Gladstone family, and the House of Commons had known for some time – that when Gladstone spoke, he spoke at length, adumbrating points under different headings, weighing moral as well as practical considerations, outlining the problem, and suggesting the solution. Sometimes his discourses with these women lasted over two hours. In a profession where time is money, his interruptions to their business cannot always have been welcome. Some of those whom he rescued were not always grateful, like the woman he persuaded to abandon 'the game' in favour of life in the Anglican convent at Clewer, near Windsor. After six months, she apologetically confided in Gladstone that she would prefer the risk of being beaten by her pimp or infected by her clients to the insufferable atmosphere of this worthy Tractarian house.

Did the ladies ever oblige Gladstone by giving him the discipline of flagellation themselves? Perhaps. Not long before he died, Gladstone emphasised to his clergyman son that he had never 'been guilty of the act which is known as that of infidelity to the marriage bed'. It is a typically Gladstonian and long-winded way of saying that he had never committed adultery. Whatever else he was, he was no liar. It would seem likely that even the flagellation happened on his own, in private, and that the encounters with these ladies were purely conversational. Though they exposed him to torments of lust, we may believe that he never compromised himself. Like everything else he ever did, his hundreds of chronicled encounters with prostitutes were motivated by a sense of Christian obligation. He had as much duty, having been enlightened with the truth, to persuade prostitutes to abandon the pavements as he had to persuade 'the West End' and the 'top ten thousand' of the population – groups whose antagonism he risked and courted – of the injustice of their privileges.

Needless to say, the hazards of his interest in the sexual underworld of Victorian London were considerable. His changing allegiance politically brought him many enemies. Just before he presented his 1853 Budget, the Chancellor of the Exchequer was seen holding an animated and extended conversation with a woman of doubtful appearance on the corner of Haymarket. No doubt he was expounding to her the eighth chapter of St John where the Saviour tells a woman to 'go and sin no more'. A Scotsman by the name of Wilson unwisely attempted to blackmail Gladstone, who instantly handed him over to the police.

Gladstone undertook the rescue of prostitutes as a charitable work in his early twenties. This picture shows girls bribing the Beadle of the Burlington Arcade, off London's Piccadilly, so that they could ply their trade in this popular shopping place.

Is it too neat to attribute, in part, Gladstone's extraordinary capacity for hard work – those endless parliamentary speeches, those long hours in committee, those thousands of words spoken, minuted and recycled – to pent-up sexual energy? In the early years of his marriage, Gladstone's wife was almost perpetually pregnant and spent much of her time in the country while he was in London. We can never imagine Gladstone relaxing. Even in extreme old age, when holidaying at Biarritz with his biographer John Morley, we find him going into shops to inquire the prices of everything; we find him mulling over textual cruces in Homer; we find him ruminating on the problems of the hour. In addition to the nation's economy, he was an efficient manager not only of his own money but that of his wife's family. His preparedness to go through everything with a tooth-comb was largely responsible for his ability, not without effort, to rescue his brother-in-law from bankruptcy. There was never a period when he was still, unless it was when he was on his knees, and even then it is all too easy to imagine the Almighty, like Queen Victoria, feeling that He was being addressed as if He were a public meeting.

Public meetings were Gladstone's forte and – in the form of them at which he excelled – it could be said that they were his invention. The Conservatives were not all wrong to think of him as a demagogue. He knew how to manage big crowds and to use the power of the crowd as an extra-parliamentary weapon.

During the election of 1868, Gladstone returned again and again to the theme of Ireland in his public speeches. He spoke of the Protestant Ascendancy there as:

> some tall tree of noxious growth, lifting its head to Heaven and poisoning the atmosphere of the land so far as its shadow can extend. It is still there, gentlemen, but now at last the day has come when, as we hope, the axe has been laid to its root. (Loud cheers) It is deeply cut round and round. It nods and quivers from top to base (Cheers). There lacks, gentlemen, but one stroke more – the stroke of these elections (Loud cheers) It will then, once for all, topple to its fall, and on that day, the heart of Ireland will leap for joy, and the mind and conscience of England and Scotland will repose with thankful satisfaction upon the thought that something has been done towards the discharge of national duty, and towards the deepening and widening the foundations of public strength, security and peace. (Loud and sustained applause).

It was a triumphant election for Gladstone. The Liberals were returned with a majority in the House of Commons of 112 seats. Gladstone (who had previously represented Newark and Oxford University) now found himself sitting for Greenwich. At the beginning of December he was at Hawarden, cutting down a tree in the park, when a telegram arrived, informing him that General Grey, the Queen's Secretary, would arrive that evening. Fully aware of the drama of the situation, Gladstone merely said, 'Very significant.' Then he resumed his work with the axe. After a few minutes he paused and said to his companion (the Hon. Evelyn Ashley, a son of Lord Shaftesbury), with a voice of deep earnestness and with an intense expression, 'My mission is to pacify Ireland.'

But how was he to do it? At nearly sixty, he could not have dreamed that he had a quarter of a century of active political life ahead of him. By the time he died, Gladstone had done all that was humanly possible to avert an Irish calamity, but he had failed; and to this hour, the people of Ireland live with Gladstone's failure.

As well as being the most dramatic arena of his political failing, Ireland was also a mirror to Gladstone's extraordinary mind. In examining his changing attitudes to Ireland, we see more clearly than anywhere else the kinds of thing which motivated him, as a politician and as a man. In the beginning, as a High Anglican bigot, he had hated the idea of Catholic Emancipation, and had felt as a matter of principle that the Maynooth seminary should not have an increase in its grant. It was, for the young Tory Cabinet minister, a resigning matter. As the years went by, however, he realised that it was not possible, nor was it even desirable, for the governing class of a country to make all its citizens follow one creed or submit blindly to a single authority. The sight of the repressive regime in Naples made him particularly sensitive to the position of the Irish. Here were citizens of the United Kingdom who had suffered religious persecution, political repression, and starvation. Not surprisingly, there had grown up a movement desiring self-government for the Irish, a movement inevitably attracting to itself hotheads, bomb-throwers, and murderers.

Justice demanded that the Irish case be met. Gladstone did what he could, in his first administration as Prime Minister, to appease the Irish, to make it clear to them that he was on their side. The trouble was to find a solution which would work, and one which would be acceptable on both sides of the Irish Sea. The crucial factor in the whole case – the position of the Ulster Protestants – was one which Gladstone ignored totally. Indeed, having only visited Ireland once for a month in the 1840s, he did not really know about it. For him, the issue was simply one of justice to the Catholics, and the pacification of the land of Ireland as a whole. So he, the High Anglican, presided over the disestablishment of the Church of Ireland in 1869. Henceforth Roman Catholics in Ireland were not in the anomalous position of having to be described as Non-conformists to a national church in which none of them believed. A year later, the Irish Land Act gave a measure of protection to small tenant farmers against the rapacity of Ascendancy landlords, to avert a repetition of the conditions which had led to the famines of the 1840s.

Gladstone had a profound personal and political antipathy to Disraeli, whose genius was the exact opposite of his own. The rivalry between the two greatest statesmen of the age was the subject of many cartoons, such as this one from Punch *in 1868.*

But Ireland was not the only thing on the political agenda in the early 1870s, and much else intervened to guarantee that by 1874 Gladstone's great adversary Disraeli would win the election and throw the Liberals out of office. By then, Gladstone was sixty-five years old. The side of his nature which craved prayer and scholarship (he used to pray that he would die in church 'though not at a time to disturb worshippers') wanted to quit the political scene altogether. He sold up his big London house, moving his vast collection of porcelain and pictures to a smaller house in Harley Street. And he retired to Hawarden. The leadership of the Liberal party passed to Lord Hartington, the heir to the Duke of Devonshire. It looked as if Gladstone's spell as Liberal Prime Minister was to have been dramatic, but brief.

His enemies, observing the huge contradictions in Gladstone's nature, dismissed him as a humbug and a hypocrite. But this is unfair. He was not one man pretending to be another. By contrast, he was many powerfully different personalities all waging war with one another. It is typical of the man that, having abandoned politics for ever, he should have been back on the hustings, more loquacious and energetic than ever, within a year.

It was a time of some of the worst trouble in the Balkans. Disraeli's government, enthusiastically supported by the Queen who pined persistently for a repeat performance of the Crimean War, supported the Turks in their hostility to their Christian minorities, and to the threatened eruption of nationalism among the small Balkan states against their Ottoman masters. The Russians, a great Christian Empire, who in Gladstone's eyes had the supreme advantage of being non-Roman but highly Catholic, protested at the treatment of Christians under Turkish rule.

Gladstone's term as Chancellor of the Exchequer in Aberdeen's Cabinet during the Crimean War had left a residual guilt about the folly and pointlessness of that conflict. Conviction told him that Christian nations should be allies and that the British should not have lined up with the Turks against the Russians. Then, in 1875, there began to emerge the terrible stories of Turkish atrocities against the Bulgarians – babies, women and children butchered in their thousands. For the Queen and Disraeli, it remained an imperial question. Which European power should dominate the Mediterranean? Should it be Russia, with its known desire to reoccupy the Constantinople patriarchate? Or should it be the weakened Turks, who would of course look to the British as their protectors? The actual fate of the Bulgarians meant less to Disraeli and to Queen Victoria than the shape of the map of Europe. How much, in the power game, did the British control?

Gladstone, who had been tormented for ten years now by thoughts of Ireland, saw this as another case of a small nation struggling for independence against the overwhelming might of ignorant imperial armies. The sufferings of the Bulgarians were, in any case, intolerable for their own sake. It sickened him that the British could regard as their allies a nation who could behave as the Ottoman Turks were behaving.

With one of the most mammoth displays of political energy of his whole life, the Grand Old Man emerged from retirement at Hawarden and made a series of speeches across the north of England. By 1879, his mind was drawn not only to the Bulgarian atrocities but also to what the British were doing, or not doing, in Afghanistan, and in South Africa. Everywhere, it seemed, there was this conflict between the desire of small nations to determine their own destiny, and the desire of Empires to crush them. This was the era when the word 'jingoism' came into the English language. The crude music-hall song was the perfect expression of that vulgar attitude of mind displayed by the Queen, the Conservative party, and the Press:

We don't want to fight but by jingo if we do
We've got the ships, we've got the men, we've got the money too!

For Gladstone, the world was not a playground in which powerful nations could tolerably behave like the school bully.

In 1879 he decided to offer himself at the next election to the voters of Scotland, the land of his high-minded Presbyterian ancestors. In the first of his legendary Midlothian campaigns he made a series of magnificent and hugely long speeches – one of the great ones was in the Corn Exchange in Edinburgh, but he followed it up, speaking to a crowd of thousands in the open air. Standing in the frosty Scottish air, he told his audience:

Remember that the sanctity of life in the hill villages of Afghanistan is as inviolable in the eye of Almighty God as can be your own. Remember that He who has united you as human beings in the same flesh and blood has bound you by the law of mutual love; that that mutual love is not limited by the shores of this island, is not limited by the boundaries of Christian civilisation, that it passes over the whole surface of the earth and embraces the meanest along with the greatest in its unmeasured scope.

In place of the commercial rapacity and sheer political arrogance of the imperial ideal, Gladstone held out a vision of something very different.

When, in 1880, the Conservative government appealed unsuccessfully to the country, they made Irish Home Rule the main issue. The Liberals won the election and Gladstone won his seat. The Queen asked Lord Hartington to form an administration. He pointed out to her – and how little she liked it – that it would be unthinkable to form a Liberal government of which Gladstone was not a member. Gladstone was approached and asked if he would serve. He replied, with his usual absence of nonsense when political power was in the offing, that he would serve in no other capacity than that of Prime Minister.

The Midlothian campaign was therefore an extraordinary demonstration of popular politicking, of demagoguery. It sits oddly beside the reclusive and quiet side of Gladstone's nature. It is hard to see the old

*The most exciting moments of Gladstone's later political life were spent
on the hustings in the Midlothian Campaigns where he addressed and enthralled
crowds of thousands, sometimes speaking for as long as five hours at a stretch.*

man, almost drunk with the sound of his magnificently resonant deep
voice and with the cheers of the Midlothian crowds, as the same person
as the scholar on his knees in the chapel at Hawarden.

The Midlothian campaign – like much else in Gladstone's life –
changed the face of British politics. It was the first election campaign
fought across the country by a senior politician. Just how strange it was
may be realised at once if we try to picture Lords Palmerston or
Aberdeen 'touring the country' in the manner of a modern democratic
leader. In so far as it was an exercise in attracting political support outside Parliament by a man who at that point held no office under the
Crown, it was not surprising that the Queen viewed the Midlothian
campaign with distaste and alarm. The waves of radicalism were riding
high. The new generation of English Liberals contained many, like
Joseph Chamberlain in Birmingham, who were anti-monarchical, and
even republican. The Queen did nothing to counteract her growing
unpopularity with many sections of the populace who resented her refusal to take part in public life while busily hoarding away her Civil List

payment from public funds. The private fortune of the present royal family in part owes its origins to the miserliness of the Widow of Windsor who for years after her husband's death never made public appearances, never attempted to meet her people, and really failed to do her job. It would not have been at all difficult for Gladstone in the 1880s to bring the British monarchy to an end altogether. As on the last occasion when it had happened, it is improbable that there would have been much, if any, protest. The popularity with which Victoria was regarded when she was a very old woman had not yet begun. Her refusal to come out of mourning and her unenlightened political views made her much hated. It was very largely Gladstone's personal devotion to the monarchy, based on his reading of the Book of Common Prayer rather than on the Queen's intolerable behaviour towards him, which saved the monarchy from extinction.

The Midlothian campaign of 1879–80 is also the key to Gladstone's Irish policy. From now onwards, it was common humanity which counted for most with Gladstone, whatever his own religious or personal preferences. Since 1875, there had been an Irish nationalist party in the House of Commons in Westminster, led by a Protestant squire by the name of Charles Parnell.

One of the greatest tragedies in the Irish situation is that Parnell was never able to trust Gladstone. As in so many of Max Beerbohm's cartoons, there is truth in his depiction of Parnell meeting Gladstone in Heaven. Parnell has his fists raised. Gladstone, with ineffable loftiness, is saying, 'If you could but give me three hours and a half of your time, I could explain *everything*!' Parnell was never able to recognise how much Gladstone, even before his mind cleared and he saw how things truly stood in Ireland, was anxious to do the right thing by that country. In exchange for some big concessions in a reworking of the Land Act – in particular, releasing tenants from arrears in their rent – Gladstone extracted from Parnell a promise that he would modify the violence of his Sinn Fein supporters. Inevitably, there had been bomb outrages not only in Ireland but in England – in London, Manchester and Liverpool. In May 1882, Gladstone sent Lord Spencer – the great-great-great grandfather of the present Princess of Wales – to be Viceroy of Ireland, and with him a nephew of Gladstone's marriage, Lord Frederick Cavendish, the brother of Lord Hartington. On 6 May, only the day after his arrival, Cavendish was walking with Burke, the head of the Irish executive, in

ABOVE Charles Stewart Parnell, the Irish Nationalist leader.

RIGHT It was the Clerkenwell bombings, when some Fenians blew up a London prison to rescue their imprisoned comrades, that panicked Gladstone into the belief that it was his mission to pacify Ireland.

Phoenix Park in Dublin when the two men were stabbed to death in broad daylight under the eyes of the Viceroy. For the rest of that summer there were incidents of murder throughout the Irish countryside. On 17 August 1882, a family in Connemara was butchered. Unlike the murderers of Burke and Cavendish, the men responsible for this crime were caught and brought to justice. At the trial, however, it was discovered that the defendants either could not or would not speak English. For the Irish, the hanging of these men, who did not even understand what was being said to them by their accusers, brought home the cruel implacability of British justice. For the English, the Irish situation called for a solution. But what was to be done? The Conservatives, and a high proportion of the Liberal party, believed that the answer was greater and greater repression of the unruly elements in Irish society. Violence must be met with violence. As for the yearning of the Irish people for nationhood, it did not *do*! The Irish were being as tiresome as those Bulgars, those Zulus, those Greeks – all those little peoples who wanted self-government. To give the Irish self-government would be to dissolve the imperial ideal, to remove a brick which might begin a process by which the whole edifice of Empire would crumble! Ireland was as much a part of the United Kingdom as was Wales or Scotland.

Gladstone, little by little, learnt that this was *not* the solution. Many things delayed his conversion; and after the conversion, there were many things which contributed to the Irish distrust of Gladstone – not least his mounting hostility to the Vaticanism, the spiritual imperialism, as he saw it, of the Papacy, rampant since the Vatican Council of 1870 of which his old friend Manning was chief architect, and which had declared the Pope, in certain circumstances, to be infallible. But since the Irish were now consistently sending back a majority of republican members to Westminster, and since all the violent agitation in town and country up and down the length of Ireland made it clear that they wanted self-government, Gladstone saw no alternative which did not ultimately have self-government as its end. He was converted at last to the view that what he believed held true for the Neapolitans and the Afghans and the Zulus was true too for the Irish. He became a convert to Irish Home Rule.

The first Home Rule Bill of 1886 was defeated in the Commons and lost Gladstone the election of that year. In the years that intervened before Gladstone was able to present the matter to the Commons a second time, a number of disasters had occurred that doomed the Irish cause to be lost for ever.

Not least of these was the rather ludicrous fact that Parnell, the leader of the Irish nationalists, had, like so many Victorian gentlemen, been leading a double life. By his enemies, Parnell was accused, quite falsely, of colluding in murder and condoning the atrocities which each month were committed in the name of Irish nationalism. A man in this position could not afford to lose the support of his friends. But this is what happened – and for the most trivial of reasons. From 1880 onwards, Parnell had been in love with Katherine O'Shea, the wife of an Irish political colleague. Her husband was prepared to turn a blind eye to what was in effect her quasi-marriage to Parnell. She shared a house with him in Surrey and bore him three children. The situation continued equably because the O'Sheas stood to inherit a small fortune from an aunt, a

*Gladstone's peroration in the House of Commons, defending against all odds
his belief that the Irish people should be allowed to determine their own
affairs. This Home Rule Bill, like its successors in Gladstone's lifetime, was defeated.*

respectable old woman who would have cut Mrs O'Shea out of her will
had the truth been known. Had that aunt been either more broadminded, or longer lived, it is conceivable that we should have peace on
the streets of Belfast today.

In 1890, the aunt died. Anxious to get his share of the inheritance,
O'Shea sued his wife for divorce and cited Parnell as co-respondent.
With a rashness which seems almost as extraordinary to us as Oscar
Wilde's determination to sue Lord Queensberry, Mrs O'Shea contested
her husband's action, and thus, in a single stroke, the cause of peaceful
Irish nationalism was destroyed. Parnell was, in the eyes of his own side,
disgraced. Many of his supporters were anxious to hold to him in disaster

as in triumph. But the priests of the Roman Church, who had been happy enough to condone the murders done in the republican cause, were unable to stomach Parnell's more venial sins of the flesh. The fact that he was a Protestant made it all the worse.

In 1891, Parnell died suddenly. By then, the forces of Irish nationalism were hopelessly divided among themselves. Gladstone, aged eighty, fought the election of the following year on the Irish question. Ever a pragmatist – what he called 'a good parliamentary hand' – he knew that he could not force a measure like Home Rule through the House of Commons on his own. He was therefore prepared to throw in his support with the English political wing who were prepared to support it: the extreme radicals. The man who had first entered Parliament as a young prig opposing the measures of the Great Reform Act found himself with some very different friends at the age of eighty. As he stood on the hustings in Midlothian he was calling for the principle of one man one vote; he had accepted the idea of disestablishing the Churches of Wales and Scotland; local government was to be reformed to allow elections to parish councils, and – for the dreary teetotallers formed a powerful group among his supporters – local councils were to be given the power to regulate and even to forbid the sale of alcoholic drink in this country. All this – much of which went against the grain – was worth it, as far as Gladstone was concerned, if it would pacify Ireland. It was not a matter of appeasement or cowardice. Gladstone did not need to be fighting an election as he entered his ninth decade of life. No one could ever accuse him of cowardice. It was a simple matter of justice. He wanted freedom for the Irish – freedom to live as they wished, freedom to live without the terror of madmen and murderers on the one hand and the oppression of Protestant landlords on the other.

It would have been so much easier for the old man to leave the problem to his successors. As it was, it propelled the break-up of the Liberal party. The most brilliant and likely of Gladstone's successors as leader, Joseph Chamberlain, joined the Conservatives, while many of the more genial souls in the Liberal party, like Lord Rosebery and Herbert Asquith, repelled by the pro-Irishry and anti-imperialism of some of Gladstone's new friends, were really preparing themselves for a split in their party. The Liberals remained, under Campbell-Bannerman and Asquith, as an uneasy coalition between those who were in favour of Empire and the Irish Union and those who were much more politically and economically radical and would one day themselves split – some behind Lloyd George, others to join the expanding ranks of the Labour Party. In this matter of Ireland, in fact, we see the whole future of the English Left in the melting-pot, and there is a strange paradox that it should have been presided over by this ancient Victorian gentleman, who went to church every day, and who would have felt no more at home in the twentieth century than would Duns Scotus or Alfred the Great.

The Queen dismissed him as 'an old wild, incomprehensible old man'. Lord Randolph Churchill in the election campaign spoke for many when he said:

> Mr Gladstone has reserved for his closing days a conspiracy against the honour of Britain and the welfare of Ireland more startlingly base and nefarious than any of those other numerous designs and plots which, during the last quarter of a century, have occupied his imagination . . . all useful and desired reforms are to be indefinitely postponed, the British Constitution is to be torn up, the Liberal party shivered into fragments. And why? For this reason and no other: to gratify the ambition of an old man in a hurry.

In February 1893, a much modified Home Rule Bill for Ireland was introduced into the House of Commons. It was merely proposed that there should be an independent legislative assembly at Dublin and that the Irish should continue to send their eighty MPs to Westminster. The debate occupied eighty-five days of parliamentary time, and the bill was *just* passed in its third reading by thirty-four votes. Needless to say, when it went to the House of Lords, it was defeated by 419 votes to 41.

Far from seeing Gladstone as an ambitious old man in a hurry, we now must see his great political failure as a piece of extraordinary quixotry. Better perhaps than anyone in England, he knew the political make-up of the House of Lords. He knew that Irish Home Rule had no chance of being allowed by a Westminster Parliament.

But, like the Trollope hero, 'he knew he was right'. He had begun to see with prophetic clarity what would happen in Ireland if the Irish were not allowed to govern themselves. He knew how much notice was taken of the House of Lords in Connemara, in Cork, and even in Dublin. His failure on a political level ws not his idealistic promotion of Home Rule. It was his complete inability to see into the minds of Ulster Protestants.

There was a sort of Olympian, donnish loftiness in Mr Gladstone which did not grow less with the years. Whether as a young Tory or an old radical, he tended to assess questions of the day against the high standards of religion and absolute morality rather than by the vulgar enthusiasms of the hour. He lacked any of Joseph Chamberlain's or Margaret Thatcher's political 'nose' – what some would call vulgarity. One sees this in the notorious incident of General Gordon's death, when Gladstone's failure to read the 'mind of the British people' cost his party an election.

Gordon, it will be remembered, was stuck in Khartoum in 1884 without reinforcement against the overwhelmingly superior opposition of the Mahdi, the self-proclaimed religious leader of a revolt against British rule in Egypt. It was the Government's indecision and prevarication that delayed the sending of a relieving expedition. When one was dispatched, under Sir Garnet Wolseley, it arrived too late. Gordon had been killed two days before. Gladstone afterwards declared himself to have been

This painting of Gordon's death at Khartoum was executed by G. W. Joy. It was fast to become an icon, reproduced in thousands of prints and engravings, hung in parlours and school-rooms, a set-piece of Victorian heroism.

'tortured' by the affair. He had never met Gordon. He had been reluctant to send him out to Khartoum in the first place. But while the Queen and the British public, with that irrational fervour that sometimes grips imperial powers (compare the popularity of Colonel Oliver North), were only able to see Gordon as a hero, Gladstone's more detached mind saw it all differently. He had the greatest objection to British soldiers being in Egypt in the first place. He did not see it as the British vocation to be the policemen to the rest of the world. Ridden with guilt as he was about his father's fortune deriving from the slave trade, he had a lifelong suspicion of interference for ultimately commercial ends in the political life of other nations. So, while the jingoistic Press proclaimed Gordon as a hero, Gladstone regarded him as a disobedient fanatic, a menace who was making a difficult situation worse.

At length, the Grand Old Man did retire from public life, and as a very old man he lived almost entirely at Hawarden, seldom venturing on to a public rostrum. But there was an exception. In 1896, when news came of yet more appalling massacres of Armenians by the Turks, Gladstone, whose deep voice was still resonant at the age of eighty-five, made a speech in Liverpool in which he described the massacres as 'the most terrible and the most monstrous series of proceedings that has ever been recorded in the dismal and deplorable history of human crime.'

And then he gave utterance to that marvellous sentence which could be said to be his creed: 'The ground on which we stand is not British, nor European, but it is human.'

It is that which coloured Gladstone's largeness of vision. Nourished by the great classics of European literature and by an intelligent exercise of religion, Gladstone was never petty-minded, never parochial, never mean.

He died at Hawarden, aged eighty-nine, on a bright May morning – Ascension Day – on 19 May 1898. All his family was kneeling at the bedside, a scene which was quintessentially Victorian. His death was felt as much in Europe as it had been in England: a sensation, it was said, as great as the death of that other great lover of liberty, Garibaldi.

His legacy to the nation is Hawarden itself, St Deiniol's Library where people may come to do what Gladstone best loved to do himself – to pray in the chapel and to read. It is partly an Oxford college and partly a Tractarian retreat house. Is Gladstone himself as quaintly irrelevant to the concerns of the generality of modern people as this place seems today? Or do his great rallying-cries, for decency in public life, and above all for liberty, have greater force now than they ever did? He wanted economic freedom – an ending of income tax was his dream. He believed passionately in the freedom of the Christian gospel against what he saw as the 'Asiatic monarchy' of the Vatican. He believed in self-determining nationhood. An enemy of Gladstone's could say that this was symptomatic of his blindness – his inability to see that these lofty-sounding ideas would turn into the rampant and selfishly destructive forces of a free market economy, into religious sectarianism and, most dangerous of all, into the rise of nationalism, the fatal effects of which in the forty years after Gladstone's death – particularly in Germany – he seems to have been entirely unable to predict. He quite failed to see the importance of Bismarck.

Certainly it is easy to see much that was unintentionally comic about a man who chewed every mouthful of food thirty-two times, and who was so prolix in conversation that he could indulge in monologues of two and a half hours with prostitutes, crowned heads, clergymen or parliamentary colleagues. The Beerbohm cartoons of Gladstone's reception into Heaven, which now adorn the walls of the Carlton Club, are the Conservative answer to the icons of Gladstone in the National Liberal Club. They hint amusingly at the sort of Gladstone we should have seen had he appeared as a character in Strachey's *Eminent Victorians*. We, with a bigger perspective than Strachey's – seventy years more perspective – may laugh at Gladstone's eccentricities but perhaps be better able to see him for what he was, just as, the further one drives away from a mountain, the better one is able to make out its mighty outline against the sky.

JOHN HENRY NEWMAN
1801-90

Poet and priest

*This picture of Newman as a Roman Catholic priest dates from the time
when he wrote his famous autobiography, the* Apologia pro Vita Sua,
which gives a moving account of his decision to leave the Church of England.

hree miles outside Oxford, in a village called Littlemore, there is a row of simple cottages which date back to the old coaching days, before the coming of the railways. Then the buildings used to serve as a staging-post to allow the coaches that made the east-west journey across England from Cambridge to Oxford to change horses.

This old staging-post was also the scene of a more momentous change. For it was here, on 9 October 1845, that the eloquent vicar of St Mary's Oxford, John Henry Newman, by far the most famous and influential intellectual leader of his generation, shocked the world by becoming a Roman Catholic.

Nowadays in England, the Roman Catholic Church numbers more regular adherents than any other Christian body; there are more Roman Catholic churchgoers than there are practising members of the Church of England. Though not all Christians accept their doctrines, the Roman Catholic Church is by far the most vigorous of all the denominations. Though pockets of prejudice against it remain, and presumably always will remain, it is now a fully accepted part of the British religious scene. As a result of the Act of Settlement at the close of the seventeenth century which determined that the British monarchy would be Protestant, the Sovereign is still forbidden either to be or to marry a Roman Catholic. But it is now a familiar part of public ritual that the Cardinal Archbishop of Westminster, or some other public dignitary of the Roman Catholic Church, will take part in such events as royal weddings, along with representatives from the Non-conformist churches.

The Roman Catholics have arrived.

So much do we take this for granted that it is almost impossible to imagine that only 140 years ago, the Roman Catholic Church in England barely existed. A very few families, mostly in the north of England, had clung to their old religion ever since the Reformation, and since the Irish famines in the early decades of the century, there had been an influx of Irish workers into the great industrial cities. But in so far as it actually affected national life in the 1830s and 1840s, the Roman Catholic Church hardly counted in England. In a town like Oxford, there might be one small Roman Catholic chapel to cater for the tiny number of local Papists who were at least (since 1778) allowed to practise their religion without infringing the law. But the scenes which are familiar today were quite alien then: several large Roman Catholic churches in every town, attracting good congregations each Sunday; Roman Catholic schools, Roman Catholic cathedrals and bishops; nuns glimpsed on a bus; monsignors, or ex-monsignors, leading anti-nuclear demonstrations.

If you had suggested to an Oxford don of the 1820s that England in the 1980s might contain so many Roman Catholics, he would have considered the proposition as fantastic. As fantastic, perhaps, as the wild notion that there might one day be a mosque in London's Regent's Park.

Ever since the Reformation, English people had nursed a dread of Roman Catholicism which might at any moment flare up in displays of irrational fear. One thinks, for example, of the Gordon riots in 1780 (described so vividly by Dickens in *Barnaby Rudge*) when London mobs, egged on by the demagogue Lord George Gordon, looted and burnt the house of supposed Roman Catholics in protest against the lifting of the legal ban against their religion. Or one thinks of the controversies which seized Oxford fifty years later in the time of Newman.

Most people arriving in Oxford for the first time are struck by the spindly grace of the Martyrs' Memorial, standing at the bottom of St Giles's. When I first saw it as a boy, and made up my mind that Oxford was the place for me, the Martyrs' Memorial struck me as the quintessence of the Middle Ages. In fact, the Memorial was erected between 1841 and 1843 to the designs of George Gilbert Scott. It commemorates the brave death, not far from this spot, of Thomas Cranmer, author of the English Prayer Book, and of Bishops Ridley and Latimer, all of whom were burnt at the stake in the reign of Bloody Mary for their refusal to accept the Roman Catholic religion and the authority of the Pope.

> Be of good comfort Master Ridley! and play the man. We shall this day light such a candle by God's grace in England as (I trust) shall never be put out.

That candle was the Protestant religion. And why did they wait until 1841 before they thought of building a memorial to the Protestant martyrs? Because in 1841 the dons of Oxford were panicked into

believing that the unthinkable was about to happen. The candle lit by
Ridley and Latimer was guttering in its socket. And the man who with
devastating logic and sleight of hand was going to snuff it out was John
Henry Newman.

The nerve-centre of the controversy was Oriel College, of which
Newman was a fellow. It was here that he and his friends – John Keble,
Edward Bouverie Pusey, Hurrell Froude and others – began their
analysis of the Christian religion and its history which was to cause so
much upset.

Very nearly all their deliberations, when read today, seem to contain
about as much matter for intellectual excitement as the controversies of
Tweedledum and Tweedledee in the works of that other Oxford clergyman Charles Dodgson, otherwise known as Lewis Carroll. Their *Tracts
for the Times*, published at irregular intervals throughout the 1830s, were
on such esoteric subjects as Fasting in the Early Church or the need for a
new translation of the Psalter.

But these tracts sold in enormous numbers up and down England. Not
only did parsons in their country rectories devour them; but all thinking

*Oriel College, Oxford, of which Newman became a fellow in 1827,
was at that period a centre of religious debate.
Newman occupied rooms just to the right of the oriel window.*

people in London rushed to buy them on their appearance, rather in the way that, in a later generation, they might have subscribed to the Left Book Club. The reason for this is partly to be found in the quite extraordinary degree of interest which early nineteenth-century men and women took in the minutiae of religious questions. But, as the Tracts continued to appear and the Tractarians, as their authors and admirers came to be known, unfolded their position, the nature of what they were saying became direly clear – clear and revolutionary.

You have to imagine a world where certain propositions were taken for granted as intellectual certainties by believing Christians: that there was a God who made the world, and declared His laws to that created world by means of a revealed religion. The first part of the revelation was through Moses and the Ten Commandments. Then, in the fullness of time, He wound up the first Testament and made a New Testament with a New Israel, the Church. He came in His own person, clothed in human flesh but fully divine, to found this society, to establish the sacraments of baptism and holy communion and to give His Church authority to teach and baptise all people in the world.

This is why people felt so passionately about religious controversies. What was at issue was the will of God Himself, who would reward those who were on His side with eternal bliss, but – as most Victorian Christians appeared to have no difficulty in believing – would consign those who got this question wrong to an eternity of damnation.

The Church of England view, in so far as it had been thought out at all, was that God, having founded His Divine society the Church, remained within it as a sacramental presence. In other words, he was there in the holy communion and in baptism. But this had not stopped the Church, over the years, becoming hopelessly corrupted, and all kinds of new doctrines, particularly doctrines about the Virgin Mary, being adopted into its system. Therefore, in the sixteenth century, when the time was ripe, it was perfectly legitimate for a more purified branch of the Church to break away from the Pope and set up on its own. The Church of England was, by this view, much purer and closer to the original Church which Christ had founded than was the Church of Rome from which it had broken away.

It would be largely true to say that for most of the eighteenth century, these questions were a dead issue in the Church of England. The origins of the Church were much less interesting to people than whether the

Church was alive at all. The controversy then was largely between those who were caught up by the fervour of the Wesleys into a lively personal faith in Christ, and those like Bishop Butler who told Wesley, 'Sir, pretending to gifts of the Holy Ghost is a horrid thing, a very horrid thing.'

A rather different sort of religious revival was to emerge through the influence of the dons of Oriel College, Oxford in the 1830s. From 1817 to 1820, Newman had been a very shy undergraduate at Trinity College, loathing the raucous behaviour of his fellow-undergraduates, and spending much of his time alone in his rooms there, playing the fiddle. All his life he was a passionate violinist. He was one of those very clever people who could not take examinations. He overworked for the Schools (as the Final exams are called at Oxford). In Mathematics, at which he was rather good, he failed, while in Classics he was placed in the lower division of the second class.

This was a shattering blow to Newman, who had no mean estimate of his own capabilities. He had set his heart on becoming a Fellow of Oriel College, for that was the place where all the cleverest men in Oxford were believed to be assembled. Different colleges acquire these reputations in different generations. When Oxford, and intellectuals generally, began to react against the interests and ideas fostered at Oriel, it was the turn of another college, Balliol – broadminded almost to the point of free-thinking and politically radical – to claim the predominance in the university.

In spite of his failure in the Schools, and in spite of the fact that he was desperately nervous about the Oriel fellowship examination, Newman managed to do justice to himself in the papers. On 12 April 1822, as he sat playing his violin in his rooms at Trinity, there was a knock at the door. It was the Provost of Oriel's butler, who said that he had 'disagreeable news to announce. Mr Newman was elected Fellow of Oriel and that his immediate presence was required there.'

The Common Room at Oriel 'stank of logic' as a contemporary remarked, but it was not what modern philosophers would mean by the word logic. Not long after his election, Newman, like the greater proportion of Oxford dons, was ordained as an Anglican clergyman, and although he was painfully shy in their presence, he settled down to get to know his colleagues. A great debate was taking place at Oriel, and neither side of the debate would immediately seem attractive to

Newman's priggish evangelical soul. On the one hand, there were men like Thomas Arnold, the future headmaster of Rugby, or Richard Whately, later Archbishop of Dublin. They were what was called liberals, arguing that if Christianity was to survive the assaults of scepticism, it was essential that it accommodate itself to the findings of modern thinking and scholarship; otherwise, Christianity would become purely obscurantist, and ultimately impossible for intelligent people to believe. These men tended to take a 'liberal' view in politics also, supporting in the fullness of time such measures as the Great Reform Bill of 1832. They were sometimes called 'latitudinarians', and they had a benign, tolerant view, for example, of Non-conformist Christians.

On the other side of the argument, there were those men who grouped themselves behind the saintly figure of the poet John Keble. These included such brilliant Hebraists as Edward Bouverie Pusey and historians like Hurrell Froude. They argued that if you took this 'liberal' view of religion, you would ultimately end up with no religion at all, since each doctrine of the Church could be scrapped if it were found to be incompatible with modern wisdom. The Church, Keble and his friends argued, was something different. It was a Divine society, instituted by Christ Himself during the days of His earthly ministry. It had been corrupted by medieval Roman Catholicism, but it was in essence Catholic, sacramental and apostolic. Indeed, it would seem that there was no purer form of Christianity, closer to the customs of the primitive Church or the intentions of its Founder, than that to be found in the Prayer Book of the Church of England.

This point of view took some arguing. It involved ignoring the historical evidence about the origins of the Church of England, and putting an imaginative interpretation upon the origins of Christianity itself. But – perhaps precisely because it was a paradoxical and difficult belief – it was the side of the argument which ultimately appealed strongly to Newman. For it was the Oriel men of the 1820s and 1830s who began to look again at the historical origins as well as the theological justification of the Church of England's existence. What became very clear, as the examination proceeded, piece by piece in the *Tracts for the Times*, was that the Church of England did not come out of it very well.

After all, no historian could claim that the Reformation had happened because of the fervour of Protestant theologians. It had happened because Henry VIII had wanted to marry his pregnant mistress, Anne

Boleyn. And as for continuity between the old Church of the first few centuries of Christendom and the modern Church, where did that lead you? However much you deplored the corruption of Popes, the super-stition of individual Roman Catholics, the inadmissibility of certain modern Roman Catholic beliefs, there was only one Church which could be seen to stretch back in an unbroken line to the time of the Apostles and to Christ himself. If God was God, and if God founded a visible Church on earth, and if he promised that this Church would never be divided, all the other churches are, by this definition, only sects, who have deliber-ately separated themselves from the parent stem.

It was this line of logic which the Tractarians started up, and which Newman was brave enough to follow to its conclusion.

No doubt, if the question had occurred in other minds, at other times, or in other places, it would have had different effects, or no effects at all. It has to be seen against the background of precisely the kind of religious enthusiasm which the Methodist John Wesley had stirred up in the eighteenth century. A few months before coming up to Trinity College at the age of fifteen, Newman had undergone an Evangelical conversion-experience. He knew that he was 'elected to eternal glory' and for the rest of his life, as he tells us in his autobiography, he rested in the thought 'of two and two only supreme and luminously self-evident beings, myself and my Creator'.

It was in such a glow of pious enthusiasm that this profoundly impres-sionable youth was exposed to Oxford. He was what we would now call an aesthete. His great passion was for music, and he was a brilliant vio-linist. But he had also, like most readers of his generation, wallowed in the poetry of Sir Walter Scott and discovered, in *The Lay of the Last Minstrel* and *The Lady of the Lake*, a vision of the past which was to trans-form the look of the British Isles.

Gothic architecture, which to earlier generations had seemed quaint, or rude, or at best picturesque, now appeared to be the quintessence of beauty. 'I think the Gothic style', Newman once told a lecture audience, 'is endowed with a profound and commanding beauty such as no other style possesses with which we are acquainted and which probably the Church will not see surpassed till it attain to the Celestial city.'

Many of Newman's contemporaries were unable to wait until they reached the Celestial city, and zealously got to work, transforming the secular cities of Manchester and Birmingham and London into neo-

Gothic paradises, with Gothic hotels, Gothic town-halls and Gothic post offices.

At Oxford, Newman found himself surrounded by genuine Gothic of intoxicating beauty. 'Beautiful city!' the poet Matthew Arnold recorded, 'so venerable, so lovely, so unravaged by the fierce intellectual life of our century, so serene! spreading her gardens to the moonlight, and whispering from her towers the last enchantments of the Middle Ages.'

St Mary's Church, Oxford, where Newman was vicar and preached his greatest sermons. 'Who could resist the charm of that spiritual apparition,' asked the poet Matthew Arnold, 'gliding through the afternoon light of St Mary's?'

Few individuals have ever been more enchanted by the Middle Ages than Hurrell Froude, the beautiful young man who became a fellow of Oriel College in 1827, and, the year following, became an intimate friend of Newman's. Froude, good-looking and aristocratic, exercised a spell over Newman by the extremism of his romantic religious faith. He practised somewhat bizarre forms of mortification, sleeping on the floor, and castigating himself with a whip for lustful thoughts or even for such heinous sins as eating too much buttered toast. He burned with the zeal of a medieval monk. His diaries are full of his hatred of the Reformation and everything which the Protestant reformers stood for. Newman, who was profoundly impressionable to male charm, lapped all this up.

He and Froude travelled in Europe together. Newman always said that he loved Hurrell Froude as a man, and that he believed he owed him his Catholic soul. They saw Rome together. 'It is the first of cities,' Newman exclaimed. 'And all I ever saw are but as dust (even dear Oxford inclusive) compared with its majesty and glory.' Newman tried to persuade himself that he still detested the *Roman* Catholic system while becoming more and more attached to Catholicism. 'I quite love the little monks and seminarists,' he wrote, 'they look so innocent and bright, poor boys!'

The year was 1833. Back in Oxford, John Keble preached his sermon in the University Church that recalled England from her apostasy. It was the day which Newman thought marked the beginning of the Oxford Movement. Significantly, he was far away at the time, in Europe, and ill. In Rome, he and Froude had gone their separate ways, and Newman had travelled down to Sicily where he became very ill and suffered for three weeks from a dangerous fever. But as he recovered and took the boat for home, he had a renewed sense of God leading him on to some task he knew not what. In the Straits of Bonifacio, his ship was becalmed, and it was there that he wrote his famous lyric, 'Lead kindly Light'. At fifteen, there had been for him only two luminously self-evident beings, himself and his Creator. Now, in the last verse, there are others – himself, yes, led on 'o'er moor and fen, o'er crag and torrent' by that unseen hand. But also, as he awaited his reunion with Hurrell Froude and his other Oxford friends, it seemed to him like an image of heaven.

And with the morn those angel faces smile
Which I have loved long since and lost awhile.

This caricature of Newman in 1841 still hangs in the vestry of his old church, St Mary's. It was in that year that he wrote his Tract No. 90 and realised that his Oxford career was in ruins. 'I fear that I am clean dished.'

In the decade which followed, Newman, who had by now been appointed vicar of the University Church, St Mary's, became the object of a besotted cult-following among the undergraduates. The poet Matthew Arnold explained his magic as a kind of silvery aesthetic charm:

> Who could resist the charm of that spiritual apparition, gliding in the dim afternoon light through the aisles of St Mary's rising into the pulpit and then, in the most entrancing of voices, breaking the silence with words and thoughts which were of a religious music – subtle, sweet, mournful?

Arnold, like so many of that generation, was bowled over by Newman's *charm*, but in later life felt quite unable to go along with his religious views – he became, in fact, an agnostic. So too did Hurrell Froude's brother James, the famous historian who in his day – like Mark Pattison and so many of the other famous unbelievers of the nineteenth century – had been drunk on what they jokingly called Newmania. James Froude attributed his attraction partly to Newman's appearance – 'his head was large, the face remarkably like that of Julius Caesar' – and partly to the bigness of his mind. Whereas most of the dons then – like most of the dons now – were content to burrow down like White Rabbits into a Lewis Carroll world of footling research and ludicrously parochial quarrels, Newman held out to the young a vision of something bigger. James Froude wrote in after-years:

> Newman's mind was world-wide. He was interested in everything that was going on, in science, in politics, in literature. Nothing was too large for him, nothing too trivial, if it threw light upon the central question, what man really was and what was his destiny.

For a few extraordinary years – agonising years as they turned out to be – this vast question of what man really was and what was his destiny, became connected in the minds of those involved in the debate with the – to us semi-comic – question of what the Church of England really was. Hurrell Froude – as beautiful young geniuses have a way of doing – died young, at the age of thirty-three, in 1836. His death left a great gap and a great sadness in Newman's heart which was not to be filled for a number of years. In devotion to his memory, Newman arranged for Froude's papers and diaries – his Remains as his friends called them – to be printed. Their publication in 1837, the very year when the Protestant succession passed into the hands of the impeccably Hanoverian Queen Victoria, caused a storm of protest.

What the world had begun to suspect was here made clear to the public! These so-called Tractarians were little better than crypto-Roman Catholics. Here were phrases out of Froude's own mouth: 'Odious Protestantism sticks in people's gizzards' and 'The Reformation was a limb badly set – it must be broken again in order to be righted.' And these sentiments were expressed by a young man who quite plainly, both in his callow pieties and his fervent devotions to his friends, was not exactly what one might call manly.

After the death of Hurrell Froude and the publication of the *Remains*, Newman became more and more addicted to exciting the young with his extreme and paradoxical religious opinions. It made him feared and hated by other dons, and he began to plan for himself some form of rear-guard action. He did not yet quite know what it should be, but in 1840 he bought the little row of cottages in Littlemore with a view to living there for periods of prayer and retreat.

Littlemore had long since been attached to the living of St Mary's.

Newman had built the church there; his mother laid the foundation stone of it in 1837. As his position as a cult idol among the undergraduates became more and more heady, and his position in the Church of England more and more doubtful, Newman found great refreshment in the simple pastoral work of a country parish priest. He was an assiduous visitor of the old, the sick, and the housebound. But although Littlemore provided him with respite, the controversies surrounding his position were not going to go away.

In 1841, Newman published the ninetieth of the Tracts. Though he claimed afterwards that he had not expected to attract any particular notice, he must have been deceiving himself. For it was in this tract that he claimed that there was nothing in the doctrinal formularies of the Church of England – in the Thirty-Nine Articles – which could not be believed by a Catholic. It is true that, in his subtle way, Newman qualified this by all kinds of tenuous arguments. It is also true that when you actually examine the contents of Tract No. 90, you realise what a very long way Newman still was from believing in Roman Catholicism. For example, he states that it would be perfectly possible and indeed desir-

LEFT *Newman built the parish church at Littlemore and his mother laid the foundation stone. He found pastoral work in a small rural parish a welcome respite from academic controversy.*

RIGHT *The cottages at Littlemore, near Oxford, converted from an old staging post, where Newman and his friends lived a semi-monastic existence while he decided whether to remain in the Church of England or join the Roman Catholic Church. It was here that he was received into the Roman Catholic Church by an Italian missionary on 9 October 1845.*

able to abolish the Papacy; and that the Bread and Wine of the Eucharist remain bread and wine in their natural substance even after being consecrated by a priest.

Such quibbles did not change the effect Tract No. 90 had upon Oxford – and upon the country at large. Here was a man who was meant to be the greatest intellect in the Church of England, which as everyone knew was a Protestant Church, saying that really, in essence, it was a Roman Catholic Church. This time, Newman had gone too far. On 12 March 1841 all the Heads of Houses in Oxford, save two, assembled in the Sheldonian theatre and condemned Tract No. 90. 'I fear,' Newman wrote to one of his beloved sisters, 'I am clean dished.'

The Bishop of Oxford was bombarded with requests from all over England to suspend this undercover Papist firebrand. He did not do so. Newman was left to work out his own salvation. By the end of the year, he had retreated to live in the cottages at Littlemore, and the world waited, nearly four years, to see what he would do.

Newman could see that the logic of his position was leading him inexorably towards Rome, but it was more than mere cowardice which held him back. Not only was he in love with the Church of England; but also, as we have seen, there was not really much of a Church of Rome to go to. In a Church which barely existed in England, what could be the place of a man like Newman, to whom all the religious minds in England looked, either with fear or respect, but with the sense that here was a

most original and important thinker?

In the cottages at Littlemore, he collected about him a group of like-minded friends, and they lived a life of the utmost austerity and simplicity, based on study and prayer. Today, it is a Catholic shrine. To one like myself, who is alas unable to accept the logic of Newman's position, it is a place of peculiar sanctity nonetheless. This meagre little place, little more than a shed, is to me – much more than the grand colleges of Oxford – a monument to intellectual integrity. Newman, like so many other men of the nineteenth century, could so very easily have put the issues of the 1830s out of his mind, and opted for a comfortable life as a much respected Oxford don. Given the quizzical and paradoxical cast of his mind, his ability to see the plausibility of other people's viewpoints, one can easily imagine him, like his friends Pusey and Keble, muddling along, trying to introduce, piecemeal and undercover, Catholic beliefs and practices into a scandalised Protestant National Church.

But that was not Newman's way. He was prepared to put aside his vast following, his glittering career, his comfort and – what perhaps mattered to him more than anything else – the feelings of his friends for the sake of what he believed to be true. In 1843, he resigned the living of St Mary's preaching a sermon in Littlemore which came to be known by the title *The Parting of Friends*. It is said that on that occasion, his own voice broke, but that the sermon was in any case inaudible, because of the sobs of his friends in the congregation. How typical, incidentally, of Newman, that he took leave of the dons not in their own home territory, but in the little country church he had built himself, surrounded by the children he had catechised, who were arrayed for the occasion in frocks and bonnets which he had bought for them himself.

Newman's life had been changed, not only by the great public drama of his resignation but by meeting a young man who to a large extent took the place in his affections of Hurrell Froude. Ambrose St John was a clergyman of twenty-eight years who came to join the community living in the Littlemore *mone* or monastery as it came to be known. 'Dear Ambrose St John,' Newman calls him in his autobiography, 'whom God gave me, when He took every one else away.' The fact that a young male friend was prepared to follow him on his journey gave Newman the strength he needed to take the plunge. For two years more, the world waited to see what Newman would do. Newspapermen hovered about outside the cottages anxious to discover bizarre monkish practices in

Ambrose St John was Newman's devoted companion from the Littlemore years onwards. 'Dear Ambrose St John, whom God gave me, when He took every one else away.'

progress, but were unfortunately unable to discover any practice odder than that Newman and his friends were always praying. Perhaps that is as odd as can be.

At long last, Newman realised that he had come to the end of his journey, the end of the period which he was later to call his Anglican deathbed. Ambrose St John went off to Bath and became a Roman Catholic on 2 October 1845. Newman immediately wrote to the Provost of Oriel to resign his fellowship. St John returned, bringing with him an Italian priest of the Passionist order called Father Dominic Barberi. It was a rainy night – 8 October – and Father Dominic arrived soaked to the skin, having travelled on the top of a coach for five hours. He was drying himself by the fire when Newman burst into his room, knelt at his feet, and begged to be received into the Catholic Church. He began to make his confession.

It went on so long that the priest had to tell him to stop, and continue it in the morning when they were both less tired. The next day they walked into Oxford in pouring rain and heard mass at the little Roman Catholic chapel in St Clements. Then they returned to Littlemore where Father Dominic heard the conclusion of Newman's confession, gave him conditional baptism, and celebrated mass on Newman's writing desk. When the ceremony was over, Newman walked down to his library at the opposite end of the row of cottages and picked up a volume of the Fathers. He kissed it and said, 'Now I belong to you.'

Newman had hardly ever met a Roman Catholic, and his future was now highly uncertain. He was forty-four years old. There was, of course, no possibility of his continuing his career at Oxford where Roman Catholics were still refused admittance. He threw himself on the mercy and guidance of the Roman Catholic authorities, such as they were. After a short period of training in Rome, it was decided that Newman and his friend should not become monks but should set up a religious house in the tradition of St Philip Neri, a sixteenth-century Roman priest who had established Oratories to house groups of secular priests living together for the purposes of instructing the faithful and attracting converts by their splendid musical tradition. As interpreted by Newman at least, the ideals of the Oratory, and the Oratorian way of life, were almost a carbon copy of an Oxford common room of the 1830s or 1840s. And the Oratory which he established with St John and his other convert friends in the Hagley Road in Birmingham has much the feel of Oxford. The room where the Oratorians meet for recreation was consciously designed by Newman to remind him of Oriel. His own library is rather more extensive than the average library in a Roman Catholic presbytery – more like a college library. And his rooms, unchanged since he left them, are the rooms of a Victorian don. It was here that, with a few interruptions, Newman was destined to spend the rest of his days, writing, instructing converts, and ministering to a large parish of poor Irish immigrants.

His conversion changed the religious complexion of England. Neither the Church of England nor the Church of Rome were ever the same again. The Church of England lost thousands of converts to Rome following Newman's agonised decision in Littlemore, and that inevitably changed the nature of the Roman Catholic Church. For instead of being a backwater Church, followed by a few heroically stubborn English families and the Irish section of the working class, it now became a Church to which clever middle-class English people felt attracted. There was no more important convert, after Newman's change of mind, than the Archdeacon of Chichester, Henry Manning, the close friend of Mr Gladstone and the very essence of an Establishment man. Manning began life as a civil servant in the Colonial Office. He always was the

Henry Edward Manning, when Cardinal Archbishop of Westminster, had the nickname of 'the Marble Arch'. His desire for a 'triumphalist' and markedly Italianate form of Catholicism was not in tune with Newman's more subtle intelligence.

brilliant civil servant and the manipulative archdeacon. Whereas Newman was the dreamer, the intellectual, the splitter of hairs, Manning was the brilliant administrator. He was the man who got the show on the road, as far as the Roman Catholic Church was concerned. And what a show it was! Thanks to Manning (and in spite of howls of protest from Gladstone and others) the Roman Catholics soon had cathedrals of their own all over England, and bishops and dioceses as if they were

Anglicans! The Roman Catholic Church as we know it in England today, with its schools, convents and hospitals, largely paid for by the addiction of the faithful to bingo, is the creation of Manning – Cardinal Manning as, needless to say, he soon became.

Nor was he content to create and organise the Roman Catholic Church in England. It was largely through Manning's influence that Pius IX established the First Vatican Council in 1870, that same council which declared that most difficult doctrine of the Pope's infallibility to be an article of faith necessary to salvation.

To some, the growth in power and influence of the Roman Catholic Church as a recognisable material institution will be seen as a sure token of Divine grace. I must confess that I am sadly blind to this fact – if fact it be. The existence of the Roman Catholic Church seems to admit of all kinds of explanations. Its being and essence seems to me no more miraculous than that of any other well-organised human institution, religious or secular. Popes, whatever their own personal qualities of goodness or wisdom, are no more likely to be infallible than any other human being. So, though I would recognise that Newman's most obvious achievement was in persuading a lot of people to become Roman Catholic who would not otherwise have dreamed of doing so, I would not think that was his greatest achievement.

In fact, by a strange sort of paradox, it could be said that after he had joined the Roman Catholic Church most of the issues which so worried him while he was an Anglican seemed insignificant, and he was able to concentrate all the powers of his delicately-honed intelligence on questions which are of momentous importance for all of us, whether we are Catholics, Hindus, or atheists.

It was the agnostic James Froude, rather than his pious brother, who put his finger on what made, and makes, Newman so compelling a writer – his unhesitating preoccupation with the big questions, with 'what man really was and what was his destiny'.

The nineteenth century is the first century in which thinking people in large numbers began openly to entertain the notion that Christianity was untrue, and that God, the all-powerful, all-loving Creator of this unhappy world, was not merely an intellectual improbability, but also a scientific and moral impossibility.

Traditional belief taught that the world could only be explained in terms of a Creator. Matter and animal life in all its varied species could not exist without Someone who made them. Charles Darwin's discoveries showed that this syllogism was simply untrue. It became perfectly possible to demonstrate how species have evolved on this planet without resorting to a theory that there is One who 'gave their glowing colours' and 'made their tiny wings'.

Then again, earlier Christian writers taught that the Bible was an infallible book, every word of which had been dictated by God Himself. This was as true of the passages which contradicted one another as of those which did not. But ever since the Germans, and in particular the Biblical scholars of Tübingen, had begun to investigate the history of how the Bible came to be composed, it had become clear that any such simple-minded fundamentalism was intellectually impossible. Like all other ancient texts, the Bible bore the traces of being the product of human beings in a particular time and place.

With the removal of these two great props – the Creator-God and the Infallible Word of God in Scripture – Christianity in Britain lost many of its adherents not to Rome but to Unbelief. Matthew Arnold, who as a young man had listened so entranced to Newman's rhetoric at Oxford, expressed the mood of a whole generation in his poem 'Dover Beach', when he saw the Sea of Faith ebbing out

> *Retreating to the breath*
> *Of the night-wind, down the vast edges drear*
> *And naked shingles of the world.*

It was to this world of intelligent, questioning people that Newman addressed himself.

Go to the spring, and draw thence at your pleasure, for your cup or your pitcher, in supply of your wants; you have a ready servant, a domestic ever at hand, in large quantity or in small, to satisfy your thirst, or to purify you from the dust and mire of the world. But go from home, reach the coast: and you will see that same humble element transformed before your eyes. You were equal to it in its condescension, but who shall gaze without astonishment at its vast expanse in the bosom of the ocean? who shall hear without awe the dashing of its mighty billows along the beach? who shall without terror feel it heaving under him, and swelling up and yawning wide, till he, its very sport and mockery, is thrown hither and thither, at the mere mercy of a power which was just now his companion and almost his slave?

Newman got small thanks for his endeavours to present the faith in a manner which might be intelligible to intelligent people. The Roman Catholic Church, with its absolutism and dogmatism, failed to appreciate him until he was more or less dead. The only great task which it asked of him was to set up the Catholic University in Dublin. The brilliant lectures which he gave there, and which were published under the title of *The Idea of a University*, filled the Irish clergy with forebodings and suspicion, and before very long, Newman, to his great relief, was sent back to Birmingham. The bishops and monsignors of Catholic Dublin were as little appreciative of the tangential subtlety of Newman's mind as had been the Protestant dons in Oxford.

But we may be thankful that Newman developed an unfair reputation for casuistry and insincerity, for it drew out of him his best-known and most passionately felt book, the *Apologia pro Vita Sua*.

That Newman had become a Roman Catholic was common knowledge. But how and why were private questions to which very few, if any, really knew the answer. It was commonly put about by Protestants that he had secretly been a Roman Catholic all along, and had merely delayed his conversion in order to undermine the Church of England. Charles Kingsley, the robust no-nonsense advocate of muscular Christianity, was one such critic. Better known as the author of *The Water Babies* and *Westward Ho!*, Kingsley, in the Christmas number of *Macmillan's Magazine* in 1863, reviewed J. A. Froude's *The History of England*. In the course of his review, he let fall the remark, 'Truth for its own sake had never been a virtue with the Roman clergy. Father Newman informs us that it need not be, and on the whole ought not to be.' Newman at once replied, demanding that Kingsley withdraw the slander. Kingsley refused. In the correspondence which followed, Kingsley attributed to Newman, while he had still been an Anglican, views which he had only developed later. 'What then,' he asked in exasperation, 'does Dr Newman mean?'

Stung by the accusations of deviousness and double-talk, Newman resolved to tell Kingsley, and the world, how he had arrived at his opinions. The result, written in a few weeks, often in tears, and always standing at his writing-desk in his room in Birmingham, was his famous

Charles Kingsley, best known today as author of The Water Babies, *prompted Newman to write his* Apologia *by his assaults on Newman's good name in* Macmillan's Magazine.

Defence of His Own Life. After twenty years, Newman returned in his mind to the events which had led up to that crisis of conscience in Littlemore. He revisited in his memory all those 'angel faces' which he had 'loved long since and lost awhile' – Pusey, Keble, the Froudes. Though nearly all the issues with which it deals are dead, the *Apologia* remains a fascinating book because its primary subject is how a mind moves and develops. What do we mean when we say that we are changing our mind, and how do we arrive at any opinions whatsoever?

> It was not logic that carried me on; as well might one say that the quicksilver in the barometer changes the weather. It is the concrete being that reasons; pass a number of years, and I find my mind in a new place; how? the whole man moves. Paper logic is but the record of it.

Newman's moving account of how, by painful steps, he came to the conclusion that the Church of England was not a part of the Catholic Church, and that he must therefore leave his friends and all that he loved, had a powerful effect on the reading public. It was immediately recognised as an autobiography of genius, and a testimony of great intellectual honesty. Strangely enough, it probably made him more friends in the Church which he had left behind than in the Church of which he was now a somewhat uneasy member. By many of his co-religionists, Manning at the head of them, Newman was regarded as a dangerous liberal, a compromiser. Before the First Vatican Council, he was quite open about his reservations concerning papal infallibility, stating that he considered it to be 'not a dogma but a theological opinion'. When the Council – the huge proportion of whose members absented themselves rather than vote for it – proclaimed the Pope to be infallible, Newman's more reasonable view of things got pushed to one side. But he had enough, when he was a Protestant, of internal squabbles among the clergy; and although the activities of the First Vatican Council, and the controversies surrounding it, caused him dismay, he managed, at least in his intellectual life, to rise above the immediate concerns of the day. For he had been planning and writing over a good many years what turned out to be his greatest book, *The Grammar of Assent*. Forgetting Roman bishops and Anglican bishops, he returns to the essence of the religious question. In a world in which, as Arnold wrote, we have 'nor certitude, nor peace, nor help for pain', how do some people – Christians – arrive at their strange and, on the the surface, improbable collection of beliefs?

If ever anyone made out a case for belief in God, Newman did so. To paraphrase it would be to make crude what is essentially delicate, to distort the very measured way in which Newman demonstrated that we assert our belief in matters for which there can never be verifiable proof. Of these, only one instance, though a primary one for Newman, is the existence of conscience, our belief in a moral law, our capacity to feel guilt when we know that we have gone against this law and the opposite when we feel that we have obeyed it. ' "The wicked flees, when no one pursueth"; then, why does he flee? whence his terror? Who is that sees in solitude, in darkness, in the hidden chambers of his heart?'

These questions of Newman's are similar to the ones that Dostoyevsky was asking in his great novels at exactly this date. If God does not exist, then is anything permitted to us? Since we feel that everything is not permitted, does this not give us pause before dismissing the notion of a Supreme Lawgiver? Newman never loses sight, though, of the extreme mysteriousness of life, the fact that with our present range of limitations and sympathies, we shall never know much.

Break a ray of light into its constituent colours, each is beautiful, each may be enjoyed; attempt to unite them, and perhaps you produce only dirty white. The pure and indivisible Light is seen only by the blessed inhabitants of Heaven; here we have but such faint reflections of it as its diffraction supplies.

It is hardly surprising that the Roman Catholic Church did not know what to do with such a man as this. For years and years, his was a strange position. He enjoyed widespread respect and enormous national popularity among Catholics and Protestants, but no kind of official recognition came to him from Rome. Nor could it be said that he did not mind, for with all Newman's sensitivity to the beauty of words and the subtlety of argument, there went an over-sensitivity in personal matters. He was touchy and awkward. I remember one of the old Oratory fathers in Birmingham telling me of a man who joined the community in the 1870s. On his very first day – and nobody knew how he did it – this unfortunate young man offended Newman. That man lived in the same house as Newman for the next twenty years without Newman addressing a single word to him.

This sort of touchiness led to a rift between Newman and the London Oratorians, and as is notorious, he got on badly with Manning. There are many stories of Manning trying to block Newman's promotion in the Church. If they were true, I would not consider them damaging to Manning, for Newman was not the stuff of which bishops or administrators are made. He was a scholar, a poet, a mystic. The humdrum chores of a diocesan bishop would not have appealed to him. His extreme readiness to take offence might well have been disastrous when trying to deal with parish priests. Newman noted in his diary the anniversaries of quarrels and disputes, the day he stopped speaking to Gladstone or Wilberforce or Pusey. How could an ordinary Irish monsignor of little education have dealt with such a person?

'Poor Newman,' Manning is supposed to have remarked, 'he is a great hater.' I am not sure that this is fair, but he certainly went in for intense feelings about other people which were not always markedly controlled.

In 1875, he lost the best of them, Ambrose St John. 'From the first,' Newman said, 'he loved me with an intensity of love which was unaccountable. . . . The Romans called him my Angel Guardian. . . . He has not intermitted this love for an hour up to his last breath.' When St John's last illness came he hugged Newman so tightly that Newman said jokingly to the doctor, 'He will give me a stiff neck,' but then as his friend's hand was clasped in his own, he realised that this was no joke. The great parting was about to happen. At midnight, Newman was summoned from his room to the sick-bed. Another priest, Father Neville, was trying to give St John some arrowroot. St John rose up on one elbow and then fell back on the pillow and died. Newman, at this date seventy-four years old, broke into a paroxysm of weeping and flung himself on to the bed. He lay there with the corpse, sobbing, for the rest of the night, only consenting to be parted from it in the morning. St John was buried in the Oratorian burial ground at Rednal. 'I trust I may now be allowed to die in peace,' Newman remarked. 'What a dream life is!'

It was 1875, and Newman had another fifteen years to live in this world without his great friend. Recognition from the Pope did come at last in 1879 when he was offered a cardinal's hat. It was a rule of the Church that you could not become a cardinal without residing in Rome unless you were a bishop. Newman was too old and too set in his ways to leave the Oratory, but when permission was granted to reside in Birmingham, he accepted the hat, and with it, two hundred pounds worth of expensive regalia. He seemed to have travelled a long way from that dark wet night in Littlemore of thirty years before.

Thereafter, Newman was a 'character', an institution, an object of curiosity whom just about everyone who was anyone reckoned on coming to hear or see. His frail figure in robes of black and scarlet was still a familiar one in the memories of old people I have met in the Hagley Road, Birmingham. With his rather wispy white hair and his curious attire he more and more came to look like an old woman. While the

Newman's sensitive nature wrestled with the profoundest religious questions. In old age he spoke and wrote less of ecclesiastical controversy and more about fundamental questions of belief.

Sovereign Pontiff heaped honours on his head, and the Church of his adoption at last began to see that he was a religious genius, the boys at the school which he founded displayed that wonderful refusal to take anyone seriously which boys will always display. One of them was the future poet Hilaire Belloc, who remembered that their nickname for the Cardinal was Jack. Every year he used to help them to produce a Latin play. The great joke for the boys consisted in trying to make 'Jack' recite particular lines of Latin poetry which would make him burst into tears.

Tears are never far from the surface in Newman's poetry or prose. It is appropriate, I think, that he is nowadays chiefly loved and remembered for his hymns and his poetry. When one of the Oratorian Fathers, Father Gordon, died in 1882, Newman was moved to write his most famous poem, 'The Dream of Gerontius', the story of a man on his death-bed coming face to face with God. Ever since, as a boy, Newman had come to believe that there were two, and two only, luminously self-evident beings, himself and his Creator, that meeting was one for which he had been preparing, the meeting when he would shake off this mortal coil and meet his Creator face to face.

Throughout his life, Newman was passionately fond of music. He once composed a violin sonata. Like Sherlock Holmes, he spent long periods of solitude in his rooms, sawing away at the fiddle. Above all, he had a taste for the most exquisitely melancholy final quartets of Beethoven – perhaps the most highly charged of all music for strings. There is much in those quartets of Newman's mysticism, of his overwrought emotions, his courage triumphing over depression, loneliness and dejection.

I think that it would have pleased him that his best poem had been transformed, by a devotee and fellow Roman Catholic called Edward Elgar, into possibly the most magnificent piece of English choral music in the repertoire: *The Dream of Gerontius*. It is not a brilliant poem, but it acquires brilliance when married to Elgar's music.

Newman was very nearly ninety years old when he died. By then, he was an eminence indeed, a prince of the Church, a much-loved institution, a name who merited a six-column obituary in *The Times*. They buried him on the outskirts of Birmingham, in the same grave as Ambrose St John.

In his memory, the Oratorian priests erected an imposing church in the Hagley Road in Birmingham, a place to match or rival the Italianate splendours of Father Faber's Oratory church in London. It feels like a

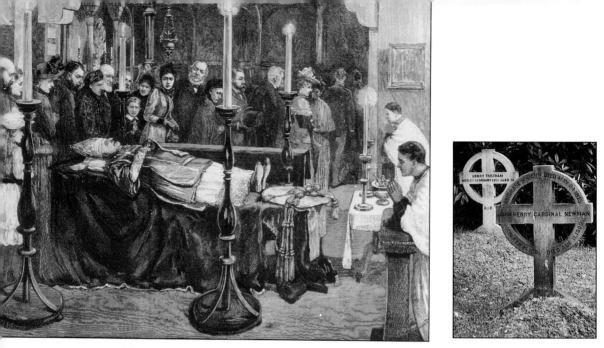

Newman insisted on being buried, not like most Cardinals in a cathedral tomb with his hat hanging above him, but in a dreary Birmingham suburb beside his devoted friend Ambrose St John.

church in Rome. So very successfully have they created a pastiche of a continental church that it is rather a surprise to emerge from the place and see the familiar old Birmingham buses making their way down to Five Ways.

It was really in the twentieth century that Newman came into his own. He has been hailed as the forerunner of modern Catholicism. I am not sure that I fully understand why this is so. But, when Pope John XXIII revolutionised the Roman Catholic Church by setting in train the Second Vatican Council, Newman was called by some the Father of that Council, the genius who was its primary inspiration. He has even been spoken of as the prophet of modern ecumenism and Christian unity, which seems a slightly strange idea to entertain about a man who suffered such pains to demonstrate the falsehood, as he saw it, of Protestantism.

If Newman was the father of modern Catholicism, it is a somewhat dubious accolade. Institutional Christianity in any form, whether in the Church of England or the Church of Rome, attracts fewer and fewer adherents, and it is doubtful whether many Roman Catholics today would share Newman's opinion that salvation outside that Church was an impossibility.

I have lately – over the last year or so – re-read most of what Newman wrote, and found it on the whole a depressing experience. We associate the one-track mind either with fools or psychopaths, and Newman was neither. But when we survey his works on the library shelf – the volumes and volumes of letters and diaries, the two novels, the works of auto-biography, the book about university education, the poems, and of course the sermons and theology – we realise that there is hardly a page in the entire oeuvre which is not concerned, obsessively so, with religion. Many of the things which mattered so much to him seem almost pathetically remote. And reading of the controversies and squabbles of the Victorian clergy I feel like Louis MacNeice reading the Ancient Greeks

> *And how one can imagine oneself among them*
>   *I do not know;*
> *It was all so unimaginably different*
>   *And all so long ago.*

And yet, for a brief period of my life – in my late teens – I was almost in love with Newman, and I read him obsessively. The first thing I did when I arrived at Oxford as an undergraduate was to walk out to Littlemore. Now, my teenage self seems almost as remote to me as the Victorians do. It is not so much that I do not believe in what Newman wrote, so much as that I cannot imagine what it was like to care about – for example – the Arian heresy in the fourth-century Church, or whether it was permissible in the nineteenth century to have a shared Lutheran and Anglican bishopric in Jerusalem. Today, invincibly ignorant as I am, I find it inconceivable that my eternal destiny might depend upon membership of any religious group. The pronouncements of the clergy, whether made as individuals or in collections of synods and councils, seem for the most part remote from the things which concern me, and remote from the New Testament. I cannot even imagine how Newman – let alone I – thought that there could be any connection between the mysterious events and personages of the Gospels and the very far from mysterious set-up in the Vatican.

'There are but two alternatives,' Newman wrote, 'the way to Rome and the way to Atheism: Anglicanism is the halfway house on the one side, and Liberalism is the halfway house on the other.' Was it this sort of extremism which appealed to me once? Peeping gingerly from the windows of my halfway house, I am rather glad not to have opted for either of Newman's bleak alternatives. Viewed from the halfway house, his life seems sad. So many of his sacrifices seem pointless. And if his conversion to Rome has meant that there are two big Churches with bishops in

England rather than one, so what? It wasn't, I now realise, his church interest which really attracted me to Newman. Was it then merely an aesthetic attraction? He still seems to me incomparably the most flawless English stylist. The music of his prose still has the power to turn me to gooseflesh. But is it that alone? 'If I looked into the mirror and did not see my face,' he wrote, 'I should have the sort of feeling which actually comes upon me when I look into this living busy world, and see no reflection of its Creator. . . . Were it not for his voice, speaking so clearly in my conscience and my heart, I should be an atheist.'

Neither as the popular vicar of St Mary's, nor as the – dare one say it – rather prissy dignitary of the Roman Catholic Church does Newman any longer attract me. But the honest man of Littlemore, who was prepared to change the course of his entire life for what he believed, will never fail to move me. And throughout his writings, every so often, one comes across a paragraph of disturbing religious power.

Do the workings of our conscience imply the existence of a moral law, and the moral lawgiver, or are they a meaningless kink in the evolutionary machine? Is our sense of awe in the presence of great art or of Nature something which has no meaning, or are such moments echoes of a homeland from which we are temporarily exiled? Above all, when we die, will the meaningless sum of all our days be blotted out, or will we, like Gerontius, open our eyes in death and wake up as one refreshed?

John Henry Newman was no more able than anyone else to give us infallible answers to such questions. But for anyone who finds it impossible, quite, to put such questions out of their mind, Newman will always be a giant, and a hero.

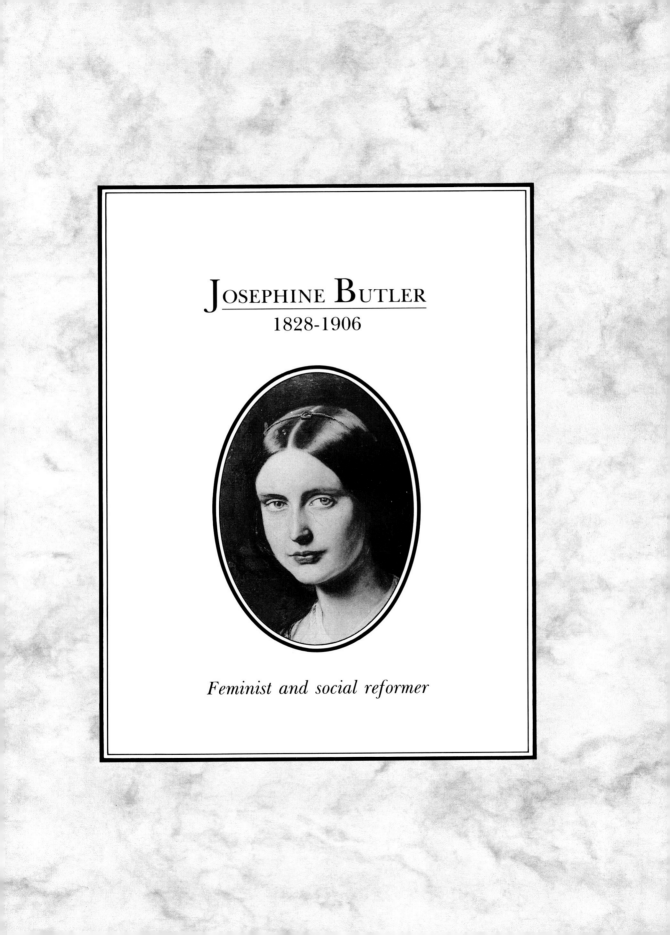

JOSEPHINE BUTLER
1828-1906

Feminist and social reformer

*A photograph of Josephine Butler in middle age. Her keen,
spiritual features are marked by sorrow and illness.*

Josephine Butler was the woman who was brave enough to defend that unmentionable class of Victorian person, the prostitute. How many prostitutes existed in nineteenth-century Britain, we shall probably never know. In 1797 it was calculated that there were 50,000 such women in London alone. Different observers calculated the figure at around 80,000 in the late 1830s and 1840s. In 1858 Whitehorne opined that one in six unmarried women between the ages of fifteen and fifty earned their living in this manner – some 83,000 women. Police estimates of known prostitutes for the period are much smaller. In 1858, for instance, it was estimated that there were 7194 prostitutes in London and 27,113 in England and Wales as a whole. How these estimates were made forms part of the story of Josephine Butler.

The actual statistics are of enormous interest, but they are not the central point at issue. What the vast number of Victorian prostitutes reveals is an attitude towards women which extended far beyond the brothels of the back street, the fumbled little encounter and the exchange of money before the man went back to his house and family in the suburbs. The existence of these women in such quantities was not, as some respectable observers of the time might have wanted to believe, in violent contrast with the respectable home life of their clients. It was merely the underbelly of the same creature. The strange, sexless heroines of Dickens's novels – sometimes like Little Nell and Little Dorrit, part child, part woman, sometimes, like Agnes Wickfield, more of an angel than a physical being – tell something of the same story. So do the paintings of Lord Leighton, Holman Hunt and Alma-Tadema. It was more than their pubic hair which the artists painted out. It was any sense of women having an independent, let alone equal, status.

The greatest single difference between Victorian times and our own is the difference in the position of women. So great is the change effected by the feminist revolution that we who live in after-times find it difficult to grasp the absolute non-status of nineteenth-century women. As we turn the pages of Jane Austen or Charlotte Brontë we do well to remind ourselves that all women in Europe – and, come to that in America – were

Wentworth Street, Whitechapel, a fairly representative London slum, is here depicted by the French engraver Gustave Doré, famous for his intricate interpretations of spiritual crisis in illustrations of Coleridge's Ancient Mariner *or Dante's* Inferno. *Like Doré, Josephine Butler found more than merely physical squalor in the lives of the poor. Her work for prostitutes was to open up infernal glimpses into the soul.*

leading lives which were every bit as restricted, legally, morally and spiritually, as those of Elizabeth Bennett or Jane Eyre. There really were two choices for women when Victoria came to the throne (unless, of course, you were of monarchical status): marriage or old maidhood.

Education for women in the early decades of Victoria's reign was limited to those few enlightened families where the male relations were prepared to share their reading-matter with their sisters. Those who survived such schools as Cowan Bridge, where the Brontë sisters were 'educated', had no chance of further education or university. It was totally unthinkable for women to enter the professions. It took Elizabeth Garrett Anderson years of heroic struggle to qualify as the first woman doctor, and it was not until the mid-1870s that she was able to set up the London School of Medicine for Women. The number of women doctors, even by the close of the century, was tiny.

It was not a question of women being denied the vote, denied education, and denied professional status, but in all other respects being regarded as human beings. In the eyes of English law married women existed only as wives, or not at all. Again, in an age when feminism has by and large achieved its objectives we can be slow to understand what this meant. The reality only comes to the surface when we read about someone desperate enough to question the system.

Take Caroline Norton, whose case came to trial a year before

Victoria's accession. A society girl, granddaughter of the dramatist Richard Brinsley Sheridan, and a writer of novels herself, she had married at the age of nineteen, the Hon. Richard Norton, who gave her three children with a great number of bruises and unpaid bills along the way. It was a disastrously unhappy marriage. After one particularly bad quarrel, Norton took the three children and placed them under the care of a cousin. It was only then that Caroline became aware of her legal status. She discovered that in the eyes of the law she was her husband's property. She had no right to see her children if he removed them from her; nor, having married the Honourable Richard, did she have any rights over her own property or even the income she derived from her writings. All belonged, in the eyes of the law, to him. He refused to let her see her children, and furthermore, sued Lord Melbourne, Victoria's beloved adviser and mentor – on preposterously unlikely grounds – for 'criminal conversation' with Caroline. Since there was no evidence for this whatsoever, the jury dismissed the case without so much as retiring from court. But the trial revealed to Caroline Norton another fact about her legal non-status. As a woman she was neither allowed to sue, nor to be sued, nor to defend her good name in a case of this nature.

Desperate to have her children returned to her, what could she do? It was only because a family friend, Sergeant Talfourd, happened to be a Member of Parliament that by 1839, there was passed into law, by a bemused House of Commons, the Infants' Custody Act, which laid down that mothers against whom adultery was not proven might be allowed custody of their children under the age of seven but only if the

An illustration to Charles Dickens's Bleak House *(1853). Dickens's novels, like the paintings of Millais or Lord Leighton, delighted in desexing women. His favourite heroines were innocents, or small women who might be mistaken for children.*

woman was of 'good character'. A woman could not sue for divorce. Divorce, which we now take for granted, was still something which women could only obtain if they were in a position to move a special Act of Parliament – in each and every divorce case. Not until 1857 could divorces be obtained though the law courts, and even then, while a man could divorce his wife on grounds of her adultery only, a wife had to prove her husband had additionally committed incest, bigamy, cruelty or desertion. And it was not until 1925 (two years after the grounds for divorce were made the same for women as for men) that women were allowed full equal guardianship of their children under English law.

'I really lost my young children,' Caroline Norton wrote, after she had obtained the right to see her two surviving sons from time to time, 'craved for them, struggled for them, was barred from them, – and came too late to see one that had died . . . except in his coffin.'

It is one of many sad stories in legal history (Annie Besant's – who lost custody of her daughter to her clergyman husband after she published a treatise on birth control with the radical atheist Charles Bradlaugh – is another). But however often a modern person reads it, she or he will still find it difficult to grasp what it means. The difference between women then and women now is as great as the difference between those who are now full citizens of the United States – as it were, senators, surgeons, professors – but whose ancestors were slaves. The difference goes to the very heart of what we mean, and what the Victorians meant, by being human. There is a strange, liberating thread which connects us here; as we see in the remarkable story of Josephine Butler. For she successfully campaigned against the laws themselves that made women the victims of the Victorian 'double standard'. The repeal of the Contagious Diseases Acts and the raising of the age of consent are both owed to her indomitable courage.

Josephine Butler was born, the seventh child of John Grey and Hannah Annett, at Milfield in Northumberland, in 1828, four years before the passing of the Great Reform Bill. She was related to Lord Grey, the Prime Minister of the day. Her cousin was Charles Grey, an equerry of Prince Albert. She grew up with all the advantages of a farflung branch of an aristocratic Whig family. John Grey made sure that all his children, including the girls, were politically educated – indeed, as cousins of the Prime Minister who had brought in the Great Reform Bill, it could

Josephine Grey was born into a land-owning family in Northumberland. Ewart Park, Wooler, was the home of her liberal-minded father.

hardly have been otherwise. As a young girl, as well as the usual accomplishments of a young lady – needlecraft, sketching, music, and a reading knowledge of French – Josephine knew all about the pioneering work of her father's friend Sir Edwin Chadwick who, the year Josephine was born, had drafted reports on the conditions of British cities which led to the passing of the Public Health Bill. It was the first step towards recognising that the State had a responsibility for the health of the nation. By growing up with a knowledge of Chadwick On Drains, Josephine learnt some of her keen sense of responsibility towards the urban poor. Her destiny was to clean up vice as Chadwick cleaned up sewage.

In addition to her political education, or rather as part of it, Josephine Grey learnt the Christian religion. That religion has at its heart the belief that God who is rich for our sakes became poor. Those who respond most vividly or affectionately to the Gospel have almost invariably been drawn to identify with the poor. This has been a fact which has linked many different Christians of widely various ethnic or cultural backgrounds. We see it in the life of Francis of Assisi, in General Booth of the Salvation Army, in Mother Teresa of Calcutta today. Because God loved the world, such Christians have always believed that it was their duty to love the world too; for 'in as much as ye have done it unto the least of these my brethren ye have done it unto me.' The dichotomy in the minds of many people between 'politics' and 'religion' does not exist for these Christians. Probably neither word plays a large part in their vocabulary. But they are living in the world which they believe God has loved and inhabited, they naturally look for justice in society, relief for the poor.

In the early part of the last century this was particularly true of the Evangelical wing of the Church of England. It was from this religious perspective that William Wilberforce brought about the abolition of the slave trade, and that, later in the century, Lord Shaftesbury prevented the use of children as what was no more or no less than a slave labour force in British mines and factories. Josephine Butler was very much the heir to this way of reading the Gospel. What she saw very clearly was that, in spite of the misogynistic traditions of Christianity, the Gospel contains within it the seeds of what was later called feminism. Just as the equality of Jew and Gentile as proclaimed in the Gospel made it ultimately unthinkable for Christians to allow the continuance of the slave-trade (though for 1800 years Christians did not *see* this!) so, for Josephine, the respect shewn by Christ for women, in spite of the social conventions of His day, led inevitably to the conclusion that women – all women, not just the prostitutes with whom her name is associated – should enjoy equal rights with men.

> Among the great typical acts of Christ which were evidently and intentionally for the announcement of a principle for the guidance of Society, none were more markedly so than His acts towards women: and I appeal to the open Book, and to the intelligence of every candid student of Gospel history for the justification of my assertion, that in all important instances of his dealings with women, His dismissal of each case was accompanied by a distinct act of Liberation.

From an early age then, radicalism and evangelical piety were in Josephine's blood. Evangelical piety, for those of us who are not used to it, can be embarrassing, even cloying. But she was never this. Feminist or political radicalism can often be strident. Josephine was never that either. For me, she is one of the most *attractive* people who ever lived: not merely beautiful, but one of those extemely rare people who is good through and through without for one second seeming 'goody-goody'.

She was twenty-two years old when she married George Butler, the son of a headmaster of Harrow, and a clergyman. Butler was very much influenced by another rich strand in the Anglican tradition, exemplified by the figure of F. D. Maurice. A friend of Tennyson's, Maurice was what that generation would have called a Christian socialist, whose faith

meant nothing to him if it was not translated into action. He was
regarded as a heretic by the Establishment, and sacked from his job as
Professor of Theology at King's College London for his doubts about
eternal punishment, that favourite doctrine of the Victorian orthodox.
(Tennyson wrote a big-hearted poem about the sacking.) Others in
roughly the same mould were Charles Kingsley and Thomas Hughes,
the author of *Tom Brown's Schooldays*. Their theology was more 'liberal'
than the Evangelicals, admitting and indeed welcoming the advances in
Biblical scholarship which inevitably modified the way in which the
Bible was viewed. But they were no less ardent in their insistence that
Christianity involves a social commitment. Josephine with her inquiring
mind and profound interest in society found no conflict of views in her
marriage to George Butler which was idyllically happy for forty-eight
years, until his death in 1890. His words to her, some four years after they
were married, are remarkable for the extent to which they recognise his
young wife's equality.

> No words can express what you are to me. I hope I may be able to
> cheer you in moments of gloom and despondency . . . and by means
> of possessing greater physical strength . . . I may be enabled to help
> you in the years to come to carry out plans, which may under God's
> blessing, do some good, and make men speak of us with respect.

One can hardly emphasise too strongly that society in the last century
was changed almost entirely by people like the Butlers – the enlightened
and educated classes, some aristocratic, mostly middle or upper middle
class. Marx could not have been more wrong in his prediction that
England would be changed by a vast proletarian upheaval. The enormous changes which took place – in attitudes to the sexes (such as that
letter of George Butler reveals), to class, to capitalism, to the conditions
of urban life, to public health, to franchise – all stemmed from the
educated classes, and in particular from the Christian educated classes.
(Of course there were many other educated reformers, from J. S. Mill
and Carlyle downwards, who were not Christian, but the point still
stands.)

The first five years of Josephine's married life were spent in Oxford,
where George had been a fellow of Exeter College. Those were the days
when fellows of Oxford colleges (but not professors) were obliged to be

Josephine Grey married George Butler, a clergyman of broad church views who came from a distinguished academic dynasty. Butler believed in marriage as a partnership between equals, and he was fully supportive of Josephine's campaigns for her fellow women. Very few of George's Oxford contemporaries shared his feminist principles. It was in the early years of married life at Oxford that Josephine came face to face with Victorian 'double standards' in sexual morality.

celibate. On his marriage, George resigned his fellowship, and set up a hall of residence for undergraduates, called Butler Hall. He combined this housemasterly duty with trying to set up a School of Geography within the University at Oxford, and hoping for a professorial job. His expertise was as a cartographer, and Josephine helped him with his maps. Oxford was not a bad place for an aspirant feminist to cut her teeth as a young wife for, even in recent years, its attitude towards married women has been not dissimilar to the Shi'ite Persians. It was only in the middle of the last century that Oxford dons were permitted to marry, and their whole lives, until quite lately, have been shaped with the assumption that they are really celibates. No woman dined in Christ Church until 1960, and it was only in that decade that the custom whereby Oxford dons dined each night in the hall of their colleges, leaving their wives behind in their dingy houses in North Oxford to eat baked beans on toast with the children, fell into abeyance.

A sympton of Josephine's quiet determination to live in a world less circumscribed than that of her neighbours was her application for a reader's ticket at the University Library, the Bodleian. It seems more than likely that she was the first woman ever to think of doing this. Certainly, at that period, the Bodleian – like everything else in Oxford, including of course the colleges – was a male preserve. Josephine got her ticket. Life among the dodos of Oxford cannot have been much fun.

An added constraint was the fact that the domestic architecture of the place was suburban and uncongenial, and the climate damp – very far from the clear skies of her native Northumberland, and the 34,356 acres of her father's estate. George's career went poorly in Oxford, too. His plans for a School of Geography there were thwarted by his colleagues, more stick in the mud than he. He applied for the Chair of Latin, and was turned down. It was at that point that he cut his losses and they moved to Cheltenham, where he became Vice-principal of the Boys' College.

Two incidents from the Butlers' Oxford life, however, are worth recording. One was a discussion arising among their limited social circle of Mrs Gaskell's novel *Ruth*. A young man seriously advanced the view that he would not 'allow' his mother to read such a book. It then emerged that the opinion of nearly everyone there was that if a young girl became pregnant, it was she and not her seducer who was to blame. This struck Mrs Butler as odd, to say the least. 'A moral sin in a woman was spoken of as immensely worse than in a man.' It was one of the first chords, very unobtrusively played, in what was to be the grand music of Josephine Butler's life. What may be called the introduction of the theme, albeit in a minor key, came at about the same time. A young woman serving a sentence in Newgate prison for the murder of her child (it is not clear whether it was a case of infanticide or abortion) was brought to the Butlers' attention. As it happened, they knew the father of the child who was a respected member of the University. But it was in keeping with their way that when the girl came out of prison, rather than expose the man as a bounder and a cad, they had her to live with them; she was the first in a succession of so-called 'fallen women' who found a welcome in the Butlers' household.

In 1857, then, they moved to Cheltenham, a place which Josephine found in every way more congenial than Oxford. The Ladies' College was still in its infancy, and its first great Principal, Dorothea Beale, was appointed in the year after the Butlers' arrival in Cheltenham. It was largely through Cheltenham Ladies' College that Josephine Butler became aware of the developments that were taking place in the education of women. Miss Beale set up the Schools Enquiry Commission in 1865, and when the Butlers moved north a few years later, Josephine undertook the same work there. The North of England Council for the Higher Education of Women was to lead to the founding of such pioneer institutions in the older Universities as Newnham College, Cambridge.

George meanwhile was happy teaching at the Boys' College in Cheltenham. By this time their family numbered four – three boys and a little girl, Eva. Had no personal misfortune befallen them, the Butlers might very well have stayed in the comfortable southern spa town for years – their benevolence towards the unfortunate doled out from a position of comfortable security and becoming, perhaps, just a trifle smug.

One evening, however, in 1863, something happened which was to change their lives for ever. Returning home from a drive, the children rushed on to an upstairs landing to greet them as they entered the hall. Little Eva fell over the banister on to the hard, tiled floor below, and lay insensible at her parents' feet. A few hours later, she died.

> Never can I lose that memory – the fall, the sudden cry, and then the silence. It was pitiful to see her, helpless in her father's arms, her little drooping head resting on his shoulder and her beautiful golden hair, all stained with blood, falling over his arm!

The torture of grief for this child was something which Josephine was unable to assuage. Never strong (she had poor lungs) she soon fell seriously ill. The house where the accident had happened became a place of dread to both the parents, and when the chance came to accept a new job in a completely different part of the country, George seized it. He became Headmaster of Liverpool College. The genteel and homogeneously cultivated atmosphere of Cheltenham was exchanged for the altogether rougher climate of a prosperous northern port – one of the biggest and most important in the British Empire. Here, the vast prosperity of Liverpool merchant families (like the Gladstones) stood in stark contrast to the plight of the poor. As in all Victorian ports, where there were families waiting to emigrate, vagrancy and homelessness were endemic. And, with a huge population of the poor, combined with a big migratory population of sailors and travellers passing through, there was a great amount of prostitution. At this date there were probably about 9000 prostitutes working in Liverpool, many of them children (1500 under 15 and 500 under 13, according to one estimate).

Josephine decided that the grief she felt for Eva could find no outlet at home.

> I became possessed with an irresistible desire to go forth, and find some pain keener than my own – to meet with people more unhappy than myself (for I knew there were thousands of such). I did not exaggerate my own trial; I only knew that my heart ached night and day, and that the only solace would seem to be to find other hearts which ached night and day.

In the Liverpool of the 1860s, she did not have far to look. She began visiting the vagrant women who had been rounded up into the notorious Brownlow Hill Workhouse, an establishment which makes the one in *Oliver Twist* seem positively benign. In exchange for a night's lodging and a hunk of bread, the girls had to work in the sheds stripping oakum (tarry hemp) from piles of rope, the same tedious and painful work – it tears all the skin off your fingers – doled out to prisoners serving penal servitude (Oscar Wilde did it in Reading Gaol). Josephine was shocked at her first sight of the oakum sheds, but her immediate and characteristic response was not to enter them as a lady bountiful, dispensing good advice or soup. Instead, she sympathised in the literal sense of the word: she suffered with these women.

> I went into the oakum shed and begged admission. I was taken into an immense, gloomy vault, filled with women and girls – more than two hundred, probably, at that time. I sat on the floor among them and picked oakum. They laughed at me, and told me my fingers were of no use for that work, which was true. But while we laughed we became friends.

The unselfconscious Evangelical felt no difficulty, in these miserable circumstances, in speaking to 'this audience – wretched, draggled, ignorant, criminal' about her Christian faith. She got one girl, tall and dark, standing up amid the heaps of tarred rope, to repeat the words of St John's Gospel – 'Let not your heart be troubled. Neither let it be afraid.' And then, they prayed. 'It was a strange sound, that united wail – continuous, pitiful, strong – like a great sign or murmur of vague desire and hope issuing from the heart of despair.' The scene reminds us of that of the prostitute reading St John's Gospel to Raskolnikov at the end of Dostoyevsky's *Crime and Punishment*.

It was not long before Josephine became aware of how easy it was for a woman to be tempted into taking apparently lighter work than picking oakum. One of the first girls whom Josephine befriended in Liverpool was called Marion. A farmer's daughter, she had been seduced when she was quite young, drifted into Liverpool, and soon been imprisoned in a brothel. By the time she met Josephine Butler, Marion was consumptive and riddled with venereal disease. Since she had nowhere else to live, the Butlers invited her to share their home. The neighbours in their comfortable bourgeois suburb of Sefton Park could hardly believe their eyes when they watched the arrival of this woman at the Butler residence. She was most visibly the sort of person whom no Victorian household would wish to 'receive'. George Butler welcomed her at the front door, showed her his arm, as if she were the grandest lady in the land, and escorted her upstairs. 'I hear that Mrs Butler takes in these creatures,' said a disgruntled neighbour to one of the Butlers' maids. 'Yes, Madam,' said the maid, 'I am proud to say she does.' When Marion died within the year, Josephine had her coffin filled with white camellias, the symbol of purity.

The story of Marion was to be typical of Josephine Butler's whole approach to her great campaigns of social reform. She was never a mere busybody who felt it was her duty to improve people. Still less was she a mere social engineer, interested in changing the condition of some impersonal thing such as 'society'. She was always an imaginative and sympathetic human being, and the end of all her work was to remind her fellow-citizens that you did not stop being human, and deserving of the honour due to all humanity, merely because you were female, or poor, or, by the rather convoluted morality of the times, a sinner.

There were far too many Marions in Liverpool for the Butlers to be able to take them all in. What was worse, the longer Josephine worked among them, the more she discovered that it was not simply a matter of reclaiming individuals. These women and children were the victims of precisely that attitude which she had heard expressed at Oxford when Mrs Gaskell's *Ruth* was under discussion: 'A moral sin in a woman was . . . immensely worse than in a man.' Women are temptresses, hoydens, harbourers of disease and corruption; men on the other hand will be men and must be indulged and forgiven. This was the 'morality' of mid-Victorian England.

This delicate portrait of Newman in extreme old age by Emmeline Deane (1889)
shows an ethereal face. At this period, hobbling along the Hagley Road
in Birmingham in his cassock, Newman was often mistaken for an old woman.

RIGHT Newman's study at the Birmingham Oratory is today preserved more or less as he left it at this death. It is called 'the Cardinal's room' but it feels less like the room of a prince of the Italian church than the book-lined den of an Oxford don in the 1830s.

OPPOSITE TOP LEFT The church at Littlemore that Newman built, and where he preached his last sermon as an Anglican – 'The parting of friends'. His words were scarcely audible above the sobs of his disconsolate followers.

OPPOSITE TOP RIGHT A design for a stained glass window, which was never made, on the theme of the Newmania, reflecting the way the cult of the Middle Ages in Oxford in the 1830s was bound up with the cult of personality surrounding Newman himself.

OPPOSITE BOTTOM Newman's room at Littlemore was as austere as any monastic cell. It was there that he wrote his book on The Development of Christian Doctrine *and prepared himself for the decision to leave the Church of England.*

My prayer for my husband. Sept. 25. 1864

My God. I pray not for myself alone,
but for him who is as dear to me as
my own soul.

Author of faith and source of strength,
give him a living faith in Thee, and
make him strong in thy might.
Confirm & strengthen him in all goodness.
Give him a self-renouncing will.
Bold to take up, and firm to sustain
the consecrated cross, which
all must daily bear who follow
Thee.
Reveal to his inmost soul the true
nature of sin, and the beauty of
holiness —
Draw near to him — nearer & nearer.
Reveal thyself to him as his
Saviour, Brother & Friend,
The Lamb slain, the immaculate

OPPOSITE *G. F. Watts's portrait of Josephine Butler was painted as part of his Hall of Fame series of those who had 'made the century'. She, in some senses, helped to unmake it by exposing the double standards of Victorian sexual morality. When it was finished, she said she felt 'so sorry' for the figure depicted.*

LEFT *Extract from a prayer written by Josephine Butler to her husband.*

BELOW *One of Josephine Butler's watercolours, depicting a family picnic in her beloved Northumberland.*

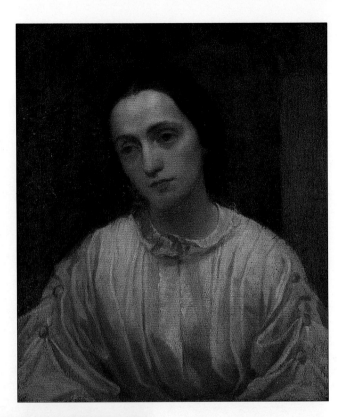

Right G. F. Watts's
*portrait of Julia Margaret
Cameron. Watts was one of
the many bearded figures on
whom Mrs Cameron doted.
She called him 'Signor' and
arranged, when he was in his
forties, for him to marry the
sixteen-year-old Ellen Terry.
Watts himself sat for many
of Mrs Cameron's*
tableaux.

Opposite 'Paul and
Virginia'. Mrs Cameron,
like many Victorians,
admired Bernardin de St
Pierre's 1787 romance of two
children leading the life of
virtuous savages in
Mauritius. The eponymous
hero and heroine are here
modelled by two Freshwater
children, Freddy Gould and
Elizabeth Keown. The
clothes, and presumably the
umbrella, which came from
India, were deemed
appropriate appurtenances.*

Left 'King David'. Mrs
Cameron greatly admired
Henry Taylor's plays, poems
and handsome bearded
appearance. He is here
representing the biblical king
and psalmist.*

Julia Margaret Cameron's photographic techniques had an influence on contemporary painters. Dante Gabriel Rossetti refused to meet her, but his canvas Beata Beatrix *reveals that he had absorbed many of her ideas. The smudgy edges of the painting, and the semi-focused close-up of the face are directly drawn from Cameron's techniques.*

It was more than a mere piece of convention which you could ignore or follow at your choice. It was written into the law of the land. The first Contagious Diseases Act was passed in 1864, with the aim of reducing the spread of sexually-transmitted disease in the armed forces. In effect it meant the establishment of state brothels for the naval and the military, but it also involved a gross violation of the civil rights not only of prostitutes but, by implication, of every woman in Britain. In 1866 and 1868, with the passing of further Contagious Diseases Acts, its original powers were extended far beyond the confines of the military encampments.

The Contagious Diseases Acts effectively abolished Habeas Corpus in Great Britain. By the provisions of these Acts, special police were empowered to arrest any woman, compel her to submit to an examination for venereal disease, and require that she should present herself to the Justice of the Peace. Her guilt was presumed unless she could prove herself innocent. No witnesses were required, and no evidence on the part of the officer making the arrest. If the woman protested or refused to co-operate with the law, she was liable to a period of penal servitude. If she did submit to the examination, it was in the eyes of many who investigated the matter little better than an 'instrumental rape'. The woman was forced into a straitjacket to prevent her from struggling. Her legs were then forced apart by metal clamps. One girl interviewed by Josephine Butler after such a 'medical' examination had rolled off the couch with a ruptured hymen. She turned out, as it happened, to be a virgin. The police paid her a few shillings' hush money, but she went at once to Josephine Butler. Another woman, walking innocently along one evening with her daughter, was arrested and charged by the special police with being a 'common prostitute'. This was how all women were now defined by the law of England unless they could prove to the contrary. This particular woman committed suicide rather than submit to the horrors of the examination.

These are matters about which many people today still find it difficult to speak in public without embarrassment. How much truer that was in Josephine Butler's day! She was not a strident, foul-mouthed woman who found it easy to mention matters normally only spoken about in the doctor's consulting-rooms (if there). But a vitally important matter of human liberty was at stake, one which would never get reformed unless someone were brave enough to challenge it. To do so would be to risk the charge of prurience and impropriety. When it was further discovered

Josephine Butler's water colours suggest an almost obsessive preoccupation with female suffering. This sketch of a young girl in chains, gazing wistfully towards her prison window, may not have been a conscious self-portrait, but it bears a strong resemblance to the artist. For much of her life, Josephine took opium, in the form of laudanum, as a relief for pain. This possibly inspired some of her stranger artistic fantasies.

that Josephine was protecting 'immoral women', she would obviously be charged with wickedness. She was an upper middle-class woman with a position to maintain. This meant little to her personally, but the reputation of her sons and her husband meant everything. George was a clergyman and a schoolmaster with responsibility for the care of the young. His entire career was put in jeopardy by the very idea of having a wife whom 'he could not control', who was prepared to peer so mercilessly beneath the respectable surface of Victorian life and reveal the cess-pit which lurked there. What should she do?

She put the problem to George. She knew that he was sympathetic to the cause, but was he prepared to risk the obloquy and anger which the campaign against the Contagious Diseases Acts would provoke? Josephine now knew more, from first-hand experience, than any other educated woman in England about the plight of urban prostitutes. The feminist campaigner, Elizabeth Wolstenholme, wrote to her in 1869 and asked her to lead the protest against the Acts. George had no doubt about where her duty lay. Quoting Saul's words to young David when he went forth to fight the giant Goliath, he told her, 'Go, and the Lord go with you.'

The Goliath whom Josephine had to fight represented almost the entire male-dominated British Establishment. This was not just a case (brave as that would have been) of standing up to the pimps, and the brothel-keepers and the madams. She had, for one thing, the medical profession against her. Since thousands of young men in the armed forces were suffering from venereal disease, it was felt that anything justified the halt of it: and for the doctors of Victorian England, who saw things from so one-sided a point of view, that merely meant controlling the prostitutes. 'It is only insofar as a woman exercises trade which is physically dangerous to the community that Government has any right to interfere,' conceded *The Lancet* of 27 November 1869. But the notion that the Contagious Diseases Acts in effect deprived women in garrison towns of civil liberty, whether they were prostitutes or not, and that it had no effect on combating the spread of sexually transmitted diseases did not seem to have occurred to the author of the article. Most doctors reacted as Dr Preston of Plymouth, who wrote on 24 June 1870

> I will pass over Mrs. Josephine Butler's address in public before men . . . because I believe that a very large majority of our sex . . . can only characterise it as the height of indecency to say the least. But it is my opinion that women are ignorant of the subject . . . but not Mrs. Josephine Butler and Company – they know nothing about it . . . Certainly if such women as Mrs. Butler continue to go about addressing public meetings – they may ultimately do so but at present I venture to say that they are ignorant and long may they remain so. No men, whomever they may be, admire women who openly show that they know as much on disgusting subjects as they do themselves, much less so those who are so indelicate as to discuss them in public.

But Josephine risked the extreme ignominy of making speeches about venereal disease because she knew she was right, even though none of the medical profession would support her. The very few women doctors who were struggling into existence at this period were frightened of their positions vis-à-vis their male colleagues. Only Dr Elizabeth Blackwell was brave enough to oppose the Contagious Diseases Acts from the first, followed eventually by Dr Elizabeth Garrett Anderson, who had been the first woman to qualify as a doctor in 1865.

Josephine Butler was eventually to collect some influential male allies – such figures as F. D. Maurice, James Stansfeld (a Liberal MP) and the philosopher John Stuart Mill. But many whom one might have thought would be sympathetic were not. None of her old friends at Oxford would lend their support. Benjamin Jowett, for example, the liberal-minded Master of Balliol, was priggish enough to say, 'Mrs Butler takes an interest in a class of sinners whom she had better left to themselves.' More surprisingly, Gladstone, himself so keen on rescuing prostitutes, was deeply unsympathetic to her cause. He considered it unfortunate that she should try to make it a political issue.

But of course it was a political issue, since her aim was to repeal a series of Acts of Parliament. This could only be done by scaring the Liberal government of the day into some kind of action. Since women did not have the vote, Mrs Butler had to appeal to men – and that meant extensive travelling around the country to speak to frequently bawdy or hostile audiences, as well as a ceaseless stream of written campaign material, largely gathered up in her news-sheet, *The Shield*. In her speeches and articles, she was punctilious in her collection of evidence; and what she began to reveal, with hideous clarity, was not the narrowly important question of the Contagious Diseases Acts and their injustice, but also the much wider question of double standards in Victorian society. This, beyond question, is why her campaigns, from the very first, got so many people on the raw. One of her friends who was sent to prison for soliciting on 2 March 1870 told *The Shield*, 'It did seem hard, ma'am, that the Magistrate on the bench who gave the casting vote for my imprisonment had paid me several shillings, a day or two before, in the street, to go with him.'

This double standard was extremely widespread. In a society where men were supposed to delay marriage until they could afford to maintain a household, and in a society where marital breakdown was not relieved by divorce, prostitutes provided an essential role in keeping the whole facade of 'Victorian values' unscathed. It was, moreover, the prostitute who supposedly made sure that the promiscuous middle-class man did not infect women of his own class – the sort of woman he might dance with, play croquet or bridge with, or escort into dinner.

In an age when there was no cure for the rampant disease of syphilis, it is easy to see how these standards grew up. It is equally easy to see how Josephine Butler's attempt to expose the standards was seen, and

Since no woman could stand for parliament, Josephine and her friends were compelled to make public speeches in their campaign for the repeal of the Contagious Diseases Acts. It required great courage to face audiences of hostile men.

intended, as a political act. She saw the Contagious Diseases Acts as 'a tyranny of the upper classes against the lower classes'. And that is why she got the Liberal Party on the run.

The first major political triumph was the Colchester by-election of 1870 when the Liberal candidate, Sir Henry Storks, was challenged by a Tory candidate who promised to work for the abolition of the Acts. When it was discovered that Josephine Butler was in Colchester, her hotel was stormed, and the mob threatened to set it alight. The manager asked her to leave, very late at night, and she was obliged to slink out with a prostitute friend who found her refuge in a grocer's shop. They hid behind piles of soap and candles until the hooligans dispersed. It was not the first time she was to be confronted with dangerous physical violence. Storks, whom she nicknamed the Bird, had been promised the War Office by Gladstone if he won the by-election. He was an experienced military administrator, and a hero of the Crimea, where he had helped Florence Nightingale set up the military hospitals at Scutari. A few days later, when the votes had been counted at Colchester, Josephine received a telegram which read simply, 'Bird Shot Dead'. Storks had been defeated by 400 votes – a big majority in those days before universal suffrage. It was a sign that the message was getting across, and that the essential injustice of the Contagious Diseases Acts was becoming intolerable to the electorate.

Realising that something had to be done, but wanting to put off the evil day, the Government set up a Royal Commission. Josephine Butler was summoned before it in 1871 to face a panel which was made up of bishops, doctors, naval and military experts and MPs. Every member of this Commission was declaredly opposed to repealing the Acts and when she stood before them, she was made conscious of their hostility. 'It was distressing to me owing to the hard, harsh view which some of these men take of poor women, and the lives of the poor generally. . . . I felt very weak and lonely. But there was One who stood by me.'

Josephine meant this sincerely and literally. She and her husband were both of the view that Christ's morality was simple, and obligatory on all Christians. They were impatient of the doctrinal wranglings which so interested Roman Catholics and High Churchmen. 'I am sure', George once wrote, 'Mary who sat at the feet of Jesus would have been puzzled by the reading over to her of the Athanasian Creed and the injunction to accept it all at the peril of the loss of her soul; but she understood what Jesus meant when He said "One thing is needful".' Josephine felt that 'those who profess the religion of Jesus must bring into public life and into the legislature the stern practical social, real side of the Gospel'. And this in turn brought the realisation that 'economics lie at the root of practical morality'.

It is for these underlying reasons that the Campaign for the Repeal of the Contagious Diseases Acts became so important. Since the Liberal Party and the Church – the two institutions to whom she would have expected to look for support – were so unhelpful, Josephine Butler looked around for any support, however heterogeneous. The friends she made in this way cut across the barriers of class, religious denomination and even of obvious political alignment. But they were united in discovering a great many things about society which had nothing specifically to do with venereal disease. They were discovering how undesirable they found an all-male-dominated, upper or upper-middle class dominated society. They wanted something different. And some of the different things they achieved – including women's suffrage itself – came about as an indirect but very certain consequence of Josephine Butler's campaigns.

The first Royal Commission on the Contagious Diseases Acts reinforced the double standard. It even published, in its report, that odious sentence which, for Josephine Butler, summed up the whole of what she was fighting against: 'There is no comparison to be made between prostitutes and the men who consort with them. With the one sex the offence is committed as a matter of gain, with the other it is an irregular indulgence of a natural impulse.'

By the time the next Royal Commission was set up, things were very different. Mrs Butler had made her point. By then, six of the Commission, out of fifteen, were abolitionists, and they were addressed by John Stuart Mill in forthright terms: 'I do not consider [such legislation] justifiable in principle, because it appears to me to be opposed to one of the greatest principles of legislation, the security of personal liberty. It appears to me that legislation of this sort takes away that security almost entirely from a particular class of woman intentionally but incidentally and unintentionally, one may say, for all women whatever.' At last the point had been made.

When Parliament opened on 28 February 1883, Gladstone was still evasive about the question of abolition, fearing it would have dangerous political repercussions. Nevertheless, the thing had by then gathered its own momentum. The end came on 20 April during a late-night sitting of the House of Commons. A Women's Prayer Meeting was held in the nearby Westminster Palace Hotel, and outside on the pavement middle-class women knelt with poor prostitutes to pray. Josephine Butler herself was inside the House in the Ladies' Gallery as James Stansfeld moved against compulsory examination. The measure was carried – and the Acts in effect neutered – by 182 votes to 110. It was at half past one in the morning that the news came. Josephine was on the terrace of the House of Commons by that time. 'The fog had cleared away and it was very calm under the starlit sky. All the bustle of the city was stilled, and the only sound was that of the dark water lapping against the buttresses of the broad stone terrace . . . it almost seemed like a dream.'

When the Repeal Bill was finally passed through the House on 18 March 1886 the full iniquity and absurdity of the Acts was shown. Before they had been brought in, in 1865, 260 in every thousand serving in the armed forces suffered from venereal disease. When the Acts were repealed, the figure was still 260 per thousand.

'Say unto Jerusalem', exclaimed Josephine Butler, quoting the Prophet, 'that her warfare is accomplished.'

But as she was almost immediately to recognise, this was only partly the case. For, in the course of her campaigns against the abuse of a particular piece of parliamentary nonsense, she had uncovered the much deeper and wider problem of prostitution itself. And this problem would not go away overnight.

From the moment she took up the challenge to fight the Contagious Diseases Acts, Josephine Butler had travelled all over Europe, collecting information about prostitution. In Paris, she saw fully-fledged state-sponsored brothels in operation and they were not very impressive. She has left a very remarkable account of her meeting with C. R. Lecours, the chief of the dreaded Agents de Moeurs. Lecours, well-groomed, harsh and cynical, had, as she pointed out, 'the keys of heaven and hell, the power of life and death for the women of Paris'. Josephine thought that 'Service de Débauche' would have been a better name for his office than 'Service des Moeurs'. The police who were supposed to be the custodians of public morals were, as she quickly found out, doing a roaring trade themselves out of the prostitutes whom they were supposed to dis-courage. It was Lecours's view, as he explained to her, that vice would go on increasing and increasing, and this was very largely the fault of the prostitutes.

> I interrupted rather abruptly by reminding him that, in this crime – prostitution – which he was denouncing, there were two parties implicated. I asked him if he had been so long at the Préfecture without it occurring to him that the men for whose health he labours – and for whom he enslaves women – are guilty.

At this point, Lecours became very angry and began to pace the room, waving his arms about like a monkey and talking about the pardonable 'carelessness' of, perhaps, a young man who had taken a little too much wine and did not know what he was doing.

Josephine Butler returned to the attack.

> Is it not the case that the woman is poor, for I know that in Paris work is scarcely to be found just now; or else she is a slave in one of your permitted houses and is sent out by her employers on what is their, other than her, business.

By the end of the interview, Lecours was shrugging, and assuring her that he was himself a highly religious man. Yves Guyot, the radical Minister of Public Works, remembered Josephine Butler addressing the Municipal Court of Paris.

Elegant, refined, of an upright figure; she gave quite an original piquancy. She expressed herself with great simplicity; but by this simplicity she reached irresistible rhetorical effects. . . . Everybody felt moved in his inmost fibres by this pathetic address which owed nothing to rhetoric, but was the spontaneous outcome of an intense feeling of justice and humanity.

She was not a fanatical man-hater, and as the depths of the problem unfolded, she even began to understand its pathos from the point of view of the clients. At a very early stage, as she had told the Royal Commission, she had braved the licensed brothels of Chatham:

I gathered the [young men] round me, or rather they gathered themselves round me, and I spoke to them as a mother to sons. I did not speak to them altogether in a directly religious manner. I spoke to them lovingly. 'Why do you come here?' I asked one of them.
  'The soldiers all come here, and these are Government women.'
  'Here is a young lad' – he was pushed forward – 'he has just joined. Couldn't you get him out of this? He doesn't understand what it means. It is a shame they don't give us some proper entertainment.'

In the case of these young men, as Josephine Butler saw, there was perhaps 'a natural impulse' – in that odious phrase – finding its 'irregular indulgence'. But as she was to discover, many clients of brothels are on the look-out for something quite other than a 'natural impulse'.

I doubt if many people have come face to face, as I have sometimes, with 'demoniacal possession' in the form of raging impurity and unconquerable lust. I have, in a sense, looked into hell. I have been filled with a deep pity for many men so possessed, rather than horror, for I felt they were themselves victims dominated and tormented like the Demoniac of Gadara. The faces of some haunt me. You will not misunderstand me when I assure you I have known men of gentle and lovable natures, 'true gentlemen' generous and ever ready to do a kind act and who at the same time have been 'possessed' by a spirit of impurity and lust so that they were driven to deep despair.

Such gentlemen were often in the grip of sado-masochistic or paedophile desires which it was quite unthinkable to gratify within the confines of respectable domestic life. As Josephine Butler discovered, England was the supplier of a vast European chain of vice, not least because it had such a low age of consent (twelve), and so persistent a habit of turning a blind eye to these problems, that it was easy to carry on the abduction, and even the sale of children, either for use in London or for export to the continent.

With the help of Alfred Dyer, a Quaker publisher, Josephine Butler exposed the trade in children which was being carried on by the Belgian Chief of Special Police, who was imprisoned in 1883. But the British Government would take no sort of action. Her son George, enlisted to help the Cause, found brothels in London where there were padded cells in which children could be tortured without their screams being heard. A certain Harley Street physician – and he was not unique – made a brisk trade in procuring under-age children for his patients. In one season, he sold over one hundred.

It was in the face of these horrors, and of an indifferent Government determined not to disturb things by mentioning the unmentionable, that Josephine Butler decided to make the matter public. She enlisted the help of W. T. Stead, the redoubtable editor of the *Pall Mall Gazette*.

Living in her house was a woman called Rebecca Jarrett, a reformed alcoholic ex-brothel keeper to whom Josephine had been introduced by the Salvation Army. She knew the ropes for procuring a child, and undertook to purchase, for the sum of £5, a girl called Eliza Armstrong, and hand her over to Stead. The girl was then smuggled out of England by a member of the Salvation Army to Paris.

As a result of this escapade, Stead was able to demonstrate, quite unequivocally, that it was possible to buy a child in London, for the purposes of sexual abuse, in the year of grace 1885. He published the story, under the title of 'The Maiden Tribute of Modern Babylon' in a sensational series of articles for the *Pall Mall Gazette* and was able to follow up his account with dozens and dozens of further examples of what was going on. 'My object throughout has been to indicate crimes virtually encouraged by the law . . .'. He then introduced his readers to 'a tiny mite' called Annie Bryant, aged five, who was in the care of the Society for the Protection of Children.

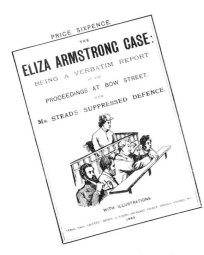

W. T. Stead, the editor of
the Pall Mall Gazette.
Stead's articles, 'The
Maiden Tribute of Modern
Babylon' provoked an outcry,
and Stead himself was
imprisoned for procuring a
child. But the articles led to
the eventual raising of the
age of consent.

She is now just five years old. Yet that baby girl has been the victim of rape. She was enticed together with a companion into a house in the New Cut on May 28 and forcibly outraged, first by a young man named William Hemmings and then by a fellow-lodger. The offence was committed and the poor little child had internal injuries from which it is doubtful whether she will ever entirely recover. The scoundrel is now doing two years' penal servitude, but his accomplice escaped. A penny cake was the lure which enticed the baby to her ruin.

Stead reckoned that there were '10,000 little girls living in sin in Christian England'. It was difficult enough to bring to justice those who abused children under the age of twelve, the legal age of consent. Once over that age, the child was more or less outside the protection of the law. Stead recounted the story of a man who had been sentenced for indecent assault on a child just under the age of twelve. In the course of the trial it became clear that he had 'violated more than a dozen children just over thirteen whom he had enticed into backyards by promises of sweetmeats, but though they did not know what he was doing until they felt the pain, they were over age and so he escaped scot free.'

Many people reacted with stark incredulity to Stead's revelations.

George Bernard Shaw, for example, who knew a certain amount about Victorian low life, dismissed 'The Maiden Tribute of Modern Babylon' article as a put-up job. But those who had dared to explore the under-world knew that Stead was telling the truth.

The *Pall Mall Gazette* articles caused an uproar. It was clearly out-rageous that the law of England allowed such abuses. The articles were published at a time when the Government's popularity was shaky as a result of its Irish policy, and it could not afford the risk of appearing to resist reform. As the articles appeared, it was rumoured that Stead knew the names of those in the House of Commons and the House of Lords whose tastes lay in the direction of sadistic paedophilia, and who had themselves been clients at the child-brothels. How many names in 'high society' were connected with these dens of vice is unclear; but Gladstone obviously felt that it was at least possible that members of his Government – certainly Members of Parliament – were implicated. This fact alone speaks volumes.

So, reform came fast. Within the same year, Parliament had rushed through the Criminal Law Amendment Bill which introduced heavy penalties for those guilty of child abuse, and which raised the age of con-sent from twelve to sixteen.

To this day, journalists still take differing views of Stead. There are those who regard him as the arch humbug, the spiritual father of those newspaper editors who profess to be horrified by what is going on in the world, but merely reveal (or invent) horrors in order to increase the circulation of their paper. Journalists like Stead, it is argued, do not really improve the world, though they may be extremely self-righteous. For others, however, W. T. Stead is a hero, and his association with Josephine Butler and Rebecca Jarrett is seen as a great example (Zola's *J'Accuse* is the greatest of all) of the power of the written word in a demo-cracy to Get Things Done. Probably neither of these extreme positions represents the full truth and Stead was, like many successful journalists after him, a strange mixture of hypocrisy and sensationalism. Whatever the fact of the matter, he had committed a criminal offence by procuring Eliza Armstrong, and he was prosecuted and sentenced to three months imprisonment. Rebecca Jarrett, however, was the one who suffered most. She was regarded as having played the most disgraceful role in the whole affair, and was awarded two years' penal servitude. Josephine Butler felt remorse to the end of her life for the trouble in which she had landed Rebecca. Jarrett herself never felt resentment against her old friend, and always spoke of Josephine Butler with gratitude and affection.

At about this time, Canon Scott Holland, the leader of the Christian Social Union, had a glimpse of Josephine Butler of which he has left a memorable account:

> A face looked at me out of a hurrying hansom, which arrested and frightened me. It was framed on pure and beautiful lines but it was smitten and bitten into as by some East wind that blighted it into grey sadness. It had seen that which took all colour and joy out of it. . . . Shortly after, all European civilisation shook with the horror of Mr. Stead's disclosures . . . I knew I had seen Mrs. Butler in the thick of the terrible work she had undertaken for God. She was passing through her martyrdom. The splendid beauty of her face, so spiritual in its high and clear outlines, bore the mark of that death upon it to which she stood hourly and daily committed. There was no hell on earth into which she would not willingly travel if, by sacrificing herself she could reach a hand of help to those poor children whom nothing short of such a sacrifice could touch. The sorrow of it passed into her being. She had the look of the world's grim tragedies in her eyes. She had dared to take the measure of the black infamy of sin; and the terrible knowledge had left its cruel mark upon a soul of strange and singular purity.

Scott Holland, famous in his day as a great social reformer and thinker in his own right, is today best known for his hymn 'Judge eternal, throned in splendour'. Those who do not know the background to the work which he, and Josephine Butler, undertook, have perhaps smiled at the language of those verses, which seem so quaintly dated today:

> *Still the weary folk are pining*
> *For the hour which brings release,*
> *And the city's crowded clangour*
> *Cries aloud for sin to cease. . . .*

But the words reflect an absolutely hideous reality which few were brave enough to face.

Josephine Butler's career shows how few people it takes to change the world. The numbers who were prepared to commit themselves to her campaigns in their initial stages were tiny yet within twenty years she had managed to organise the repeal of the Contagious Diseases Acts and to raise the age of consent. But these legislative reforms, although they did a certain amount to reduce human misery, had also uncovered an amount of wretchedness and sheer evil which could not be reformed by any Act of Parliament. As a young girl from a prosperous and high-minded Northumberland family, it had seemed to Josephine that England could be changed by extending the suffrage and passing laws to produce a juster society. She had assumed that the level of decency which her own family took for granted was one on which everyone was agreed, even though certain individuals, perhaps through little fault of their own, were not yet in a position to pursue it. Her journeys through the dark places of English cities had uncovered something infinitely more troubling. Her career exemplified in the most painful way a dilemma which was one of general application for the decent, or culti-vated, classes of Victorian England. Matthew Arnold, as a schools inspector, had not seen the horrors which confronted Josephine Butler, but he was aware that decent values were not, in fact, accepted, or even known about, by the generality of his fellow countrymen. It was the underlying point of his great essay on *Culture and Anarchy*. With terrifying speed, Great Britain had been transformed in a few generations from a small island with trading interests around the world into a great Empire, sustained and paid for by an ugly and entirely inequitable industrial expansion at home. The imperial glory which haunted Disraeli's fantasy-life, the commercial prosperity on which Gladstone's Liberalism depended, were both alike covering over the grisly reality of what Vic-torian cities in fact were – seething hotbeds of vice and disease, where the poor had no status whatsoever, and where one half of the population, however rich or comfortable they might be, had no status either in the eyes of politicians or the law. Josephine came to believe, and write:

> Womanhood is *solidaire*. We cannot successfully elevate the stan-dard of public opinion in the matter of justice to woman, and of equality of all in its truest sense, if we are content that a practical, hideous, calculated, manufactured and legally maintained degra-dation of a portion of womanhood is allowed to go on . . . 'Remem-ber them that are in bonds as being bound with them.'

The generations immediately following Josephine Butler looked to her as a heroine of social reform, and of the feminist movement; both of which she was. Blake's prophetic lines

The harlot's cry, from street to street
Shall weave old England's winding-sheet

was a favourite among early twentieth-century socialists. The capitalist with his big cigar and his top-hat was seen as the creator of the poor harlot in the gutter. But this was not really Josephine Butler's view, even though she had done so much to point out that no woman would *choose* to become a prostitute if all the economic circumstances of her life would allow her to do something different. If it was economic necessity which determined that there would always be fresh supplies of girls for the brothels, it was not economic necessity which meant that these girls would have clients. The existence of the clients said sadder and more far-reaching things about that much cherished Victorian institution, the family. The very values which Josephine had grown up to cherish – chastity and decency among them – were those which had helped to create a climate in which quite a number of men felt driven to some form of release outside the stifling confines of 'decency'.

What singles Josephine out from the run of do-gooders and reformers is that she had such a very human understanding of this. She was a tough fighter, but there was nothing self-righteous about her, nothing strident. And though she was intelligent enough to see the economic causes which led to the abuses she attacked, she had an ultimately larger scale of values by which to assess the whole problem. From the rescue of one

By the end of her life, Josephine Butler had become associated with almost every 'good cause' in the world, from the plight of the Russian Jews to that of Dreyfus in France. She travelled constantly.

Liverpool prostitute, she moved on to the larger question of prostitution, of the Contagious Diseases Acts, and of what that told her about the position of women in society; it led her to a form of socialism, and to a belief that men and women must change their whole attitude to each other. But, ultimately, her feeling that society was out of joint derived from the impulse which had led her, in the first place, to help those less fortunate than herself. That is, it derived from her Christian belief. There were many things, from the death of her own daughter onwards, which contributed to moods of doubt and despair, when she felt tempted to 'a hopeless and final denial of the Divine goodness'. But she repeatedly returned to the central notion that the world fell out of joint when it departed from the purposes of that Divine Goodness itself. At the heart of her practical concerns for others there remained something like a mystical love of God. Although it was refined by much suffering and fre-quent doubt, she could say,

> as we get nearer to God, all prayer resolves itself into *communion*. To the Holy of Holies, face to face with Jesus, all perplexities vanish. No difficulties can live. If I may dare to tell a little of what He has taught me, even in days and weeks of bodily suffering, it is this; that in prayer I am still, silent, waiting for the Spirit and the Spirit is granted, so that He prompts every request.

The overtly religious tenor of her utterances, and her motivation, is poss-ibly one of the things which enabled Josephine Butler's name to sink into some obscurity after the early years of this century, when other feminist heroines could be less embarrassingly quoted. Among her co-religionists, on the other hand, her name became forgotten for subtly different reasons. Prostitutes and venereal diseases did not cease to be unmentionable subjects. In Anglican folk-memory, however, she has always occupied a much-loved place. When Liverpool Cathedral eventually came to be built, a window was erected there to her memory. Being represented in stained glass is only a short step away from being made a saint. The Church of England does not have a Process, like the Church of Rome, by which individuals can be declared saints, but when the new Prayer Book of 1980 was compiled, provision was made on 30 December, the anniversary of her death, to commemorate Josephine Butler. It is hard to know what she would have made of that.

Josephine Butler and her family. There is no doubt that Josephine Butler's family suffered as a consequence of her campaigns. Her son's career at the Bar became impossible, and George Butler was compelled to resign his post as Principal of Liverpool College. But they all supported her because they knew she was right.

In the notoriety of her campaigns, George Butler had felt it better to resign his position as Principal of Liverpool College. 'He was even more to me in later life than a wise and noble supporter in the work which may be called especially my own', she remembered. Much to the credit of the established Church – which is not always to be relied upon to be unstuffy – they made him a canon of Winchester Cathedral. It was in that beautiful and gentle southern town that the Butlers were able to live for the five years following the *Pall Mall Gazette* furore. When George died in 1890, Josephine's home life, and her happiness, had in some ways been brought to an end.

Though she had nursed George Butler throughout his last illness, she was unable, quite, to remain a purely domestic creature, even in this sorrow. Life had made her into a supporter of Causes, and the remaining sixteen years of life were to see her name being added to those who continued to fight for the reform of vice in European towns. She was pro-Dreyfus, pro-Boer, pro any good cause you could mention until her death. There is a haunting photograph of her taken in old age, a lace cap on her head, a pen in her hand: a strange link between the high-minded generation who grew up after the Great Reform Bill, and the 'modern' women she helped to liberate. She died, where she had begun, in Northumberland, at Wooler, on 30 December 1906.

Some years before, in the 1890s, the prolific painter G. F. Watts was engaged in his great 'Hall of Fame' series of portraits of those who had 'made the century'. He asked Josephine Butler to sit for him. He told her to 'look into Eternity, looking at something no one else sees'.

When he had finished the picture, she told him that she felt inclined to burst into tears.

> I will tell you why. I felt so sorry for her. Your power has brought up out of the depths of the past, the record of a conflict which no one but God knows of. It is written in the eyes and in the whole face. Your picture has brought back to me all that I suffered, and the sorrows through which the Angel of God's presence brought me out alive. I thank you that you have not made that poor woman look severe or bitter but only sad and purposeful.

The sorrow which the portrait reveals was, as she confided, a deeply personal one. But it was also one which her whole class, and all decent-minded people, must have felt when surveying Great Britain and the British Empire. She was one who 'made the century' in one sense. In another, she helped to unmake it, because it did not deserve to be, and in unmaking it, she and her like were to unpick the very fabric of so much that they took for granted and loved. 'God and one woman make a majority', she had once said. It turned out to be true, and it was a devastating combination.

Julia Margaret Cameron
1815-79

Pioneer of portrait photography

This picture of Julia Margaret Cameron was taken by her fellow enthusiast Lewis Carroll. She and Carroll belonged to the small band of Victorian photographers who saw the imaginative and artistic potential of the camera, and stood apart from the dull conventional work of the studio photographers.

*T*wo years after Queen Victoria came to the throne, some small boys were playing near the foot of Charles I's statue at the Trafalgar Square end of Whitehall. Since that statue was first erected close to the site of the king's execution, thousands of children must have sat there in the hot weather to play marbles, spun hoops there in the bracing mists of spring, or scooped up snowballs from its iron railings on winter days. There was nothing different about this particular group of boys – Artful Dodgers in top hats – but there was something exceptional about the moment they had chosen to play there. For on the other side of the road, in Trafalgar Square, a Frenchman called de St Croix was tinkering with a mysterious piece of equipment. He was in the process of taking a daguerreotype on that autumn day in 1839. Those boys must be among the first people in England to have been photographed.

The first real photograph may be said to have been produced in 1827 by Nicéphore Niepce, a Frenchman who pioneered methods of fixing the image obtained by a *camera obscura*, or pin-hole camera. His techniques were developed by his fellow-countryman L. J. M. Daguerre who, as a painter, had been famous since 1823 as the man responsible for the striking topographical views displayed in the Diorama he had opened on the edge of London's Regent's Park. It was de St Croix who first demonstrated Daguerre's discoveries to a London audience at 7 Piccadilly on 13 September 1839. The technique exploited the sensitivity of silver salts to light. A polished and silvered copper plate was made light-sensitive with iodine vapour and, after exposure in the camera, was developed with mercury vapour and fixed into a permanent image with hydro-sulphite of soda.

Quacks and mountebanks, showing off their latest invention, were a familiar part of the London scene. Gullible invited audiences must often have been ushered into such rooms as these, to be entertained with the latest developments in phrenology (the science of telling character from the bumps and lumps on your skull), the mysteries of psychic research (as demonstrated by Mr Sludge the Medium), hydropathy (the application of water to cure almost every known ailment, as pioneered by the celebrated Dr Gully and practised by almost every intellectual of note in the mid-nineteenth century) or genetics (as expounded in 1859 by Charles Darwin). As the list suggests, some of these 'discoveries' have affected the way we look at the universe today. Most of them – like the huge majority of scientific 'discoveries' in history – have been shown to be purely bogus.

The discovery of photography, however, changed the world in a manner with which, even now – 150 years later – it is not always easy to come to terms. Questions about the nature of time, and of reality itself, are raised by the figure of M. de St Croix, standing in Trafalgar Square with his little box. Until then, each moment had been essentially evanescent. The only media in which a moment could be 'frozen' or the past be 'captured' were manifestly interpretative – through the written word, or the painted or sculpted image. It was taken for granted that the here and now – the particular minute or two in the gardens of Westminster Abbey, for example, it took for a man in a peaked cap and a frock coat to walk along with a woman who could be Dora Copperfield – would pass by for ever. Men and women no more thought of holding such moments than a butterfly would so think. But there it remains for us, in a famous calotype of around 1845, taken by William Fox Talbot.

The arrival of the camera had an almost immediate effect on the other arts, which by the end of the century had diverged into many fascinating reactions and counter-reactions. It more or less goes without saying that the history of painting after 1840 is haunted by the knowledge that pencils, brushes and crayons are no longer the only means of representing reality on paper. The extreme, detailed 'realism' of Dominique Ingres, or of John Everett Millais or William Holman Hunt, owed something to the existence of M. Daguerre's box. So, obviously, did the opposite development in painting, the discovery that a painter was now liberated from being a mere recorder and could become an interpreter of the world, as all great artists always had been. Impressionists could look at light, not as the camera artificially freezes it, but as the eye sees and feels it. Post-Impressionists could convey, as poets can, what landscape feels like, not just what it looks like. Liberated from representationalism, painters and sculptors could begin to experiment, as Cézanne did in his later canvases, with form which is of interest for its own sake. Cubism is only a step away in one direction, and non-representational painting in another. Without the camera there would be no Picasso, no Braque, no Mondrian, no Miró.

Literature, either consciously or subliminally, is influenced by the discovery of the camera, too. The neo-realism of such childhood-recreations as *Jane Eyre* and *David Copperfield* provides in prose what a family photograph-album was soon to give every middle-class household in England: an exact representation of the self at its most ephemeral period. It was, however, abroad that these tendencies, hinted at by English novelists, were taken to their greatest extreme. Proust is the most obvious example, his great *roman fleuve* attempting to provide a series of endless inner photographs, reclaiming something which, until that point of history, could never, by definition, be reclaimed: time itself.

All this has had a disconcerting effect upon our idea of reality. The audience at 7 Piccadilly on 13 September 1839 were not being tricked. M. de St Croix really had, by employing the ingenious methods of M. Daguerre, produced photographic images of the streets of London. In another sense, however, it could be said that he was unfolding the most fraudulent of all illusions; no greater untruth was ever uttered than the saying that the camera cannot lie.

The nineteenth century, so unlike other eras in history in so many ways, apparently distinguishes itself yet again by being the first which we can apparently *see*. Our vision of the Napoleonic Wars, and of all the previous European conflicts, we believe, would be quite different if, as during the Crimean campaigns, photographers had been present on both sides. If it is arguable that Samuel Johnson, Voltaire or Frederick the Great, familiar to us through the portrait artist's eye, would be discernibly different historical figures if we knew them through photographs, how much more would Mary Queen of Scots, Shakespeare, Francis of Assisi be. Photography increases our sense of life's vividness, but it also diminishes. Scientific perusal of the Turin Shroud prompts the apparently profane, actually religious, question, whether the doctrine of the Incarnation itself could ever have been formulated had the Romans invented photography, and had the *Ecce Homo* been preserved on daguerreotype.

The invention of photography advanced the severance which had already begun between what was 'imaginary' and what was 'real' in the human mind. For many, it confirmed the notion that there was such a thing as 'objective' or 'scientific' reality. Photography became a stan-

The nineteenth century is the first epoch in history which we can see.
This photograph by Roger Fenton shows Lt Gen Sir George Brown and his staff in the Crimea
in 1856. It is interesting to reflect on how differently we would regard earlier
wars if we had photographs of Marathon, Agincourt or Waterloo.

dard, a criterion of objectivity – something which political propagandists in the early decades of the twentieth century were not slow to exploit. It is surely no accident that most of the footage of film which documents the Russian revolution was not newsreel but posed and invented stuff by Eisenstein. Those crowds sweeping into the Winter Palace, for example, which for many of us are the image of the October Revolution of 1917, were filmed in the 1920s. The reality of the coup was undramatic; no crowds, few shots fired. The film-makers and photographers needed to create something as vivid as, say, Carlyle's *French Revolution*.

The history of photography-as-history is full of such cases: either of photography being used fraudulently to convey reality, or, much more disconcertingly, of people assuming it to be real merely because it is on film, and regardless of the photographer's motive. Photography, as most of the great early examples of men like William Fox Talbot show, is an extremely unrealistic medium. True, on an obvious level, it can record the shapes of buildings, the clothes people wore, the existence or non-existence of a particular landmark (though these can be easily altered in the darkroom). But, in various quite important degrees, common sense shows that photography, unlike painting, can never be completely true. For one thing – to limit our discussion to still photography – the world never has been still. Most Victorian photographs had to be taken on a long exposure, so that the faces of the sitters had to be frozen for anything up to ten minutes or quarter of an hour. No wonder one gets the impression that they were a gloomy crowd (besides, saying 'cheese' was an embarrassment in an age when dentistry simply meant drawing rotten teeth, and when most people aged forty were by modern standards almost toothless). Fox Talbot tells us a certain amount about the look of Victorian England. But the painter William Frith with his crowded *Derby Day* or seaside scenes tells us much more. His canvases move with life and colour.

Eyes, as opposed to cameras, interpret, quickly and changeably, the images which are played upon the retina. No eye has ever seen the same image for ten minutes without movement, which is why slowly-exposed photographs always have an air of unreality. By contrast, no eye has ever frozen one single image from a split second, which is why modern fast-exposed photographs, however vivid or beautiful, also have an air of unreality.

> He thought he saw an Elephant,
>   That practised on a fife:
> He looked again, and found it was
>   A letter from his wife.
> "At length I realise", he said,
>   "The bitterness of life".

Such moments of 'double-take', to which eye and brain constantly readjust in the course of an ordinary day, are impossible for the camera. Filmed from the wrong or right angle, the letter from the wife always looks like an elephant. It was no accident that such an *aperçu* should have come to one of the most distinguished amateur photographers of the Victorian age, Lewis Carroll.

Carroll's photography of children sets up an awkward set of responses in the modern observer. Rather than enjoy the haunting beauty of his frames, we are more inclined to pose as guardians of Carroll's morals, or at least of his *psyche*. A dangerous game, whether you play it with the dead or with the living.

> *Then they joined and all abused it –*
> *Unrestrainedly abused it –*
> *As 'the worst and ugliest picture*
> *That could possibly be taken . . .'.*

Carroll belonged to that early generation of photographers who saw at once that, whether you use a pencil, a brush or a camera, it requires human imagination to make pictures. While the majority of 'studio photographers' in the nineteenth century set out to make their living (quite understandably) from dull posed family groups standing by potted plants, or from cartes de visite, there was a handful of genuine artists who immediately saw the point of photography, its imaginative potential.

To emphasise the contrast between these artists and those who merely took photographs, you only have to turn the pages of some Victorian family album in which the compiler has forgotten to label the images. Nothing is deader than these faces. A silhouette or a sketch of their grandparents, executed in the days of the Regency, has a thousand times more animation! The slow exposure and the bad studio lighting so often contrived to deprive their features of character. This is oblivion indeed; for we really feel that these nameless images could be *anyone*. Far from emphasising the distinctiveness of their subjects, as a true portraitist or artist would do, these depressing productions – like the faces on passports or ID cards today – make one doubt the very existence of human individuality. An album of cats and dogs, if we are being candid, would contain more variety. It is in the light of these pictures, and not with thoughts of modern child pornography, that one should look at Lewis Carroll's photographs, or at those of an even better photographer, Julia Margaret Cameron.

Julia Margaret Cameron's interest in photography was first aroused at the age of twenty when, recuperating from an illness at the Cape of Good Hope, she met the astronomer Sir John Herschel, one of the pioneers of photographic processing. It is to Herschel that we owe the first use of the terms 'negative' and 'positive' as applied to this process, 'snap-shot', and the word 'photography' itself. Mrs Cameron did not, however, take her first picture until she was forty-eight years old. Before that momentous day on the Isle of Wight in January 1864, there stretched 'a life crowded with incident'.

She was born Julia Margaret Pattle, in Calcutta on 11 June 1815, a week before the Battle of Waterloo. It was a big family – ten children, of whom Julia Margaret was the fourth. Her father was a senior official of the East India Company, and the saying out there – originating with Lord Dalhousie – was that society divided into 'men, women and Pattles': not that there was anything androgynous or hermaphroditic about the Pattle girls, but – like many large families – they to a certain extent devised their own patterns of behaviour, often at variance with those of the rest of the world. 'Pattledom' became a term synonymous with oddity. They were a family about whom tall stories were told, and they all appear to have been happy to live up to their reputation as originals.

Julia Margaret Cameron came from a famously peculiar Anglo–Indian family called Pattle. She was unfortunate in being the only Pattle sister who was not beautiful.

When James Pattle died in 1845, his body was preserved in alcohol and put on a ship bound for England. He had expressed a wish for interment in his native soil. Mrs Pattle (the daughter of a man who had been one of Marie-Antoinette's courtiers, the Chevalier de l'Etang) accompanied her husband on his last journey. Rounding the Cape of Good Hope, the ship ran into a storm. The cask of alcohol containing Mr Pattle rolled over and burst, and his widow, having heard the explosion, went next door to see what was happening. The sight of her husband's pickled corpse bursting from its cask is said to have driven her mad. Two months later she too died, 'Raving . . . the shock sent her off her head.'

Her daughter Julia Margaret – never far, it would seem, from the mental condition in which her mother died – had married Charles Hay Cameron when she was twenty-two and he an extremely elderly forty-three. He had a distinguished career in India, rising to become President of the Calcutta Council of Education. His chief passions were Ceylon, where he owned considerable estates, Homer, whose poetry he liked to read aloud, and liberalism. He was a follower of the great utilitarian philosopher, Jeremy Bentham, and a keen supporter of good causes. Despite her Pattle eccentricities, Julia Margaret could contrive great feats of organisation. We have an early glimpse of her energies when news reached Calcutta of the Irish potato famine in 1845. She managed to raise £14,000 for the relief-fund; and she ran the campaign more or less single-handed.

By the time Charles Cameron was fifty-four, he felt ready for retirement and the family (by then there were six children) decided to return to England. Since they had no idea where, eventually, they would settle, the journey assumed an almost Abrahamic feeling of caravan as they loaded on board ship their children, together with trunkfuls of belongings – fabrics, rugs, carvings, spices, curry-powder and coffins (mindful of her parent's unhappy experience at the Cape, Mrs Cameron never went anywhere without taking something to be buried in).

She was a short woman, and unlike her sisters, rather plain. Her olive complexion and dark hair were a throwback to her French ancestors. A pronounced mole or wart dominated the left-hand side of her face just next to the nostril, and her eyes were too small for her brow. Undeterred by these aesthetic disadvantages, she enlivened her appearance with a quantity of brightly coloured shawls, mantillas, and festoons of velvet drapery. Since her husband had shoulder-length, prematurely white hair and a long beard which would have done credit (indeed, *was* to do credit) to Merlin or King Lear, the couple must have made a striking entrance into the drawing-rooms of London.

Arrived in England, Julia Margaret happily falling back into Pattledom, made contact with her sisters. She made the hottest bee-line for Sara, also married to an elderly Indian civil servant, called Thoby Prinsep, and the centre of an artistic coterie which included the Pre-Raphaelite painters John Everett Millais, Dante Gabriel Rossetti, Edward Burne-Jones, William Holman Hunt and G. F. Watts. He was to become Julia Margaret's favourite. Sara Prinsep inhabited a residence known as Little Holland House – rented from Lord Holland, who lived in Italy – and Watts, nicknamed Signor by Sara, who 'came for three days and remained thirty years' had a room there where he could paint, pontificate and entertain his friends. Sara and Julia Margaret were responsible some years later for urging Watts, when quite a grey-beard, to marry the sixteen-year-old Ellen Terry. It is one of the more chilling little episodes in the history of 'Pattledom'. Ellen, though beginning to make her way on the stage, was emotionally immature, and even after her marriage liked to play, as one of the children, with Mrs Cameron's offspring. After a year, her unconsummated union to Signor was allowed to be deemed a failure.

As well as painters, Mrs Cameron liked to cultivate poets. The most famous of her poets was Alfred Tennyson: it was because he resided for a while at Putney that the Camerons found themselves taking up brief residence on Putney Heath. But a poet she admired with equal fervour was Henry Taylor. Nowadays, he is little more than a footnote in the history of literature, but in his day he was an enormously prolific playwright and epic poet. Like most of the men Mrs Cameron admired, Taylor had a beard which grew generously over his chest. Taylor and his wife soon learnt what it was to be the devotees of Julia Margaret's generosity. She liked to shower her friends with gifts, and Indian shawls, bracelets, ivory, inlaid portfolios poured on to the doorstep of their house at Mortlake, as did huge letters at least six pages long. On one occasion, Henry Taylor and his wife were sitting in a railway carriage, about to leave Waterloo Station, when a dishevelled lady rushed up at the last moment and flung a Persian rug through the window. Just as the train began to move, Taylor had the presence of mind to roll up the rug and plop it back on to the platform. Refusing her bounty was not always that easy. Mrs Taylor once returned an extravagantly valuable shawl which Mrs Cameron had forced upon her. Many months later, when visiting the hospital for incurables at Putney, she was surprised to see an invalid sofa inscribed as a gift from herself. Mrs Cameron had sold the spurned shawl and given the money to the hospital in Mrs Taylor's name.

All this sounds as though it has something about it of the intrusive; as though Julia Margaret was a tuft-hunter. That is to mistake the exuberance of her generosity altogether. It applied to everyone, not just the famous. Years later, when police in the Isle of Wight informed her that trippers and locals were picking the flowers in a rose hedge which ran along the road at the bottom of her garden, she replied that was why she had planted the hedge in the first place – so that people could pick the flowers.

It is with the Isle of Wight that we most associate Julia Margaret Cameron. After a peripatetic existence, and an attempt to make a life for themselves in Tunbridge Wells, the Camerons heard, in 1860, that the Tennysons had moved to Farringford House on Freshwater Bay at the western end of the island. That summer, Mrs Cameron visited Tennyson. (She was, incidentally, the only woman apart from his wife whom he ever called by her Christian name.) The cliffs, the sea air, the colour, the proximity of a great, heavily bearded poetic genius all determined Mrs Cameron. She immediately bought the two cottages adjoining Tennyson's extensive grounds, erected a tower between them, and named them, after her husband's estates in Ceylon, 'Dimbola'.

The Camerons arrived in Dimbola with their strange caravan of belongings and offspring. A new individual had been added to the throng, an Irish girl called Mary Ryan, one of the most noted beneficiaries of Julia Margaret's strange, swooping possessively exuberant heart. Mary had been a little vagrant girl until her mother, an Irish tinker, had been unguarded enough to knock at the door of Mrs Cameron's cottage in Putney and beg for alms. Mrs Cameron immediately decided that she was not prepared to give mere gifts of money to the pair. They must come and live with her. Unsurprisingly Mrs Ryan beat a hasty retreat, preferring the hardships of hedgerow and heath to the oppressive attentions of Mrs Cameron's good nature. Mary, however, stayed. Not quite a daughter and not quite a parlour-maid, she was kept in Mrs Cameron's household, her hour not yet come. Once adopted, Mary received no particular affection from Mrs Cameron. She

Farringford House, Freshwater Bay – the home of the poet laureate,
Alfred Tennyson, and his family.

collected people rather as she collected objects, largely because their looks were appealing. For example, though she had almost no garden during the last years of her life in Ceylon, she employed a gardener there because she liked the shape of his back. Before the arrival of the camera in her life, Julia Margaret was a natural photographer, taking, we may believe, a myriad plates inside her highly distinctive brain.

Mary Ryan was destined to become one of her most remarkable photographic subjects, and with far-reaching consequences for herself.

215

Dimbola, the Camerons' house on the Isle of Wight,
named after Charles Cameron's estates in Ceylon.

Her sad eyes, her full lips, her thick hair, made a lasting impression on one of the visitors to an early Cameron exhibition in London. He was a young Indian civil servant called Henry Cotton. With long hair and wild eyes, he made the journey to Dimbola and, having sent in his card, announced to Mrs Cameron, 'I have come to ask for the hand of your housemaid. I saw her at your exhibition and have all the time kept the bill she wrote out for me next to my heart.'

Objections from the Cotton family were eventually overruled. Only the vagrant Mrs Ryan protested at the unsuitability of the match. Under the benign eye of their patroness, the young people were married at Freshwater in 1867. Within eight years, he was Sir Henry Cotton with a salary of £2400. 'What is more important,' said Mrs Cameron, 'it was a marriage of bliss.' And how is this defined? 'With children worthy of being photographed, as their mother had been, for their beauty.'

Julia Margaret kept tirelessly in touch with her circle of friends and family. She never sent less than six telegrams a day. 'Let out all Henry's throats' was one wire she bafflingly dispatched to the wife of Henry Brotherton, the artist. 'I had a dream my Henry was suffocating,' she explained in a letter which followed, 'and in case my dream were to come true, I telegraphed Mary to make his throats (i.e. shirt collars) bigger.' Increasingly, Mr Cameron found it necessary to attend to his estates in Ceylon, leaving his wife behind on the Isle of Wight. Since their children were now all grown up, or on the verge of being so, she spent much of her time in the post office, sending them letters or telegrams. When two of her sons accompanied her husband on a prolonged visit to Ceylon, she would sit in the post office until the last minute before the departure of the Indian mail, scribbling her interminable missives to them. 'How much longer?' she would ask the clerk. 'Five minutes madam.' Scribble, scribble, scribble. 'How much longer now?' 'Two minutes, madam.' And so on, until the moment that the last mailbag was closed.

Three of her sons eventually settled in Ceylon, to grow coffee on their father's estate. Her daughter Julia, distressed by her mother's loneliness, was aware of how much she minded the boys' absence. 'The more it is prolonged,' Mrs Cameron admitted, 'the more the wound seems to widen.' It was at this point that Julia and her husband Charles Norman thought of a present to revive Julia Margaret's spirits. They gave her a large wooden camera (the plates it took were 9 in × 11 in) and all the necessary dark-room equipment. 'It may amuse you, Mother, to try to photograph during your solitude at Freshwater.'

The coalhouse at Dimbola was instantly transformed into a dark-room, and Mrs Cameron set to work. She made mistakes; but from the first, there was a distinctiveness about her way of looking at people which immediately communicated itself. At first, she concentrated on por-traits. She paid 'Farmer Rice' half a crown to pose for her, and it was not a great success. Then in January 1864, she found a little girl called Annie who made a much better subject. 'I was in a transport of delight,' she tells us in *Annals of My Glass House*. 'I ran all over the house to search for gifts for the child. I felt as if she entirely had made the picture. I printed, toned, fixed and framed it, and presented it to her father that same day.'

The result was the picture inscribed, 'Annie – My First Success'. Much of the success, as even Mrs Cameron's gushing prose allows us to recognise, is her competent grasp of the photographic medium. The chemistry of the art was something she mastered at once, and she was to exploit it as she matured. But a mere knowledge of how to develop a picture would not have produced 'Annie'. We can see an understandable wariness in the sitter. Who would not have been wary of this lady, described by William Allingham, at about the same date, as 'shrieking' and wearing 'a funny red openwork shawl'. But beneath all the 'Pattledom' there was an extraordinarily sympathetic imagination. We feel we *know* Annie.

One of the reasons for Mrs Cameron's success as a portraitist is that she boldly employed the use of close-up. She refused to enlarge, using only her 11 in × 9 in plate negatives, going on in 1866 to 15 in × 12 in ones. Often she is so close to her subject that it is out of focus, causing the famous Cameron 'imperfect vision'. But there are no better Victorian portraits than hers. She seems to see into the souls of her subjects. And because of her irrepressible boldness, she managed to capture many of the most eminent Victorians of them all.

Anthony Trollope, the novelist, was an early *trouvail* – he came to the Isle of Wight in 1864. Here, Julia Margaret's 'imperfect vision' has made of the borders of the picture what Sir Joshua Reynolds would have made in one of his oil sketches. They are just a smudge, leading our eye directly into the features of the subject. In her portrait of Benjamin Jowett, the famous Master of Balliol College, taken the following year, she has brilliantly caught the contradictory qualities of that fascinating man. The neat Oxford MA hood has become a fuzz, and the translator of Plato comes before us, as is appropriate, in a kind of spiritual emanation. The face, however, has only half glimpsed the wisdom of the Greeks. The superciliousness of the mouth tells us of Jowett the snob, the social climber, the cultivator of the society of duchesses. The clever eyes are both amused at the absurdity of undergraduates, and meditating upon the mystery of things.

If her Jowett is on the edge of being a comic figure, her Carlyle is pure, unremitting tragedy. The historian of *The French Revolution*, Thomas Carlyle's increasingly desperate vision of the human condition was blackened by a crushingly depressive temperament, exacerbated by the fact that he had no gift for marriage. It was Tennyson's surprising malice which thanked God for making Carlyle marry Mrs Carlyle – thereby making two people unhappy instead of four. In 1866 Carlyle's clever and long-suffering wife Jane died, quite suddenly, of a stroke while in her carriage going round Hyde Park Corner. Mrs Cameron captures Carlyle a year after this melancholy event, his face full of the remorse which he felt for the rest of his days, for the deliberate withholding of affection from a woman to whom he owed so much. He used to go and stand on Hyde Park Corner to do penance for the sufferings he had caused her; and he made sure that his biographer, J. A. Froude, knew the whole miserable story, so that he should not be allowed to escape the judgement of posterity.

The melancholy of Lord Tennyson's face, by comparison, is much more showy. We notice here (particularly in the famous picture which he nicknamed 'The Dirty Monk') how Mrs Cameron liked not merely to take close-ups, but to see her subjects in an informal, intimate way. 'Although I bully you, I have a corner of worship for you in my heart,' she told Tennyson, who for some time had resisted posing before her camera.

The 'bullying' certainly took intrusive forms, even by her bossy standards. Since they were her immediate neighbours at Freshwater, the

Tennyson with his wife Emily and sons Lionel and Hallam in the garden of Farringford House on the Isle of Wight. It was here that Julia Margaret Cameron attempted to photograph Garibaldi and was impatiently dismissed as a beggar.

Tennysons bore the brunt of her generosity. 'She is more wonderful than ever in her wild beaming benevolence,' Tennyson said to his wife about Julia Margaret one night after dining with her. He was less sanguine when she decided that he should undergo a vaccination against small-pox. Tennyson locked himself in his tower at Farringford when he heard that Mrs Cameron was on her way with the doctor. She stood at the bottom of the staircase and shouted, 'You're a coward, Alfred, you're a coward!' until he opened the door and submitted to the needle. The vaccine was past its best, and Tennyson was confined to his bed until the effects had worn off.

On another occasion, long past the ordinary hour when the Tennysons normally dined, Mrs Cameron decided that they should eat a leg of mutton, and pushed her way through to the kitchens, insisting that their cook put the meat in the oven straight away. Again, Emily Tennyson was surprised to come downstairs one morning to find her hall heaped with rolls of fashionable new 'Elgin Marbles' wallpaper which Mrs Cameron – without consulting the Tennysons – had decided would be an appropriate adornment to the Poet Laureate's household. At least she did not hang the paper – unlike the occasion when she stayed with the Henry Taylors and covered their spare bedroom, furniture and walls, with floral transfers during the night.

As well as loving Tennyson as a dear neighbour, Mrs Cameron saw him as an admirable 'bait' to attract subjects for her portraiture. Many of the Poet Laureate's distinguished visitors were resistant to Mrs Cameron, but she was hard to deter. When she heard that Garibaldi, the great hero of the Italian Risorgimento who was being feted wherever he went in England, had arrived at Farringford, she rushed round to persuade him to be photographed. He was sitting in the garden, and was astonished by the advance of someone he took to be a gipsy woman, her hair awry, he hands blackened by silver nitrate, her shawls and mantillas stained and dishevelled. She threw herself at his feet. He dismissed her with a wave of the hand, assuming her to be a beggar.

Another visitor to Tennyson's house who refused to be photographed was Edward Lear, the nonsense poet and watercolourist, no great lover of women. 'Mrs Cameron came in only once – with feminine perception, not delighting in your humble servant,' Lear told Holman Hunt. Knowing Lear's fondness for music, and hearing that the Tennysons' piano was out of tune, Mrs Cameron hit upon what seemed like the per-

Alfred Tennyson, c. 1867. Tennyson was Mrs Cameron's neighbour at Freshwater on the Isle of Wight and he was her most celebrated subject.

fect way of winning his heart – or at least his willingness to sit for his portrait. She ordered eight men to carry her own piano around to Farringford and offer it to Lear for his use while staying on the Isle of Wight. He still refused to have his picture taken.

Nevertheless, she managed in the end to have an impressive gallery of characters in her portrait collection – as well as Tennyson, G. F. Watts, Henry Taylor, Thomas Carlyle, Benjamin Jowett, and Anthony Trollope there were the poets Robert Browning and Henry Longfellow, Charles Darwin, William Holman Hunt, the sculptor Thomas Woolner, and the historian William Lecky, not to speak of Ellen Terry and Alice Liddell of *Through the Looking Glass*. This was surely an impressive collection of 'Eminent Victorians'.

One of the reasons why her portraits are so lively is undoubtedly the simple fact that her sitters were with *her*. You could not be in Mrs Cameron's company and not react to it in some manner or another, even if your reaction – as so many of her sitters' reactions seem to have been – was absolute incredulity that anyone could be quite so extraordinary as the lady behind the camera. She did not need to tell *them* to watch the birdie, as she swirled to and fro between their chair and the camera, ruffling their hair with silver-nitrate-stained fingers, and talking poetic nonsense in a loud voice. Sometimes, as is the case with Trollope I think, her sitters registered intolerance, the sense that being 'a character' was one thing, but that Mrs Cameron went too far. Sometimes, as in Jowett's case, there is barely concealed amusement in the features. What they perhaps did not realise until they saw the results (and not always even then) was that she had an extremely intelligent and penetrating eye. There is no doubt, as we survey her portfolio, that she was in control of her subjects and, when we consider the eminence of the subjects, that is in itself sufficiently remarkable. She was in control because she did not consider herself her subjects' superior. Not in the least. She was a genuinely humble person. When she went down on her knees to Garibaldi, there was nothing false in the gesture. She believed herself to be in the presence of a giant, but when he dismissed her, she was defiant. Waving her filthy hands, she remonstrated, 'This is Art, not Dirt.'

As well as being a portraitist, however, she was also an imaginative artist, a Pre-Raphaelite with a camera. Roger Fry, the Bloomsbury artist and art critic, believed that she was in fact the greatest artist of the Victorian age. 'Mrs Cameron's photographs already bid fair to outlive most of the works of the artists who were her contemporaries,' he wrote. 'One day we may hope that the National Portrait Gallery may be deprived of so large a part of its grant that it will turn to fostering the art of photography.' Fry was being deliberately provocative, and he praised Mrs Cameron partly because he admired her but chiefly as a way of expressing contempt for the productions of Millais, Holman Hunt, Rossetti, Lord Leighton or Alma-Tadema. It is indeed hard to believe that some of her Tennysonian *tableaux*, for example, are meant seriously, rather than being satires on the subject-matter and composition of her contemporaries in the field of painting. But such pictures as her 'Gareth and Lynette' or her 'Passing of Arthur' are offered in the same spirit of artistic seriousness as masterpieces like the portraits of Carlyle. The contrast between the two, however, to a modern eye is so glaring that some comment seems to be necessary.

I think one should not be too beguiled by the word 'serious'. The

Pattles, like most big families until the invention of wireless and tele-vision, enjoyed parlour games, charades, and amateur dramatics of a more or less formal character. Julia Margaret had grown up with the idea, now lost to us, that it was fun to dress up, pose and act for a small circle of family and private friends. Even when the subject of the charade or tableau was 'serious', it would be a mistake to think that the game was played with no sense of fun. It is heavy-handed, perhaps, even to say so, but when some modern commentators poke fun at Mrs Cameron's 'Pre-Raphaelite' scenes, they do not give sufficient attention to the fact that these scenes were often executed in a spirit of fun, though not of course meant to be 'funny'. Plenty of people found them unintentionally comic at the time. We need not think that because they raise a smile on our lips, this somehow proves our emotional sophistication or aesthetic superiority to Mrs Cameron and her generation.

The tableau-photographs, however, cannot really be defended on aes-thetic grounds, but they do, unintentionally and fascinatingly, raise all sorts of questions about Victorian aesthetics and, indeed, Victorian sexuality. Nor was the influence all one way. Mrs Cameron did not merely draw inspiration from Pre-Raphaelites; she herself created images which the painters tried to copy. Dante Gabriel Rossetti's *Beata Beatrix* in the Tate Gallery, with its smudged background and artificial glow around the head, surely owes much to Mrs Cameron's techniques (though in fact Rossetti refused even to meet her). But you only have to look at a picture where she herself has imitated Rossetti (her 'Too Late! Too Late!' of 1868 owes much to his *Rosa Triplex* of 1867) to see where the difficulties arise. The whole point about Rossetti's maidens (as that great admirer and collector of his work, L. S. Lowry, observed) is that they are not real. 'They are dreams,' as Lowry said. You can paint a dream, but you cannot photograph one. The girls in 'Too Late! Too Late!' just look like real girls who are horribly bored. (For a picture called 'Despair' Mrs Cameron was reputed to have locked the sitter in a cupboard for several hours to obtain the appropriate expression.) Moreover, by taking her camera so close, and by exaggerating the muddiness and tactility of her girls' complexions and expressions, Mrs Cameron vividly presents us with the very thing which mid-to-late Victorian painters all sought so strenuously to exclude from their canvases: female sexuality. No wonder Henry Cotton fell in love with Mary Ryan from her photograph. Here, unlike anything you would see in a gallery of contemporary paintings, is an overpoweringly attractive woman with real skin, real hair. Rossetti, and even more Lord Leighton and Alma-Tadema, removed the least vestige of human texture from their female subjects' limbs. Their nudes have no pubic hair. Their faces are vacuous, purely receptive. The messages given out by these, in many ways repugnant, canvases are quite clear. Women – and by implication sexual relations – have to be presented with the same kind of saccharine unreality as the heroines of Dickens and Thackeray. These pretty-pretty beings are in the greatest possible contrast to *real* girls, like Mrs Cameron's models. Florence Anson in 'Girl Praying' is probably trying to look soulful. She fills the male observer of the photograph with other than soulful thoughts. Mary Hillier in such pictures as 'The Kiss of Peace' or Alice Liddell in young adulthood, are full of fleshy reality.

The critic John Ruskin hated Mrs Cameron's pictures as much as she idolised his writing. Both reactions were quite appropriate. She, as a committed and passionate aesthete, naturally drew inspiration from the

'The Gardener's Daughter,' 1867. This illustrates Tennyson's poem of the same title. It is an unusual Cameron picture, being taken out-of-doors, probably in the garden of Dimbola, her house on the Isle of Wight.

greatest aesthete of the age. Ruskin could plainly see that her photographs gave the lie to many of the modern paintings of which he had been the godfather or inspiration. Ruskin, we remember, was the man who was incapable of consummating his marriage because of his appalled sense of shock, on the wedding night, at the discovery that women had pubic hair. He was to move on, living frequently on the borders of insanity as well as having periods of raving madness, to a besotted devotion to a pubescent girl called Rose La Touche. Yet, the Victorian male devotion to young girls seems vaguely obscene in a picture like Cameron's 'The Whisper of the Muse'. She is trying to convey to us a face of great genius – G. F. Watts – being visited by angel voices. We see only a slightly unsavoury man with a beard being whispered to by a Muse whose name in real life was Lizzie Keown. Freddy Gould, the other muse, 'spoils' the effect of the picture (but actually makes it) by cheekily refusing to act, and staring instead at the photographer. His look speaks volumes about what it was like to know Mrs Cameron.

Victorian women were only meant to have hair, abundant, flowing, hair, growing from the top of their heads. All other parts of the body had to be rendered with marbly smoothness by the painters. The men who feasted on these images, however, sported more facial hair than at almost any other time in post-Merovingian European history. In the eighteenth century, men were clean-shaven unless, like George III and other poor creatures of that kind, they could not be trusted with a razor. By the reign of that bearded monarch, Edward VII, it had once again become normal for men to be clean-shaven; street urchins liked to call out 'Beaver!' in Edwardian England, if they saw a bearded man walking down the street. Forty years earlier, there were so many bearded men about that the boys would have been shouting all day long. Mrs Cameron's gallery of men is a positive Valhalla of Gnomes: Signor (G. F. Watts) himself, Longfellow, Trollope, Darwin, William Michael Rossetti, Tennyson, Henry Taylor – all sprout, not just beards, but flowing beards. Set beside the women (or the faintly androgynous Jowett) these men seem not to be just of a different sex but of a different order of being. Whatever psychosexual explanation (if any) we may wish to produce for the conspicuous Victorian cult of beards, it is certainly something which, on a visual level, distinguishes them from the previous and subsequent generations.

Their predilection for beards is only one of a number of matters – their attitude to the family, to religion, to money are others – on which the

Victorians taken as a whole seem unlike any other cluster of generations in history. That is why 'parallels' between the Victorians and our own generation are so seldom successfully drawn. How can you compare a culture such as our own in which few people have even read the Bible, and one in which the majority of educated people knew much of it by heart and believed it to be not merely an infallible guide to morals, but also to physics and biology? How can a generation such as our own which takes for granted the findings of psychology to such a sophisticated degree that we can afford to be post-Freudian, or post-Jungian – how can such a generation be compared with one which knew almost nothing of such matters, and therefore, in their attitudes to sex, will always seem like innocents? (Nowadays, the Church would feel the need to justify or suppress Newman's wholly 'innocent' expressions of adoration for his friend Ambrose St John; just as the University Proctors would have complaints if Christ Church dons such as Charles Dodgson chose to photograph the children of North Oxford in a state of undress.) How can a western democracy – let alone any other country in the world – begin to understand the political atmosphere of a country where the Prime Minister spent five months of each year outside the political arena, cutting down trees and reading Dante? There are no parallels. Mrs Cameron's photographs, which seem to be depicting a different world, almost a different species, perhaps really were doing so. The world changed deeply, fundamentally, at the time of the First World War, leaving the Victorians to seem as obsolete as the dinosaurs.

Julia Margaret Cameron's true period of activity as an artist was from the end of 1863, when Julia and Charles Norman gave her her first camera, to 1875 when the Camerons finally left Freshwater. During this period, she said herself (it is thought that she exaggerated, but not much) that she produced over 500 plates each year. At first, she exhibited her work widely – in Dublin, Berlin, London and Paris. After 1873, when her daughter Julia, the donor of the camera, died in childbirth, a shattering blow for Mrs Cameron who plunged herself thereafter more and more deeply into work, she tried to develop her charade-style tableaux into book illustrations, abandoning exhibitions. Two volumes of Tennyson's *Idylls of the King* were published with Mrs Cameron's photographs: 'The Passing of Arthur' is typical of these illustrations. Quentin Bell comments on this picture, '"So like a shattered column lay the King".

ABOVE '*Connor of the Royal Artillery, winner of prizes at the RA Games at Freshwater, October 1864*'.

RIGHT '*Annie, my first success, January 1864*'.

He looks as though he might easily be sick. They are going to lose an oar. Something unexpected has happened to the moon, and to the water. In fact Mrs Cameron has more poetry than she can deal with.'

Since love of family was as strong in Mrs Cameron as love of art, it is perhaps not surprising, after half a lifetime in England, that she eventually felt drawn to Ceylon. Her husband was by now an invalid, Ceylon was always his first love, and it was the residence of their three coffee-growing sons (their fourth son, Hardinge, accompanied his parents on the journey). It was no mere matter of loading a few cases into the hold of a ship. There were the coffins to take on board in case any member of the party should die at sea. Then – how to avoid tuberculosis on a sea-voyage? Why, take your own cow, of course, to ensure fresh milk each day. The number of crates, boxes and packing-cases which accompanied the Camerons seemed to be without number, and the long-suffering porters, carrying all the stuff on board, were surprised to discover, when their labours were complete, that they were tipped not with cash but with original Cameron photographs. Those short of money would probably have preferred sixpence to one of Mrs Cameron's bored-looking entourage posing as Tennyson's Princess with a banjo. But those whose families kept these remarkable gratuities may have been grateful: not because of their financial value, but because sixpences come and go, but Mrs Cameron is unique.

They did return to England once, in 1878, 'a visit of turmoil, sickness, marriages and deaths', Mrs Cameron called it. For the rest of her life, however, she was marooned in Ceylon. She liked the inhabitants but, strangely enough, her inspiration seems to have left her under the tropical skies. She took some photographs in Ceylon, but the distinctive Cameron touch is absent in these plates.

In January 1879, when she was staying at the house of her son Henry Herschel Cameron, soon to become a professional photographer himself, she became ill, and took to her bed. Henry arranged it so that his mother could see through her window and across a balcony. One evening, the stars were particularly bright. 'Beautiful', said Mrs Cameron, and died. Surely nobody could possibly have invented for her a more appropriate last word.

Perhaps the most striking faces in Julia Margaret Cameron's plates are those of the children – sometimes bored stiff, sometimes suppressing the giggles, very frequently looking as if they want, by some means or another, to get their own back. Well, they did. One of the pieces of family business which Julia Margaret Cameron wanted to discuss on her last visit back to England in 1878 was the fate of her newly-widowed niece Julia Duckworth, daughter of her sister Mia. Mrs Cameron's idea was that she should marry poor Charles Norman, the widower of her own daughter Julia. But Mrs Duckworth married instead the morosely agnostic ex-clergyman and man of letters Leslie Stephen. When we see Mrs Cameron's statuesque portraits of Mrs Duckworth we do not need

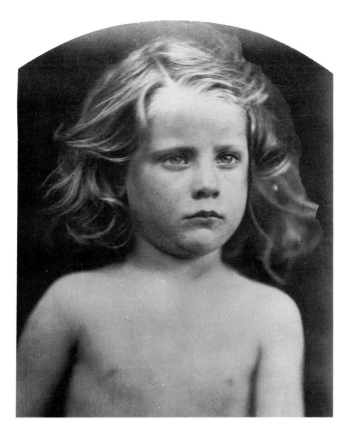

'Young Astyanax', 1866. This is a rare excursion for Mrs Cameron into classical literature. Astyanax, or Scamandrius, was the younger child of King Priam of Troy, who was killed by being thrown over the battlements by Agamemnon. He is here represented by Freddy Gould who looks bored and cold.

to guess whose mother she was destined to become: the resemblance to Virginia Woolf is uncanny.

Within a generation, the sniggering sophisticates of Bloomsbury were gathering in the studio of Vanessa Bell, Julia Stephen's other daughter, to see enacted a play by Virginia, entitled *Freshwater: A comedy*. In Virginia Woolf's casting list, we read that Mrs Cameron was played by Vanessa Bell herself, Charles Hay Cameron by Leonard Woolf, G. F. Watts by Duncan Grant, Alfred Tennyson by Adrian Stephen and the young, exploited Ellen Terry by Angelica Bell, Vanessa's daughter by Duncan Grant. In the light of all that we know about Bloomsbury there seems something almost ghoulish in this *jeu-d'esprit*. The vaguely obscene jokes about Ellen Terry and G. F. Watts, instead of making us titter, as they doubtless made the Bloomsbury set titter over their cigars and lemonade, strike a chilling note: Angelica Bell's own memoirs reveal that the emotional torture of growing up in an emancipated post-Victorian world could be every bit as dreadful as the supposed troubles of Ellen Terry matched to the Signor.

> NELL: *My name is Mrs George Frederick Watts.*
>
> JOHN: *But haven't you got another?*
>
> NELL: *Oh, plenty! Sometimes I'm Modesty.*
> *Sometimes I'm Poetry. Sometimes I'm Chastity.*
> *Sometimes, generally before breakfast I'm merely Nell.*

Now that we know more than we would ever have asked to know about the Bloomsbury families, we might very well echo the servant Mary's words in the final act of *Freshwater* – 'Gorblime! What a set! What a set!'

Yet Bloomsbury, particularly through the malicious wit of Lytton Strachey, was very largely responsible for shaping twentieth-century attitudes to the Victorian Age. *Freshwater* is a joke, and a private family joke; it would be heavy-handed to build too much upon it. But it reveals in caricatured form the impish, mischievous belief that everything about the Victorians was essentially ridiculous. Beneath the giggling, there are serious political and religious feelings. The generation of which Bloomsbury were the most articulate and amusing mouthpieces had watched 'Victorian values' take their effect, and it is not particularly surprising that they were unimpressed. The combination of unchecked industrial expansion with Gladstonian economics had led to conditions of poverty and squalor which (in numerical terms) were without equal in civilised history. As members of the Fabian Society, or readers of Beatrice Webb's *My Apprenticeship*, could observe, there were children starving on the streets of London at the turn of the century. That was the achievement of Victorian capitalism.

In terms of family life – that other supposed bastion of Victorian virtue – we have only to read the Bloomsbury memoirs themselves, or, say, the novels of Ivy Compton-Burnett, to discover what emotional havoc can be wrought by growing up in a family, particularly in one of those large, prosperous middle or upper-class families which were supposed to be the finest flowering of the English system. The Wilde trial and its aftermath (1895) had revealed the depths of ignorance which existed of human character and variety, just as the Dilke and Parnell scandals had uncovered the extent of English humbug. To the pains of growing up in one of those Victorian families was often added the pure horror of a public school – again the product of Victorian thinking, and Victorian values, particularly those of Dr Thomas Arnold.

Nor did the enlightened reformers of the Victorian age seem to have achieved all that much. The 'liberalism' advocated by such as Matthew Arnold had no effect in dispelling the 'philistinism' which hung over the suburbs and guided the way the British thought about sex, politics, or religion. Though Darwin on one level and the historians of the Bible texts on another had exploded any possibility of clinging to orthodox Christianity in its unreconstituted, fundamentalist form, there seemed no shortage of people who were prepared to assert the truth of things which had been – as it seemed to the next generation – manifestly proved false. Arnold's 'sweetness and light' seemed to make no more headway in the world than Gladstone's innocent nationalism. Nationalism itself, far from being a peaceful desire for self-determination, had taken on Nietzschean, Wagnerian overtones of doom and strength.

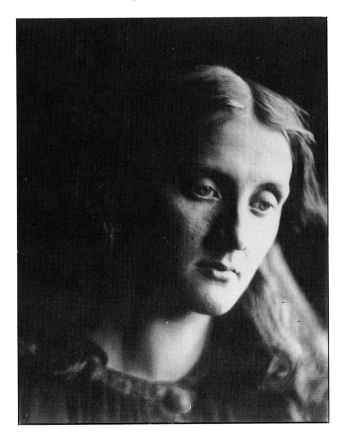

'My favourite picture. My niece Julia,' April 1867. Julia Jackson's second husband was Sir Leslie Stephen by whom she bore two daughters – the painter Vanessa Bell and the writer Virginia Woolf. Julia's resemblance to Virginia is very strong as this 'favourite picture' shows.

Between Gladstone and Disraeli the debate had appeared to be between innocent nationalism and jingoistic imperialism. By the end of the century these no longer seemed like alternatives. Instead, they were both capable of fuelling the suicidal urge which overcame the great European powers in the decade after Queen Victoria died. No wonder, as Russia, Germany, France and Britain prepared to fight the most pointless and the most destructive war in history, if the children of the Victorians saw the whole sorry struggle as a tragic enactment of the 'values' cherished and built up by the 'eminent Victorians'. Sending young men to their death in the mud of Flanders was all part of the same silly ideal of personal heroism, detatched from political common sense, which had inspired such famous Victorian set-pieces as the death of General Gordon of Khartoum or the Charge of the Light Brigade.

Those who protested against the First World War found themselves treated with great harshness. Bertrand Russell, as a conscientious objector, was in Brixton Gaol in 1918 when his wife Alys brought him a copy of a recently published book by Lytton Strachey. It was called *Eminent Victorians*. 'It caused me to laugh so loud', Russell remembered, 'that the officer came to my cell, saying I must remember that prison is a place of punishment.'

It is that story, to my mind, which illustrates better than any other why *Eminent Victorians* had such an overpowering effect when it was first published. Strachey had conceived the idea of the book in 1912 when he was thirty-two. The timing of the publication had much to do with its effect. But so, too, did Strachey's manner, the elegance of his satire, the refusal to take his Victorian idols remotely seriously. Just as the Victorians had enjoyed huge stodgy meals, multiplied themselves in vast families (like the Stracheys themselves) and lived in big, lumpy houses, so they had written monumental biographies of their great men and women. Strachey immediately cut them down to size by presenting four such idols – Dr Arnold, Florence Nightingale, Cardinal Manning and General Gordon – in minimal caricature. He does not need to say what he thinks about 'Victorian values' by the time he has finished making these four ridiculous. The release from those values is made by the most liberating means of all: laughter.

In Strachey's dismissal of his subjects, however, as in a rebellious child's rudeness about his parents, there is more than a little love mingled with the hatred. We see this even more strongly in his life of

Queen Victoria, published in 1921, where the affection for his subject –
indeed, identification with her – is very marked. We see it, too, perhaps
in the rather trivial but possibly significant fact that Strachey, unlike
most men of his generation, chose to grow a long flowing beard, so that
the famous Henry Lamb portrait, now hanging in the Tate Gallery in
London, looks less like a scourge of the Victorians than the last etiolated
specimen of their kind.

We are different. We do not need to score points off the Eminent
Victorians as if (or as in the case of Bloomsbury, because) they were
embarrassing members of our family. From our more distant perspective, we can see that, for all the horrors of life in the nineteenth century, it
did throw up figures of a stature not easily rivalled in the post-Strachey
years. With the exception of Churchill – and only then in a wartime con-
text – there simply have been no twentieth-century British statesmen to
match Peel, Gladstone, Disraeli or Lord Salisbury. There has been no
theological figure of the stature of John Henry Newman, either in the
Church of Rome or in the Church of England. He outsoars them all. Few
modern engineers have ever matched the sheer energy and expertise of
Isambard Kingdom Brunel. And think of the great Victorian architects!
Where is there in the twentieth century an architect who can come near
them for the scale, majesty and self-confidence of their achievement? I
am thinking of the front-rank architects – George Gilbert Scott,
Augustus Welby Pugin, Charles Barry, William Butterfield, George
Edmund Street, G. F. Bodley – but there are a whole host of lesser ones
who produced buildings, each one of which, when it has been allowed to
survive into our own day, provides us with something like a reproach.

It should not be supposed that I am trying to make some sweeping or
indefensible suggestion (except perhaps in the case of architecture where
the temptation to do so is almost insuperable) about the superiority of
nineteenth over twentieth-century taste or achievement. That is not
what I am suggesting at all. In terms of paintings, for example, admirable as individual canvases are, I find my taste for the High Victorians
ebbing away to the point where it has almost vanished, whereas the
twentieth century seems full of excitement. Likewise, if I am honest, I
find the twentieth century (in Britain) a much more exciting one in the
history of literature than the nineteenth. What I am talking about is the
size and self-confidence of the Victorian achievement. There might, for
example, be better historians writing nowadays (though I somewhat

*'Faith', 1864. The first of
the theological virtues is here
represented by Mrs
Cameron's long-suffering
maid, Mary Ann Hillier,
who posed for many of her
most successful plates.*

doubt it) but there is no one writing on the massive scale and with the
grandly self-confident poise of Macaulay, Froude, Lecky.

No one will ever write a funnier book about the Victorians than Lytton
Strachey did, nor one more elegant. What I have tried to suggest in this
book is that there really were 'giants in those days'. It does not mean that
they were without foibles, sometimes hilarious ones. But their stature is
unquestionable. Virginia Woolf mocked 'Aunt Julia' Cameron, Lord
Tennyson and the others because by implication they embodied a set of
'Victorian values' which the Bloomsburyites were too sophisticated any
longer to accept. Strachey even more, in his selected four 'Eminent'
Victorians chose figures who may be said to have exemplified values
which modern people might hope to have outgrown.

In latter years, we have seen a reaction, and 'Victorian values', far from being things to snigger at, appear to be vote-winning concepts in the minds of politicians. Usually, it turns out on examination that the cherished values concerned are no more 'Victorian' than they are 'modern'. It is simply that, in an age of Laura Ashley wallpaper and successful Dickens movies, we might also be expected to admire politicians and journalists more if they, too, dress up their ideas as 'Victorian'.

My purpose in this book has been much simpler, much less propagandist, much more like that of Julia Margaret Cameron in her close-up portraits. I have done my best to look at six individuals, Mrs Cameron included, with the sole aim of finding out what they were like. I have not been trying to make a point, either about our own age, or about theirs. As it happens, far from being six exemplars of 'Victorian values', I find that I have chosen six people who, in one way or another, turned supposed 'Victorian values' on their head. Prince Albert was a foreigner who never came to terms with England or the English. As it happened, he defended the monarchy, but only by unintentionally making it into something more modern, and wholly unpolitical. Gladstone – a figure synonymous in many ways with the Victorian Church and State – was a man whose mind was awake, and who therefore went on changing, and went on upsetting people, to the end. Newman, too, was brave enough to change his mind: not just before he became a Roman Catholic, but afterwards, too. No one could call him a defender of 'Victorian values'.

The three women in my collection have a more ambivalent relationship with the society in which they found themselves. Charlotte Brontë led a life which was almost buried, hidden from the world. And yet her private fantasy, fashioned into art, became one of the most popular novels of the age. She is a good example of the private and public faces of art. The artist is always a hermit; but unless what she creates is of interest to the outside world, then her labour is vain.

Josephine Butler, beautiful, 'fulfilled', with a good husband and children, devout, might seem at first sight to be a 'typical' Victorian woman. But capitalist society in its most corrupt manifestations had fewer more devastating opponents. In spite of sex, let alone venereal diseases, being unmentionable words, she managed to change the conscience of society. She looked at it without illusions, for what it was. There was tremendous heroism in her opposition to the Contagious Diseases Acts, and in her more generalised defence of feminism and women's suffrage. She is a good example of why Lytton Strachey's satirical approach to the nineteenth century is misleading. She saw more clearly than Strachey did what was wrong with Victorian England. So did Gladstone and Newman. But they all in their vigorous way did something about it.

Mrs Cameron, her hands black with silver nitrate and the other chemicals of her strange alchemy, took an altogether less sociological view. She was through and through an aesthete. But it is thanks to her, more than to her great-niece Virginia Woolf and the Bloomsbury circle, that we have some of the most memorable images of the Victorian age. She believed in divinity. So, strangely, did all the six in my book, and I think this would have been true, even had I chosen another six, with a few carefully selected atheists or agnostics, such as Charles Bradlaugh, J. A. Froude or George Eliot. Long after they had abandoned a belief in a personal Creator, such people continued to believe in a moral law, in duty, and in the divine potential of human beings. It was this divine potential which got lost during the First World War, and led to so much literature of despair, of which Strachey's *Eminent Victorians* is but one, elegant and hilarious example. The world has not got any nicer since Strachey wrote his book – in fact, the reverse. But somehow, it is no longer possible to dismiss anyone, whether dead or alive, in quite the debonair spirit in which he caricatures his subjects. We share a common humanity with people in the past, even when they baffle us, and puzzle us. It is common humanity with the Victorians which we have recovered. In recovering it, we also recover no small sense of their greatness.

Index

PICTURE CREDITS

Colour Photographs

Page 81 Tate Gallery; 82 National Portrait Gallery; 83 *top* The Royal Collection, *bottom* Deene Park; 84 *top* Brontë Society, *bottom* National Portrait Gallery; 85 *top, bottom left* and *right* Brontë Society; 86 National Portrait Gallery; 87 *top* Andrew Anderson, *bottom* The Mansell Collection; 88 Illustrated London News; 177 National Portrait Gallery; 178 Canon Bartlett; 179 *top left and right* Magdalen College Oxford; 179 *bottom* Canon Bartlett; 180 *top and bottom* Mary Evans Picture Library; 181 and 182 *top* National Portrait Gallery; 182 *bottom* and 183 National Museum of Photography; 184 Tate Gallery.

Black-and-white Photographs

Page 2–3 Hulton Picture Company; 7 Illustrated London News; 11 Greater London Photograph Library; 13 *and* 14 Hulton Picture Company; 19 Her Majesty The Queen; 23 Victoria and Albert Museum; 26 Punch; 29 Hulton Picture Company; 31 Her Majesty The Queen; 34 English Heritage; 35 *and* 36 Her Majesty The Queen; 39 Illustrated London News; 41 Hulton Picture Company; 45 National Portrait Gallery; 49 Hulton Picture Company; 50 Brontë Society; 52 British Library; 55, 57, 60, 61, 63, 65, 68, 73, 77, 93 *and* 95 Brontë Society; 99 *and* 100 Hulton Picture Company; 102 Julian Selmes; 105 Illustrated London News; 107 *and* 111 Hulton Picture Company; 115 *left* Mary Evans Picture Library, *right* Illustrated London News; 117, 120 *and* 123 Mary Evans Picture Library; 125 *left* Hulton Picture Company, *right and* 127 Illustrated London News; 130, 133 *and* 134 Hulton Picture Company; 137 Royal Commission on Historical Monuments; 142 Bodleian Library (G A Oxon a 68, page 17 item 23a.); 144 Hulton Picture Company; 146 *and* 147 Oxfordshire County Libraries; 149 Birmingham Oratory; 151 National Portrait Gallery; 155 Hulton Picture Company; 158 The Mansell Collection; 160 *left* Mary Evans Picture Library, *right* Birmingham Oratory; 163 *and* 164 Fawcett Library; 166 The Mansell Collection; 167 Hulton Picture Company; 169 Mary Evans Picture Library; 172 *left* Illustrated London News, *right and* 186 Fawcett Library; 189 Salvationist Publishing; 195 Hulton Picture Company; 199 Mary Evans Picture Library; 201 Fawcett Library; 203, 204, 208 *and* 211 Hulton Picture Company; 215 *and* 216 Joy Lester, 219 Lincolnshire County Council; 221, 224, 227 *left and right*, 229, 231 *and* 234 National Museum of Photography.